Sage ACT! 2012 Cookbook

Over 90 advanced recipes for power users of ACT! 2012 for increasing the efficiency of your business

Karen Fredricks

[PACKT] enterprise
PUBLISHING   professional expertise distilled

BIRMINGHAM - MUMBAI

Sage ACT! 2012 Cookbook

First published: September 2011

Production Reference: 1190911

Published by Packt Publishing Ltd.
Livery Place
35 Livery Street
Birmingham B3 2PB, UK.

ISBN 978-1-84968-250-3

www.packtpub.com

Cover Image by Artie Ng (artherng@yahoo.com.au)

Credits

Author
Karen Fredricks

Reviewers
Len Kamerman
Roy Laudenslager
Keith Wilson

Acquisition Editor
Stephanie Moss

Development Editor
Susmita Panda

Technical Editor
Ajay Shanker

Project Coordinator
Vishal Bodwan

Proofreader
Aaron Nash

Indexer
Rekha Nair

Production Coordinator
Arvindkumar Gupta

Cover Work
Arvindkumar Gupta

About the Author

Karen Fredricks began her life rather non-technically growing up in Kenya. She likes to say that she developed her sense of humor while dodging bombs in Beirut where she attended high school. She graduated from the University of Florida and holds degrees in English, Theatre, and Accounting. She settled in Boca Raton where she includes tennis, trips to the gym, and cheering for the Gators in her busy schedule.

A true CRM expert, Karen is the author of more than 10 For Dummies books, including titles on ACT!, SugarCRM, Outlook, Business Contact Manager, Office Live, and Marketing with Microsoft Office 2007. This is her seventh book devoted to ACT! and her second book written for Packt.

Karen's firm, Tech Benders (www.techbenders.com), customizes popular contact management, and CRM software to help businesses grow by being more productive, efficient, and profitable. Karen believes in working smarter in order to have the time to enjoy life and tries to instill that philosophy in her clients.

It may not take a village to write a book, but it does take a number of helpful people! This is my second Packt book and the staff was a pleasure to work with. I'd like to thank Stephanie Moss, my Acquisition Editor, who saw the need for an ACT! title on the new and more powerful features of ACT! Susmita Panda had the task of making sure my writing would be easily understood by readers. Vishal Bodwani took care of the scheduling of the book.

Gary Kahn was always there to support me, offer an occasional back rub, feed me lots of red licorice and help keep me on track.

And to my daughters, Andrea, and Alyssa: I love you both!

About the Reviewers

Len Kamerman is a CRM consultant in Toronto, Ontario and is the owner of Hero Technical Solutions, focusing on helping small businesses take advantage of technology including ACT! and Microsoft CRM. He has been working with ACT! for the last nine years and often writes custom software to extend ACT!'s capabilities. Len lives in Hamilton, Ontario with his wonderful wife, three month old son (who sleeps like a champ), and energetic dog. He has written guest articles for the Sage ACT! community and has a blog that can be found through www.yourcrmhero.com.

Roy Laudenslager has spent his entire career working on computers. He likes to say he barely missed the vacuum tube computers. He's repaired them, written numerous training manuals about them, and spent many years troubleshooting them. He began working for Symantec, when they combined all their technical support in a new site in Eugene, Oregon. When they acquired the ACT! program, he was one of the first ACT! support agents. He was already familiar with the ACT! program having used the DOS version at another company. He spent the next 10 years supporting the ACT! program for Symantec, then InterACT Commerce Corporation, and finally for Sage Software. By the time he left, he was the lead support agent for ACT escalations. Escalations are the problems that the regular support agents are unable to solve; his job was to solve the unsolvable. He also trained new support staff on database field modifications, reports, and synchronization. His expertise in the area of synchronization led to the Knowledge Base document that he wrote for setting up synchronization, making it possible to synchronize ACT! 3 through 6 reliably. After 10 years in ACT! technical support, he wanted to become an ACT consultant, so he left Sage and joined Karen Fredricks as part of Tech Benders, allowing him to do what he loved to do: work with ACT! users!

Roy has worked with the ACT reports since ACT! for Windows 2.0 and is known around Sage as the ACT report writer guru. He wrote the 12 new reports that first appeared in ACT 2010/12.

In the early part of his career, Roy spent several years working as a technical writer and authored many training and reference manuals.

While working in technical supports for Symantec and later Sage, he contributed one or more articles monthly to the Easy ACT! newsletter. This body of work took place over a 7-year period and represented over 100 articles.

Most recently, he was the technical editor for the Dummies books on ACT! versions 7-11 and the report chapters in the Dashboards and Reports Cookbook.

Keith Wilson has worked with ACT for nearly 20 years and has developed a global following of raving fans and constantly receives fantastic recognition for his obvious ability to teach all levels of the Sage ACT system.

His unique Academy Coaching Program (ACT) (www.TheACTAcademy.com) has subscribers from all over the world learning the skills required to get the maximum output from this amazing software.

Many testimonials are available both at the preceding main website and also his active blog at http://theactacademy.wordpress.com.

In addition to his extensive ACT knowledge, Keith is also a very experienced Internet marketer and because ACT is primarily a sales/marketing solution, this knowledge helps compliment what he teaches on ACT, and therefore adds even more value to his products and services.

In a previous book review, I extensively thanked my father for giving me the confidence to be the person I am today, but there are two other people in my life that also deserve huge recognition.

My dear mum Brenda and my darling wife Karen.

Without the grounding and constant unconditional love given by my mum, both when growing up as a child to now as a 37 year old adult, life would definitely not have been as fun or happy without her constantly being there for me, especially when I needed her most.

Add to that my 14 years of being very happily married to Karen, my soul mate, my partner, my friend, my lover, and most of all, the mother to my two amazing children.

You are both truly amazing individuals and I thank you for everything you've done for me in the past, and continue to do today.

Plus with the inclusion of my two fantastic sisters, I genuinely couldn't be happier with my life.

So for all the support and guidance you've given me over the years, I thank you all from the bottom of my heart and love you very much.

---

www.PacktPub.com

Support files, eBooks, discount offers and more

You might want to visit www.PacktPub.com for support files and downloads related to your book.

Did you know that Packt offers eBook versions of every book published, with PDF and ePub files available? You can upgrade to the eBook version at www.PacktPub.com and as a print book customer, you are entitled to a discount on the eBook copy. Get in touch with us at service@packtpub.com for more details.

At www.PacktPub.com, you can also read a collection of free technical articles, sign up for a range of free newsletters and receive exclusive discounts and offers on Packt books and eBooks.

 PACKTLiB®

http://PacktLib.PacktPub.com

Do you need instant solutions to your IT questions? PacktLib is Packt's online digital book library. Here, you can access, read and search across Packt's entire library of books.

Why Subscribe?

- ▶ Fully searchable across every book published by Packt
- ▶ Copy and paste, print and bookmark content
- ▶ On demand and accessible via web browser

Free Access for Packt account holders

If you have an account with Packt at www.PacktPub.com, you can use this to access PacktLib today and view nine entirely free books. Simply use your login credentials for immediate access.

Instant Updates on New Packt Books

Get notified! Find out when new books are published by following @PacktEnterprise on Twitter, or the *Packt Enterprise* Facebook page.

Table of Contents

Preface   1

Chapter 1: Working with the Welcome Page and Navigation Bar   5

  Introduction   5
  Using the Welcome Page   6
  Changing the Startup view   8
  Working with the Navbar   10
  Changing the Current view   13
  Customizing the Navbar   15
  Connecting ACT! to other services   16

Chapter 2: Jotting Down your Notes Using Scratchpad   19

  Introduction   19
  Adding an item to the Scratchpad   20
  Making changes to Scratchpad items   22
  Changing the order of the Scratchpad items   23
  Transferring Scratchpad items to an ACT! database   24
  Marking a Scratchpad item as complete   26
  Printing the Scratchpad list   27

Chapter 3: Using Queries to Find Data   29

  Introduction   29
  Performing a basic lookup   30
  Looking up by Example   34
  Creating an Annual Event lookup/search   35
  Creating a lookup by Contact Activity   37
  Creating an Advanced Query   39
  Searching on keywords   42
  Using the universal search   44

Chapter 4: Relating Contact Records   49

Introduction   49
Adding the Relationship tab   50
Adding a Related Contact   52
Adding multiple Related Contacts   54
Changing a relationship   55
Creating a Secondary Contact   56
Promoting a Secondary Contact   58

Chapter 5: Integrating Contact Information with Websites   61

Introduction   61
Understanding the Web Info tab   62
Editing an existing web link   65
Creating a new web link   67
Deleting a web link   69
Creating an Internet link   70
Adding a website link to the History tab   72

Chapter 6: Grouping your Contacts   75

Introduction   75
Creating a Group   76
Adding Static Members to a Group   79
Removing Static Members from a Group   81
Adding Dynamic Members to a Group   82
Creating a Group from the current Lookup   84
Using the Group tab of the Contact Detail view   85
Working with Groups   88

Chapter 7: Working with Companies   93

Introduction   93
Learning about Company views   94
Creating Companies from the Companies   95
Detail view   95
Creating a Company from a Contact record   97
Adding a Division to a Company   98
Deleting a Company   100
Linking Contact and Company Records   101
Adding a Contact to a Company   103
Working with a Company Record   103
Linking Company and Contact Fields   106
Creating a Lookup of Company Contacts   109

Chapter 8: Creating Golden Opportunities   **111**

Introduction   **111**
Working with the Opportunity View   **112**
Adding processes and stages   **114**
Adding products and services   **118**
Working with opportunity fields and layouts   **121**
Creating an opportunity   **124**
Editing an opportunity   **127**
Working with the Opportunity List   **129**
Creating an Opportunity Graph   **132**

Chapter 9: Integrating with Microsoft Outlook   **135**

Introduction   **135**
Setting up Outlook as your ACT! e-mail client   **136**
Sending an Outlook message to a single contact   **141**
Sending an Outlook message to multiple contacts   **143**
Sending an e-mail to an ACT! contact in Outlook   **144**
Linking incoming Outlook e-mail to ACT!   **146**
Creating a new ACT! contact from Outlook   **148**
Synchronizing your ACT! calendar to Outlook   **150**
Synchronizing your ACT! contacts to Outlook   **154**

Chapter 10: Integrating with Google   **161**

Introduction   **161**
Setting up Google and ACT! integration   **162**
Synchronizing your ACT! calendar to Google   **164**
Synchronizing your ACT! contacts to Google   **167**
Setting the Record History options for Google   **172**
Setting up automatic integration   **175**

Chapter 11: Performing Routine Maintenance   **177**

Introduction   **177**
Performing routine maintenance   **178**
Creating a backup   **179**
Restoring a backup   **181**
Using the ACT! Scheduler   **183**
Applying ACT! updates   **187**
Removing old data   **190**
Merging duplicate records   **191**
Deleting a database   **195**
Performing a global edit and replace   **196**

Chapter 12: Creating an E-marketing Campaign   **199**

Introduction   **200**

Adding your E-marketing account credentials   **201**

Moving a template to the local library   **204**

Editing a local template   **206**

Importing an existing HTML template   **214**

Sending an E-marketing pieces   **216**

Updating ACT! with E-marketing history   **218**

Analyzing an E-marketing campaign   **219**

Creating a Lookup of your Campaign Results   **222**

Creating a survey   **225**

Creating a web form   **229**

Chapter 13: Working Smarter with Smart Tasks   **233**

Introduction   **233**

Learning about the existing Smart Tasks   **235**

Editing an existing Smart Task   **237**

Creating a Smart Task template   **243**

Adding a Smart Task step   **246**

Changing Smart Task steps   **249**

Setting a Smart Task to Auto-Run   **250**

Running Smart Tasks manually   **253**

Checking the status of a Smart Task   **256**

Index   **259**

Preface

ACT! is the best selling contact manager software on the market today. This cookbook is full of immediately applicable recipes covering advanced features of ACT! 2012, with a particular emphasis on those new to this forthcoming release. Many recipes will be relevant to users of ACT! who have not upgraded since 2009 or 2010 as many advanced features originate from these releases. The content will familiarize you with the new startup options and a new design to better navigate the product. You will also learn to use ACT!'s E-Marketing and Opportunity features, so that you will be able to easily build your business and keep track of your profits.

This practical cookbook provides numerous recipes that will take you from being an ACT! novice to a CRM pro in no time, as you learn to utilize all of the advanced functionality of ACT! 2012 added in the most recent ACT! versions.

The recipes begin by covering the most basic elements of opening an ACT! database, and advance to include several recipes that will guide you through powerful CRM functionality, including creating E-Marketing Campaigns and sending them off to specific segments of your database. If you have information in your ACT! database, you need to be able to use it quickly and logically—this book will help you do just that.

What this book covers

Chapter 1, Working With the Welcome Page and Navigation Bar, explains what to expect when you first open ACT!, how to change the various startup options, and how to navigate around the ACT! software program.

Chapter 2, Jotting Down Your Notes Using Scratchpad, shows you how to use Scratchpad to keep a list of tasks that you need to do or notes that you want to jot down.

Chapter 3, Using Queries to Find Data, covers how to perform lookups based on various contact information including fields, notes, histories, and activities. It'll also walk you through running advanced lookups or queries which allow you to find contacts based on multiple criteria.

Chapter 4, Relating Contact Records, shows you how to cross-reference two existing ACT! contacts by creating a relationship between the two contacts.

Chapter 5, Integrating Contact Information With Your Websites, shows you how to use the existing links on the web info tab, which pull ACT! contact data directly into popular websites including Google and weather.com. You'll learn how to edit the existing links and create new links to your favorite web and social networking sites.

Chapter 6, Grouping Your Contacts, teaches you how to make groups and sub-groups, how to create dynamic groups that automatically populate based on your search criteria, and how to create quick lookups based on the contents of a group.

Chapter 7, Working With Companies, teaches you how to create companies and divisions to create an account-centric database. The chapter will show you how to link existing company and contact records, update all related contact records from the company record, and add new contact records to a company record.

Chapter 8, Creating Golden Opportunities, teaches you how to create a sales pipeline by adding a sales process, related stages, and a list of products to ACT!. You'll learn how to create a new opportunity, edit it to reflect its progression through your sales funnel, and report on the final outcome of the sale. You'll also be able to access, filter, and sort all of your opportunities from one centralized location.

Chapter 9, Integrating With Microsoft Outlook, shows you ways in which you can integrate Microsoft outlook with ACT!. You'll learn to send and receive outlook e-mail and have the history automatically recorded in ACT!. You'll learn how to synchronize the outlook and ACT! calendars and contacts, and learn how to create a new ACT! contact directly from an incoming e-mail message.

Chapter 10, Integrating with Google, covers setting up Google and ACT! integration, synchronizing your ACT! and Google calendars, synchronizing your ACT! and Google contacts, setting the Record History options for Google, and setting up Automatic Integration.

Chapter 11, Performing Routine Maintenance, shows you how to use the ACT! scheduler to create automatic procedures to run periodic backups and maintenance routines. You'll also learn to access the ACT! diagnostic utility to perform advanced maintenance, if needed and run reports on the inner structure of your database.

Chapter 12, Creating an E-Marketing Campaign, explains the difference between ACT! e-mail and E-Marketing. You'll learn how to design HTML e-mail templates, send out marketing pieces, and analyze the results of your E-Marketing campaign.

Chapter 13, Working Smarter with Smart Tasks, explains how to edit the existing Smart Tasks as well as create brand new ones to automate your sales and marketing efforts. You'll learn how to add additional Smart Task steps to automatically send out e-mails and remind you of important follow-up activities.

What you need for this book

No prior ACT! knowledge is necessarily required; however, you'll find it helpful to have good working knowledge of how to add data into ACT!, or to work with an ACT! database that has already been populated with data.

Who this book is for

This is an advanced cookbook of easy-to-follow recipes about ACT! 2012 designed to transform you into an ACT! power user. If you are an ACT! end user who wants to learn about the advanced functionality of ACT! 2012, then this book is for you. It will also be useful if you are a 2009 or 2010 user, as many advanced features originate from these ACT! versions. If you are an ACT! administrator who needs to administer an ACT! database or understand outlook integration, you will also find this book helpful.

Conventions

In this book, you will find a number of styles of text that distinguish between different kinds of information. Here are some examples of these styles, and an explanation of their meaning.

New terms and **important words** are shown in bold. Words that you see on the screen, in menus or dialog boxes for example, appear in the text like this: "Click the Write menu and choose **Manage ACT! Services**".

Warnings or important notes appear in a box like this.

Tips and tricks appear like this.

Reader feedback

Feedback from our readers is always welcome. Let us know what you think about this book—what you liked or may have disliked. Reader feedback is important for us to develop titles that you really get the most out of.

To send us general feedback, simply send an e-mail to feedback@packtpub.com, and mention the book title via the subject of your message.

If there is a book that you need and would like to see us publish, please send us a note in the **SUGGEST A TITLE** form on www.packtpub.com or e-mail suggest@packtpub.com.

If there is a topic that you have expertise in and you are interested in either writing or contributing to a book, see our author guide on www.packtpub.com/authors.

Customer support

Now that you are the proud owner of a Packt book, we have a number of things to help you to get the most from your purchase.

Errata

Although we have taken every care to ensure the accuracy of our content, mistakes do happen. If you find a mistake in one of our books—maybe a mistake in the text or the code—we would be grateful if you would report this to us. By doing so, you can save other readers from frustration and help us improve subsequent versions of this book. If you find any errata, please report them by visiting http://www.packtpub.com/support, selecting your book, clicking on the **errata submission form** link, and entering the details of your errata. Once your errata are verified, your submission will be accepted and the errata will be uploaded on our website, or added to any list of existing errata, under the Errata section of that title. Any existing errata can be viewed by selecting your title from http://www.packtpub.com/support.

Piracy

Piracy of copyright material on the Internet is an ongoing problem across all media. At Packt, we take the protection of our copyright and licenses very seriously. If you come across any illegal copies of our works, in any form, on the Internet, please provide us with the location address or website name immediately so that we can pursue a remedy.

Please contact us at copyright@packtpub.com with a link to the suspected pirated material.

We appreciate your help in protecting our authors, and our ability to bring you valuable content.

Questions

You can contact us at questions@packtpub.com if you are having a problem with any aspect of the book, and we will do our best to address it.

1
Working with the Welcome Page and Navigation Bar

In this chapter, we will cover:

- ▶ Understanding the Welcome Page
- ▶ Changing the Startup view
- ▶ Working with the Navbar components
- ▶ Collapsing and expanding the Navbar
- ▶ Changing the Current view area
- ▶ Customizing the Navbar
- ▶ Connecting ACT! to other services

Introduction

By default, the Welcome Page is the first page that, well, welcomes you when you open ACT! The purpose of the Welcome Page is to acquaint you with some of the more common ACT! features. Although some of the links found on the Welcome Page are nothing more than shameless plugs to entice you to purchase more ACT! services, there is a lot of great content to be found on the Welcome Page.

The Welcome Page holds four main categories of information:

1. Links to ACT! help screens
2. Links to ACT! training videos
3. Links to specific ACT! features
4. Links to various areas on the Sage website

Theoretically, the Welcome Page will help you get up and running very quickly in ACT! However, although you can't change the information on the Welcome Page without some advanced knowledge of JavaScripting, you can choose to *not* use it because most of the information that it contains is also found elsewhere in the ACT! program.

Using the Welcome Page

Getting ready

You can only get to the Welcome Page by opening up an ACT! database. If you don't have a database open in ACT! you'll see an abbreviated version of the Welcome to ACT! screen like the one shown below, which allows you to either open or create a database:

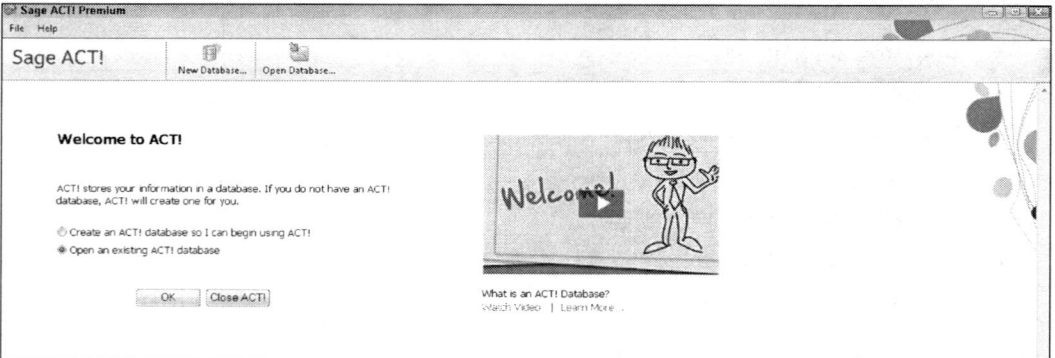

How to do it...

1. Open a database to see the complete Welcome Page.
2. The Welcome Page is divided into several areas which you can navigate to. Click on any of the areas as shown on the Welcome Page in the following image:

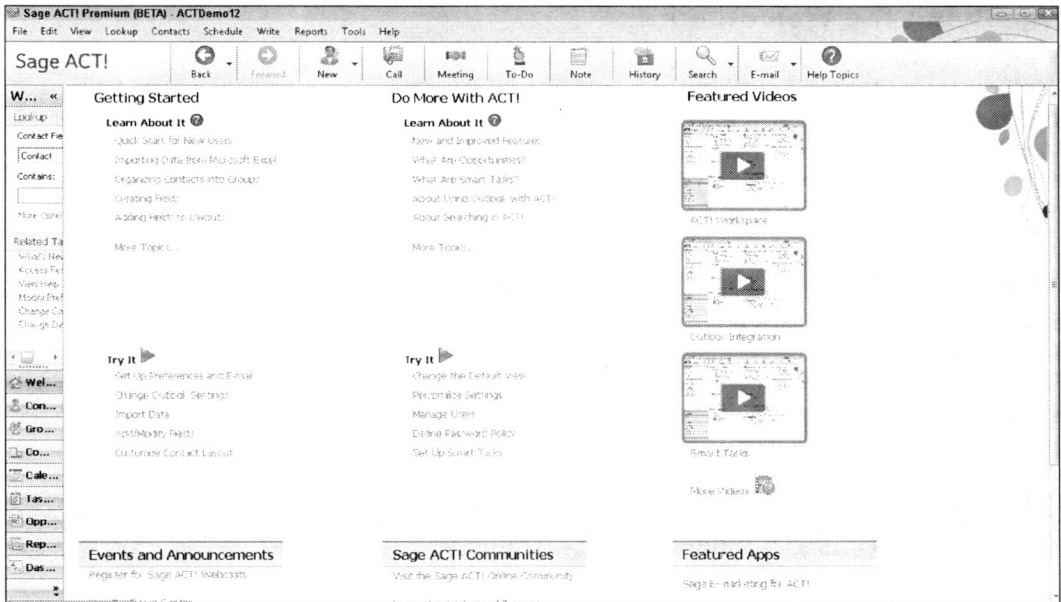

How it works...

The tasks displayed on the Welcome Page vary according to your user permissions. For example, if you are logged on as an Administrator your Welcome Page will include tasks such as **Creating Fields** and **Importing Data**. However, because you must be an ACT! Administrator to create a field, you won't see that option listed if you sign on as a standard user.

The areas labeled **Learn About It** include links to the help screens of various features. The **Try It** area links will actually take you to the feature itself. For example, clicking the **Import Data** link will open the **Import Wizard** and the **Add/Modify Fields** link will open the **Define Fields** dialog window.

In addition to the links to the help windows and feature dialog windows, the Welcome Page also includes links to Featured Videos and a variety of websites, including links to the **ACT! Online Community** and the **ACT! e-store**.

There's more...

Perhaps this section should be entitled *There's No More* because unfortunately the Welcome Page is not easily modified.

Modifying the Welcome Page

If you really want to explore the possibility of modifying the Welcome Page you'll find its contents located in the `Program Files/ACT!/ACT! for Windows/Home/XML` folder in the `Data.xml` file. Although you can make simple changes to the heading and graphics of the Welcome Page by opening the `data.xml` file in an XML editor, making changes to the links themselves requires knowledge of JavaScripting and is probably not worth the effort to edit. You may need assistance from an ACT! Certified Consultant to modify them.

Seeing changes in the Welcome Page

Because the `data.xml` file is stored outside of your database, it is associated with your ACT! installation. And, because so many of the links are attached to specific Sage websites, the Welcome Page presents a great opportunity for Sage to supply you with information. Don't be surprised, therefore, if the contents of the Welcome Page change as you apply update patches or upgrade to newer versions of ACT!

Changing the Startup view

Most ACT! users have a love/hate relationship with the Welcome Page. It seems like for every ACT! user who loves the helpful links found on the Welcome Page, there's another user who wants to simply "cut to the chase" and start using their database.

If you've outgrown the functionality of the Welcome Page, or you just want to plunge headfirst into your contact when you fire up ACT!, then there are a number of options available to you for changing the default startup option.

Getting ready

The startup options for an ACT! database are found in the Preferences. In order to get to the Preferences, you must have an ACT! database open.

How to do it...

1. From the **Tools** menu, click **Preferences**.
2. Click the **Startup** tab. You can see an example of the **Startup** tab in the following screenshot:

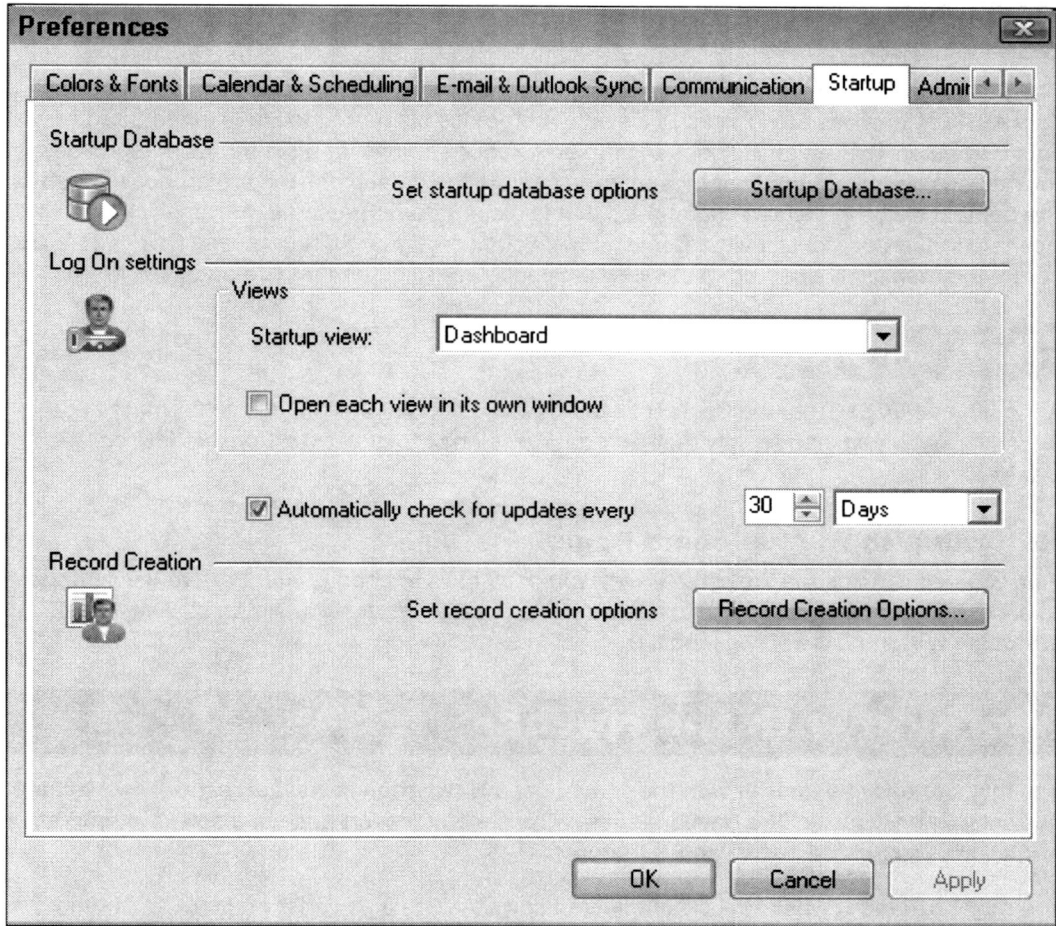

3. Select a view from the **Startup view** list in the **Log On settings** section of the **Startup** tab. Your choices include **Welcome**, **Contacts**, **Contact List**, and **Dashboard**.

4. Click **OK**.

How it works...

The Startup view preference is machine specific and not user or database specific. All of your ACT! preferences are located in a single preference file that lurks deep in the heart of your computer. This single file contains the preference settings for all of the ACT! databases located on your computer. That means if you change the default startup preference to open the Contact List, then all ACT! databases that you open from that same machine will also open up to the Contact List view. Conversely, if you access your ACT! database from a different computer, then it will open up to the view previously specified on that computer.

There's more...

Although opening ACT! to the Contact Detail view is a popular startup choice for most ACT! users, you can also specify that your database open to either the **Contact List** or **Dashboard** view.

Returning to the Welcome Page

Find yourself missing the Welcome Page? You don't have to change your Preference settings to access it. You can manoeuvre to the Welcome Page at any time by simply clicking the **Welcome** button on the Navigation bar.

Working with the Navbar

You might already be familiar with the concept of a **Navigation** or **Navbar**, especially if you are currently using Outlook. The Navbar generally runs along the left edge of a software program and allows you to access the various features.

You might use the Navbar as a placeholder of sorts. ACT! is a powerful program and offers lots of functionality. Unfortunately a new ACT! user (or even a fairly accomplished one) might occasionally get lost. For example, the Company List view can be easily confused with Contact or Group List views because they look pretty much the same. As you move from one ACT! function to the next, you'll notice that the corresponding button on the Navbar lights up. In addition, if the ACT! function offers both a **Detail** and **List** view you'll notice that the corresponding button (located near the top of the ACT! window) lights up as well.

The following figure shows you what the ACT! Navbar looks like:

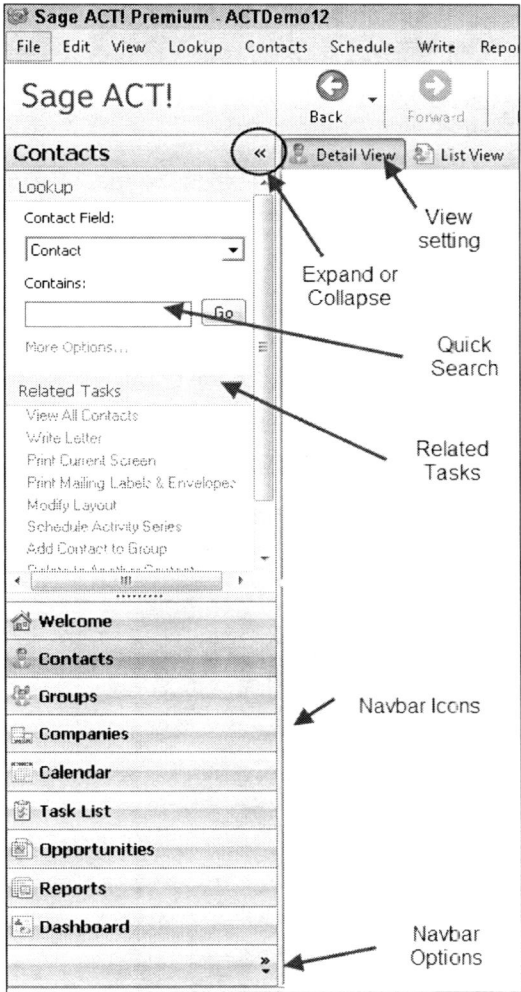

You'll notice that the Navbar actually includes several areas:

▶ Current view: lets you know whether you are currently in the Detail or List view

▶ The Navbar Lookup area: allows you to quickly access a specific record

▶ Related Tasks: offers suggestions for functionality based on the current area of ACT!

▶ Navbar buttons: allows you to quickly move to other areas of ACT!

Depending on your ACT! layout, you might feel that the Navbar is intruding on your available screen space. Some of you might not like the Navbar, or prefer to access the various parts of the ACT! program directly from the Menu Bar. If that's the case you might want to minimize the Navbar.

There are not a lot of times that we can boast that using a feature is as easy as "clicking a button" but this is one of those times.

Getting ready

Make sure that you've started ACT! and that a database is open. If you don't see the Navbar running along the left side of the screen it means that ACT! is running but you haven't as yet opened a database.

How to do it...

1. Click the collapse icon (**<<**) located at the top of the Navbar to collapse it.
2. To expand it, click the expand icon (**>>**).
3. The Navbar should look like this after you've collapsed it:

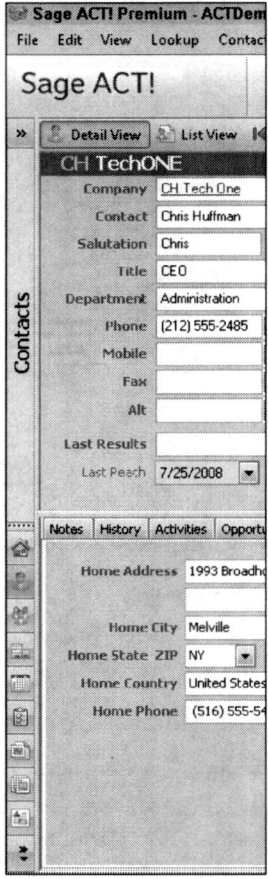

How it works...

It is not possible to totally remove the Navbar from ACT! When you collapse the Navbar you are in essence replacing the Navbar with a much thinner version. The Navbar buttons no longer show labels, just the graphic associated with each button. However, you can also resize the Navbar by dragging the Navbar's right edge to the left or right.

There's more...

Although you might find that the minimized Navbar better suits your needs there are a few things to consider.

Unfortunately, the folks at Sage must not have thought that many people would actually minimize the Navbar; no mouse-overs appear as you hover your cursor over the Navbar buttons. You're left to your own devices in terms of knowing which button is which unless you memorize the Navbar icons.

When you minimize the Navbar you also lose the ability to perform a Navbar lookup; you'll have to create your lookups using an alternative method.

Changing the Current view

A **Detail view** is a layout which has fields and tabs that you can customize. You use the **Detail view** to add and edit information about a single entity. The **Detail view** provides functionality including the ability to:

- Create new records or edit existing ones
- Link various records together
- Add notes, histories, and activities

The **List view** displays the data contained in the fields on the Detail view in columns that you can sort, move, or hide. You can even export all of your records from the List view by clicking the Excel button on the List view's icon bar. The List can display all of your records, or only those records that match your latest query.

Throughout the course of a day, you'll find yourself moving back and forth between the Detail and List views. Fortunately, you can do it with one click each way.

Getting Ready

Make sure that ACT! is open to a database and that you've already added a handful of Contacts, Groups, Companies, and Opportunities. After all, it doesn't make a lot of sense to look at an empty list!

How to do it...

1. Click the area of ACT! that you want to use from the Navbar.
2. Click the **Detail View** or the **List View** button.

How it works...

ACT! often works quietly in the background to make your life as simple as possible. A case in point is switching between the various elements and views. For example, you might look at the Opportunity List that you've filtered down to just include one specific stage. You then click the **Detail View** button so that you can view each of those opportunities in more detail. From the Detail view you click on the **Contact** tab and then click on the name of the person that is associated with the current opportunity. At that point you might be interrupted and need to quickly look up the phone number of another contact. When you're ready to return to the opportunity that you were working on, you can simply click the **Opportunities** button on the Navbar; ACT! will automatically return you to the Detail view of the last opportunity that you were working on.

There's more...

Although many ACT! users associate the List view with Contacts and Opportunities, there is also a Company List view and a Group List view. However, these views are not used as often as the Contact List view because the Company and Group Detail views already include a **tree** running along the left-hand side that displays the hierarchy in alphabetical order, like the one you see in the figure below:

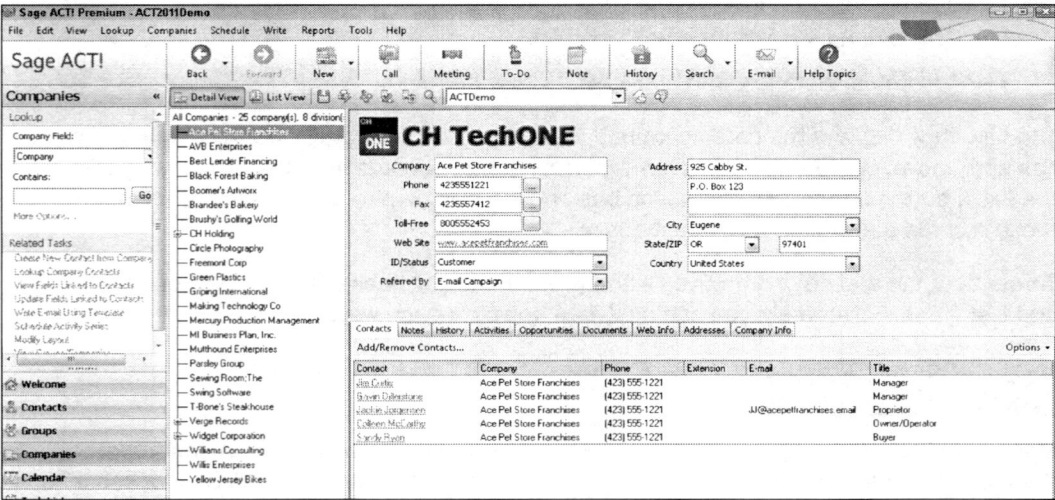

Customizing the Navbar

Most of us are quite content with the Navbar but it's always nice to be able to tweak it if the mood hits you, by either adding or removing buttons. For example, you might not use the Opportunity functionality and want to remove it from the Navbar.

Getting Ready

Make sure that you've already fired up ACT! and that you have a database open.

How to do it...

1. Click the **Configure** (double right-pointing arrows) button on the bottom right corner of the Navbar.

2. Choose **Navbar Options** from the contextual menu. The Navigation Pane Options box opens like the one you see in the following figure:

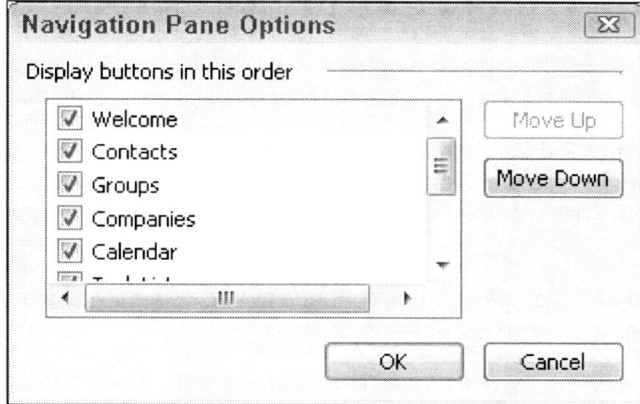

3. By default, all available options are already on the Navbar.

4. Remove the checkmark next to any item that you'd like to remove from the Navbar.

5. (Optional) To change the order of the Navbar items, select an item and then click the **Move Up** or **Move Down** button.

6. Click **OK** to save your Navbar changes.

There's more...

Once you've added or removed an item from the Navbar you might want to either increase or reduce the amount of room devoted to the Navbar buttons. You'll notice a slider (the line with several dots on it) immediately above the Navbar buttons. You can drag the slider up or down to change the area that appears on the Navbar.

You might have noticed two other options on the Navbar's Configure button: **Show Fewer Buttons** and **Add or Remove Buttons**. Unfortunately these two options lack the flexibility of the Navbar options. The **Show Fewer Buttons** option removes a single button from the icon bar, starting with the **Reports** button. Although the removed items then appear to the left of the **Configure** button, they are very small and hard to identify.

The **Add or Remove Buttons** option lists all of the Navbar buttons; supposedly the ones that you're not currently using are "dimmed". However, because it's so hard to tell exactly which icons are dimmed, you'll probably find it much easier to use the **Navbar Options** button covered earlier.

Connecting ACT! to other services

Having a variety of unrelated software programs can often lead to duplication of work. Fortunately, ACT! can connect directly to two popular email clients: Outlook and Google.

In addition, Sage Connected Services for ACT! is a portfolio of subscription-based services and productivity tools that integrate with Sage ACT! and are designed to grow your business and work more effectively. Prices for the Connected Services products vary; some come with trial periods or free levels.

Although it is likely that Sage Software will continue to add new service offerings to ACT!, as of this writing the three Connected Services products are:

 ▸ Sage Business Info Services for ACT! – connects with Hoover's to allow you to obtain more information about your existing contacts, or purchase and download a new list of prospects directly into ACT!.

 ▸ Sage E-marketing for ACT! – links ACT! to an e-mail marketing service. You can learn more about this service in *Chapter 12* of this book.

 ▸ Sage ACT! Connect – synchronizes your ACT! data with BlackBerry, Android, and Windows Mobile devices.

Getting ready

To set up and access Sage Connected Services for ACT!, you need:

▶ An Internet connection.

▶ Your Internet browser configured to accept cookies.

▶ An e-mail address in the E-mail field of your Sage ACT! My Record. The information in your My Record will be used when you set up an ACT! Connected Services account.

If you already have a Sage E-marketing for ACT! account (formerly known as Swiftpage), you can use it as your Sage Connected Services for ACT! account.

How to do it...

1. Click **Connections** on the Navbar.

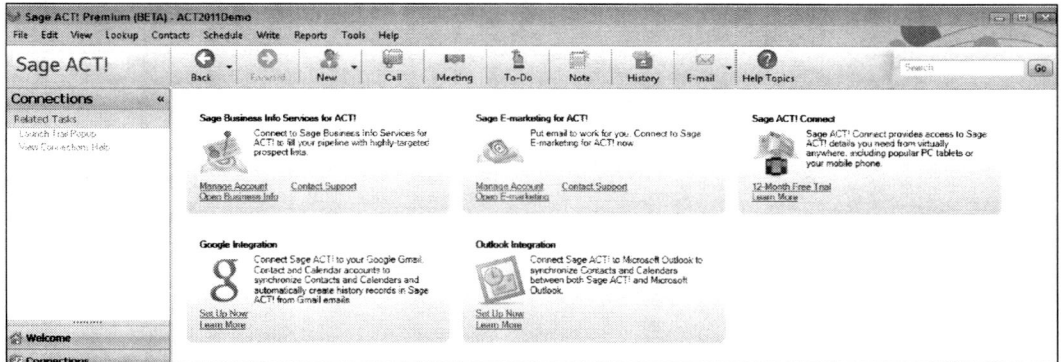

2. Click the **Sign Up Now** link to start a trial version of one of the services.

3. Follow the prompts in the Account Management dialog window to either create a new account or to sign in using your existing credentials.

4. You'll be prompted for various pieces of personal information depending on the service you are signing up for.

5. When you are finished, click **OK** to save your changes and close the Account Management dialog window.

How it works...

Once you've signed up for one service you can easily add additional services by clicking the Manage Account links that now appear next to each of the service offers. You can also use the Manage Account links to quickly increase or decrease your current level of service.

There's more...

The Connections page also includes links to Outlook and Google. You can use the **Configure Settings** links to set up your connection to either of these services. Or, if you have already completed the setup, you can click on the **Synchronize Now** links to start a manual synchronization. *Chapter 9* will give you detailed instructions on setting up the Outlook configuration, and *Chapter 10* will guide you through the Google setup.

Linking to Accounting Software

Although not listed on the Connections page, there are a number of third-party products that link ACT! to accounting software, including QuickBooks, Peachtree, and MAS. These products require that you establish the connection from the linking software itself rather than from ACT!; consequently you will not find the connection information on the Connections page.

2
Jotting Down your Notes Using Scratchpad

In this chapter, we will cover:

- ▶ Understanding the Scratchpad
- ▶ Adding an item to the Scratchpad
- ▶ Making changes to Scratchpad items
- ▶ Changing the order of Scratchpad items
- ▶ Transferring Scratchpad items to an ACT! database
- ▶ Marking a Scratchpad item as complete
- ▶ Printing the Scratchpad list

Introduction

ACT!'s **Task List** is a great way for you to access all of your tasks ncluding your scheduled Calls, Meetings, and To-Do items. However, some ACT! users don't like ACT!'s Task List because it has to be related to a specific contact record. In addit on, they find it difficult to reprioritize their various tasks.

The older versions of ACT! (those versions prior to ACT! 2005) included a standalone program called **SideACT!**. SideACT! gave users a place to quickly jot down miscellaneous thoughts and notes in the same way you routinely write them down on the scratchpad that you probably have sitting on your desk.

The Sage ACT! Scratchpad is a new addition to ACT! 2012. It provides users with a handy way to keep a list of tasks that they need to do or notes that they want to jot down. You can enter personal or work items, and you can use the Sage ACT! Scratchpad whether Sage ACT! is open or closed. You can easily reorder or edit the items that you've listed on your Scratchpad. In addition, you can easily transfer the important items on your Scratchpad into your ACT! database, and delete other items that are less important or that you no longer need.

The Sage ACT! Scratchpad installs automatically when you install ACT! 2012 and a shortcut is placed on your desktop. You can see what the shortcut icon looks like in the following figure:

There are a number of ways to open Scratchpad, including:

- ▶ Double-click the Sage ACT! Scratchpad icon on the desktop of your computer
- ▶ Click the **Start Sage ACT! Scratchpad** link in the **Try It** section of the Welcome Page
- ▶ Click the Windows Start button, point to **Programs**, choose **Sage ACT!**, and then click **Sage ACT! Scratchpad**
- ▶ Choose **Sage ACT! Scratchpad** from ACT!'s Tools menu

All of these options will result in the opening of the Scratchpad. Once opened, you can close, maximize, or minimize Scratchpad exactly as you would any other software. However, although you can drag any of the Scratchpad borders to make the Scratchpad larger, you cannot make the Scratchpad any smaller.

Adding an item to the Scratchpad

Adding items to ACT!'s Scratchpad is much less formulaic than adding an item to ACT! itself. The whole idea of the Scratchpad is to use it to jot down unstructured notes, exactly as you would on a piece of paper. Keep in mind, however, that you can convert the Scratchpad items into corresponding ACT! activities should you want to in the future.

How to do it...

1. Open the ACT! Scratchpad.
2. Place your cursor in a line of the Scratchpad and begin typing.

3. Click on another line of the Scratchpad to save your entry and start creating a new one.

The following screenshot shows you exactly what the Scratchpad looks like:

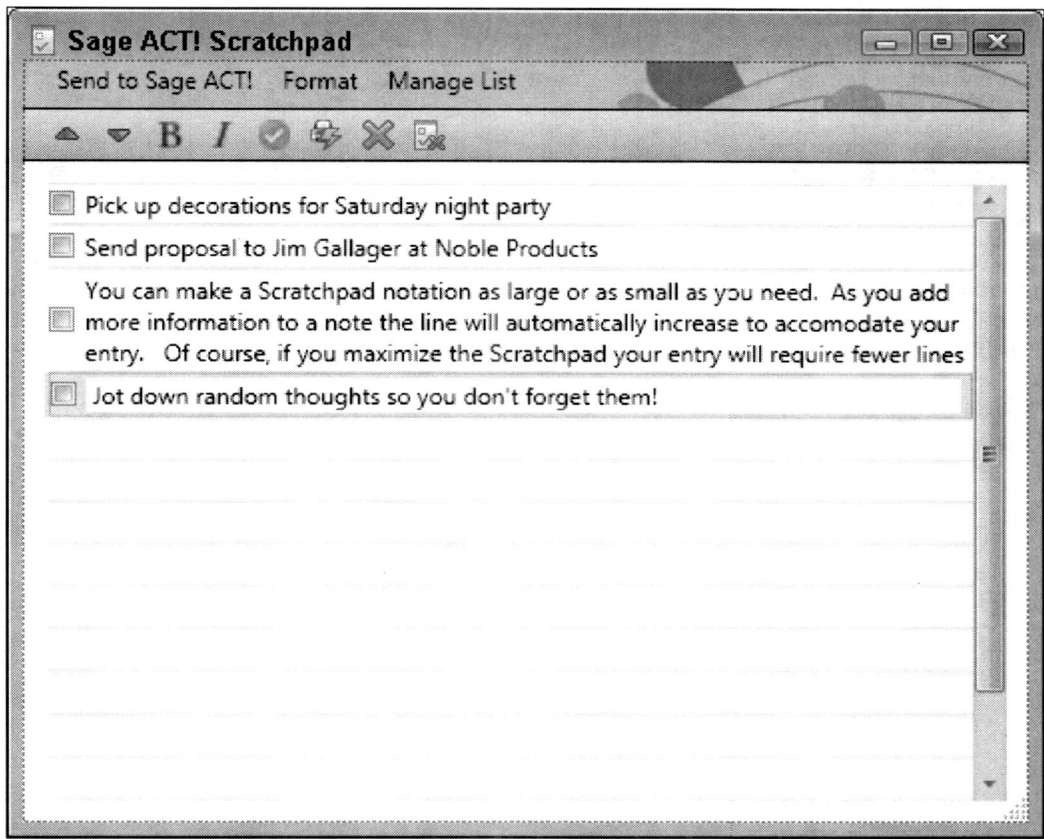

How it works...

The Scratchpad item is automatically saved as you move to another line in the Scratchpad. Alternatively, you can hit the *Enter* key to start another entry. You'll also notice that a check box appears in front of the item so that you can clear it later.

There's more...

You can make a Scratchpad notation as long or as short as you need. If your Scratchpad entry is fairly long, you might think that you need to manually drop your cursor down to the next line by hitting the *Enter* key. Fight that urge! If you run out of space at the end of a line, the cursor will automatically drop down to the next line and the Scratchpad item will expand to accommodate all of your text. And, if you maximize the Scratchpad you'll notice that the item will expand horizontally to make use of the extra space.

Making changes to Scratchpad items

If you're used to making notes using a traditional scratchpad you know that it can be difficult to read your own handwriting—particularly if you have attempted to make changes to your original note. The beauty of the Sage ACT! Scratchpad is that you can edit as often as you like and still be able to decipher the final entry.

How to do it...

1. Open the ACT! Scratchpad.
2. Place your cursor in the item you wish to modify.
3. Use the *Delete* or *Backspace* keys to remove existing text.
4. (Optional) Select the text in a Scratchpad item by using one of the following methods:
   - Double click on a word to select it
   - Hold down the *CTRL* key and hit the *A* key on your keyboard to select the entire item
   - Place your cursor at the beginning of the phrase you wish to select, hold down the *Shift* key, and tap the right pointing arrow to select a portion of the entry
5. Type in your changes.
6. (Optional) Click the **Bold** or **Italicize** icons on the Scratchpad toolbar to bold and/or italicize an entry.
7. Press *Enter* to create a new item or click on another line to save your changes.

There's more...

You edit your Scratchpad entries in much the same manner as you edit any other word processing document. However, one thing you cannot do is drag your mouse across an entry to highlight it.

Deleting a Scratchpad entry

The Scratchpad also provides you with an easy method to delete items that are completed or no longer relevant. You can remove a Scratchpad entry by selecting the item and then clicking the **Delete** button on the Scratchpad. Alternatively, you can also click the **Manage List** menu and select **Delete**. The item will immediately disappear from the list of Scratchpad items; you will not receive a warning prompt. If the item had other items below in the list, these items are moved up the list to replace the deleted entry.

[**Important note:** Deletions are permanent; unfortunately there is no way to retrieve a mistakenly deleted Scratchpad item.]

Changing the order of the Scratchpad items

When you create a task in ACT! you can sort your activities in a number of ways including by date, priority, and contact. However, when faced with a long list of tasks you might find that your priorities change as you rush to fulfil your various obligations.

One of the great features of the Scratchpad is the ability to sort your list by impulse instead of by set values. For example, if you know an item on your list is time sensitive, you can move it immediately to the top of the list.

How to do it...

1. Open the ACT! Scratchpad.
2. Place your cursor in the item in the item you wish to move.
3. Move the item to a new location by following one of these methods:
   - Drag the item to the desired location in the list.
   - Select the item and then click either the **Move Up** or **Move Down** arrows on the Scratchpad toolbar.
   - Select the item. On the **Manage List** menu, click **Move Item Up** or **Move Item Down**.

How it works...

The item will now appear in the new location. If you prefer, you can also move items further down the list to make room for new Scratchpad additions.

Transferring Scratchpad items to an ACT! database

So far we've been looking at ways that the Scratchpad can be used as a standalone product. However, some of you might still be thinking that you can get by with a traditional pad of paper or some other software product. That's probably because you haven't as yet discovered the most powerful Scratchpad feature: the ability to convert your notations into ACT! histories, notes, and activities.

Getting Started

You must have ACT! open in order to convert an item into an ACT! activity, note, or history.

How to do it...

1. Open both ACT! and the ACT! Scratchpad.

2. Select an item from the Scratchpad list.

3. Click **Send to Sage ACT!** on the Scratchpad menu; the following screenshot shows you what the menu looks like:

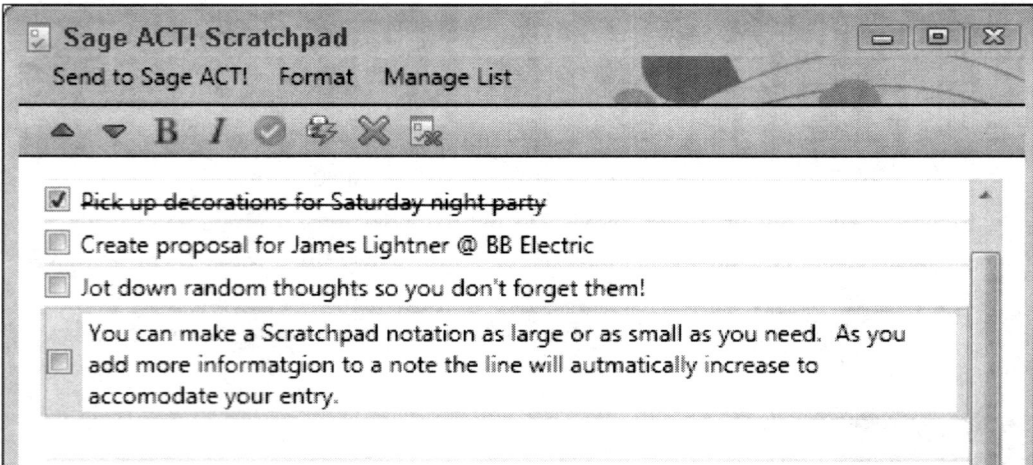

4. Choose from the following choices:

   - **Insert Note**: ACT!'s Insert Note dialog window will open with the contents of your Scratchpad entry already added to the body.

   - **Record History**: ACT!'s New History dialog window will open; the contents of your Scratchpad entry will appear in the **Regarding** field.

❑ **Schedule Activity**: this will allow you to schedule a Call, Meeting, or a To-do; the contents of your Scratchpad entry will already appear in the **Regarding** field.

5. The following figure shows an example of a To-do item that was created from a Scratchpad entry:

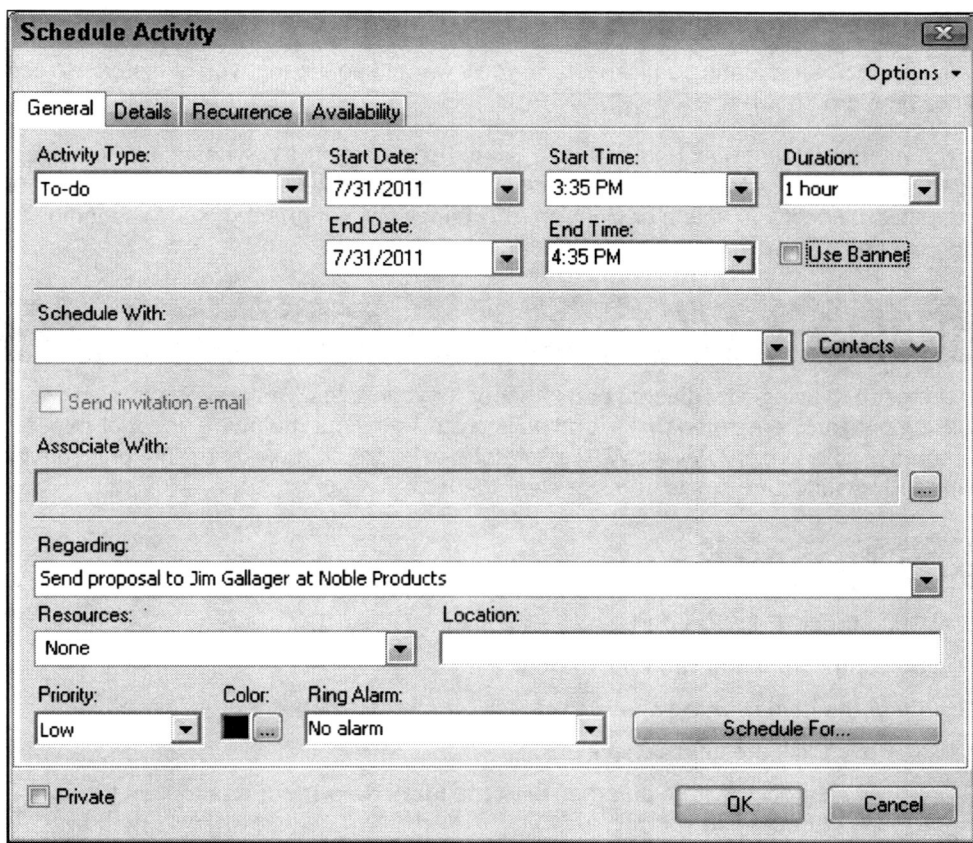

6. Complete or make changes to the remaining fields in the dialog box that appears.

7. Click **OK** to save the ACT! activity, note, or history.

How it works...

You new item will now appear in ACT!.

There's more...

Although the Scratchpad provides you with an easy method to create a new ACT! item, you will still need to verify that the dialog window is properly filled in. For example, you'll want to make sure that you select a contact for the note, history, or activity. In the **Contact** or **Schedule With** field, click the down arrow to select the contact that should get the note or history, or the scheduled activity.

In addition, if you are creating a history item, you'll want to select the type of history to record from the **Type** drop-down box.

Once you've created a new ACT! item from a Scratchpad entry, the two items are no longer linked together in any way. If you delete or clear a Scratchpad item it will still remain in your ACT! database. And if you delete or clear an ACT! item it will not affect the corresponding Scratchpad entry.

Marking a Scratchpad item as complete

If you are used to using a traditional pad of paper for your notes, you're probably also used to crossing out your completed tasks, and possibly throwing out the entire sheet of paper if its contents are no longer relevant. ACT!'s Scratchpad works on the exact same principle by allowing you to both clear single items or clear the list entirely.

How to do it...

1. Open the ACT! Scratchpad.
2. Select the item that you wish to clear.
3. Clear the item by using one of the following methods:
   - Click the item's check box.
   - Select the item and then click the **Mark Item Complete** tool on the Scratchpad toolbar.
   - Click the **Manage List** menu and choose **Mark Item Complete**.
4. (Optional) Remove the checkbox to unclear an item that you cleared by mistake.

How it works...

A checkmark appears in the item's check box and the item has a line through it to indicate it is complete. You can see what this looks like in the following image:

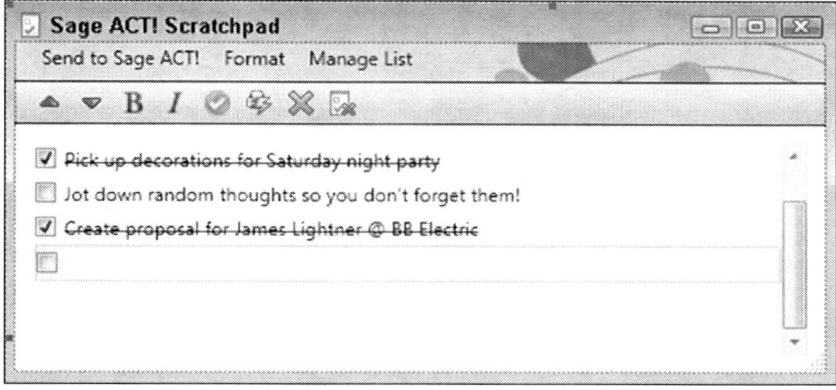

There's more...

If you wish to clear the entire contents of the Scratchpad you can do so by clicking the **Clear List** tool on the Scratchpad toolbar or by clicking the **Manage List** menu and then choosing **Clear Sage ACT! Scratchpad**.

Printing the Scratchpad list

The only problem you might have with using a computerized scratchpad is the fact that you might need to access a copy when you are away from your computer. Fortunately, it's easy to print out a copy of the ACT! Scratchpad. The Scratchpad printout actually includes faint lines similar to the ones you see in the background of the Scratchpad. They are ideally suited to making manual notes on the hard copy of your Scratchpad.

How to do it...

1. Open the ACT! Scratchpad.
2. Print the Scratchpad by using one of the following options:
   - Click the **Print** tool on the Scratchpad toolbar.
   - Click the **Manage List** menu and then select **Print**.

How it works...

The hard copy version of the Scratchpad includes all the checkmarks, formatting, and grid lines that you see on the computer version.

3
Using Queries to Find Data

In this chapter, we will cover:

- ▸ Performing a basic lookup
- ▸ Looking up by example
- ▸ Creating an Annual Event Lookup/Search
- ▸ Creating a Lookup by Contact Activity
- ▸ Creating an Advanced Query
- ▸ Searching on Keywords
- ▸ Using the Universal Search

Introduction

In ACT!, a **lookup** is a way of looking at only a portion of the contacts in your database, depending on your specifications. A good practice in ACT! is to perform a lookup first and then perform an action second. For example, you might perform a lookup and then print some labels. Or you might do a lookup and then perform a mail merge. Need a report? Do a lookup first!

The theory behind the lookup is that you don't always need to work with all your contacts at one time. Not only is working with only a portion of your database easier; at times, doing so is absolutely necessary. For example, if you were changing your mailing address, you might want to send notice to everyone in your database. Alternatively, if you're running a special sales promotion, you probably only want to contact your prospects and customers. And, if you really want to get the best results, you might send your promotion out to just those contacts in your database who have previously expressed interest in your product.

Some ACT! users think they need to create multiple databases to store information about various types of contacts; for example they might create one for customers and another for prospects. However, it's probably a better idea to include both your customers and prospects in one database. All you need to do is make sure that each contact is identified in some specific way; for example you might use the ID/Status field to differentiate between your customers and prospects. At that point you can simply perform a lookup to work with just your customers or with your prospects.

In this chapter, you'll learn how to perform lookups based on various contact information including fields, notes, histories, and activities. I will also walk you through running advanced lookups or **queries** which allow you to find contacts based on multiple criteria.

Performing a basic lookup

How to do it...

1. Click the **Lookup** menu from the Contact Detail or List view. The following screenshot shows you the menu options:

2. Choose one of the criterions listed on the **Lookup** menu to create a basic lookup. You'll notice that all the options at the top of the menu refer to contact fields, and the items on the bottom of the menu refer to Group, Company, and Opportunity fields.

3. (Optional) Click **Show more options** in the **Lookup Contacts** dialog window if the dialog window doesn't have two rows of options like the one you see in the following figure:

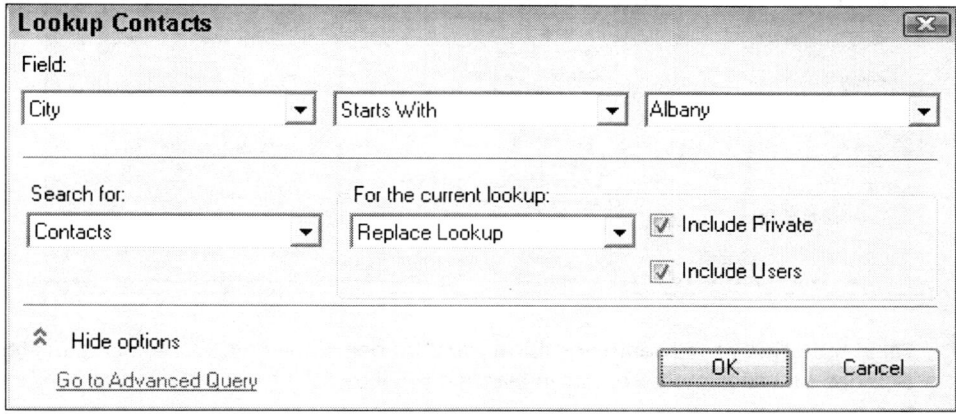

4. (Optional) Select an option from the **Search for**: drop-down box if you want to search for a Group, Company, or Opportunity field.

5. (Optional) Click the drop-down arrow and select a field if the field you're searching for does not already appear in the **Field** box.

6. Select a search operator from the second drop-down box. As you can see in the following screenshot, there are a number of options. A few of the more common ones include:

   ❑ **Starts with**: This operator will only return contacts that have the exact same value in the beginning of the given field; for example, if the Company name is "The Miami Herald" and you fill in the value as "Miami Herald", you will not come up with any matches.

   ❑ **Contains**: This operator will return contacts that contain the value searched anywhere in the given field; for example, if the Company name is "The Miami Herald" and you fill in the value as "Miami Herald", you will come up with a match.

   ❑ **Contains Data**: This operator will find only those contacts that have data in a given field; for example, you might be looking for all contacts that have an email address.

- ❑ **Does Not Contain Data**: This operator will return a list of contacts that don't have any data in the given field; for example, you might be looking for all contacts that don't have an email address.

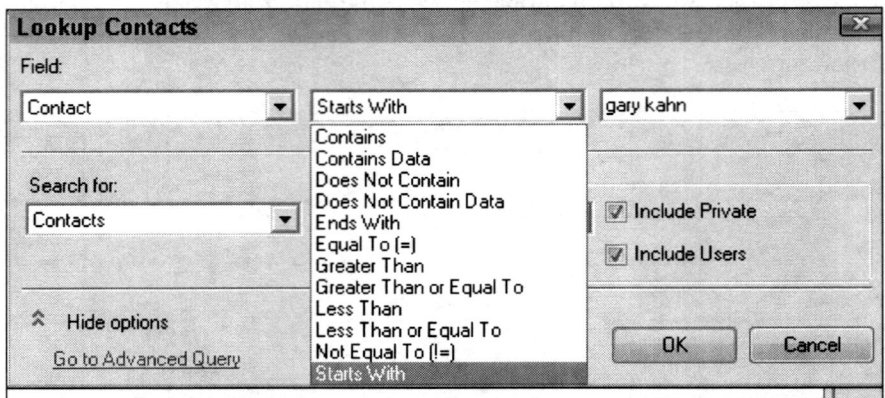

7. Fill in the value you're searching for in the third box. If the field you selected in steps 2 or 5 has an associated drop-down list then you'll be able to select from those items in this drop-down.

8. Select an option from the **For the current lookup** drop-down box:

   - ❑ **Replace Lookup**: Creates a brand-new lookup based on your criteria and overwrites the current lookup.

   - ❑ **Add to Lookup**: Adds the contacts to a current lookup based on your criteria. For example, if you create a lookup for your contacts based in Chicago, select this option to add your New York contacts to the set of Chicago contacts.

   - ❑ **Narrow Lookup**: Refines a lookup based on a second criterion. For example, if you create a lookup of all your customers, you could select this option to narrow the lookup to only those customers based in London.

9. (Optional) Check one or both of the check boxes in the **For the current lookup** area:

   - ❑ **Include Private**: Includes Private records in your search.

   - ❑ **Include Users**: Includes users of the database in your search.

   - ❑ Click **OK**.

How it works...

If only one contact record matches your search criteria, that record will display in the Contact Detail view. However, if several contact records match your criteria, the Contact List appears with a list of all your matching results. In either case, the record counter now reflects the number of contacts that match your search criteria.

By default, ACT! automatically searches by the beginning of your string unless you change the operator. You'll also want to remember that with ACT!, less typing often produces the best match. For example, typing "Tech" for the company name returns Tech Benders and Technology Consultants. However, typing "Technology" returns only Technology Consultants.

There's more...

1. If you like to right-click to access a contextual menu, you might prefer to simply right-click the field for which you want to create a lookup and then click **Lookup**. That will open up the **Lookup Contacts** dialog window with the name of the field already in the **Field** box.

2. ACT! has **view specific** menus. That means that the menus change slightly as you move around in ACT! to reflect the tasks that are most specific to that view. You'll notice, for example, that the **Lookup** menu that you access in the **Groups Detail View** varies slightly from the menu you see in the Contacts, Companies, or Opportunities Detail views.

Returning to a previous Lookup

Many ACT! users like to return to viewing all contacts once they've finished working with a lookup. To do that click the **Lookup** menu and choose **All Contacts**. However, you might find it just as easy to remain in your existing lookup until you need to search for another contact record.

Sometimes you might experience an interruption while you're working with a lookup that necessitates leaving the current lookup. For example, you might be working with a list of your best customers in Paris when one of your hot prospects calls. It's easy to return to that previous lookup by returning to the **Lookup** menu and choosing **Previous**. There you'll see a listing of your last nine lookups if you need to return to one of them.

Creating a group from the current lookup

You might think of the ACT! group as a useful bookmark that will hold your place—or at least your contacts—within your database. Once you create a lookup you might need to revisit it again at frequent intervals. Later in this chapter you'll learn how to save advanced queries but for now you might find it useful to know how to move all the contacts in your current lookup into a group.

Once you've created a lookup, simply click the **Lookup** menu, choose **Groups**, and then select **Save Lookup as a Group**. You'll be taken to the Groups Detail view where you need to assign a name to your new group. As soon as you do the Group will automatically populate with the contacts in your current group. And, best of all, the group will be a **dynamic** one, which means it is based on your query criteria and will update automatically when additional contacts meet those criteria.

Looking up by Example

If you need to base your lookup on multiple criteria, you can perform a basic lookup and then use the **Narrow** or **Add to** lookup options in the **For the Current Lookup** drop-down list in the **Lookup Contacts** dialog box to create a more specific search. This option works fine if you're willing to create several lookups until you reach the desired results. A better alternative is to create a lookup **by Example**. This simple but powerful lookup allows you to specify multiple criteria and then creates a lookup of contacts that match all of those criteria.

The Lookup by Example function allows you to create an exact profile for the contacts you're hoping to find. For example, you might want to have a look at all customers in the state of Arizona who originally found out about you through a phone book advertisement.

How to do it...

1. Click the **Lookup** menu and choose **By Example...** The **Lookup by Example** dialog window opens, which is a replication of your current layout with one big difference: all the fields are blank.

2. Click in the field that you want to query.

3. Fill in the value on which you want to search. You can see an example of the **Lookup By Example** dialog window in the following screenshot:

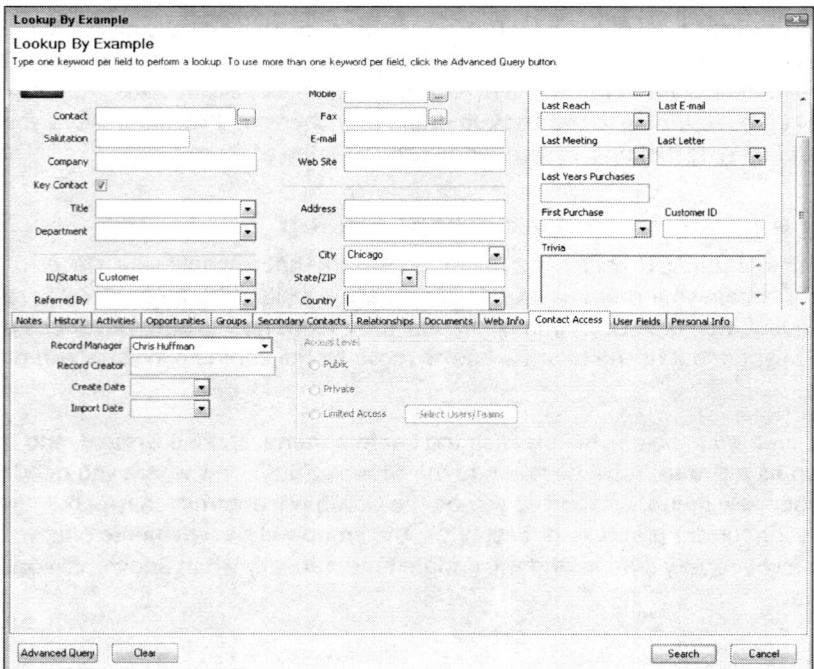

4. (Optional) Repeat step 3 as many times as you'd like.

5. Click the **Search** button when you're ready to find the matching contact records.

6. Click **OK** at the prompt asking if you'd like to Replace, Add to, or Narrow the current lookup.

How it works...

Although you can fill in as many criteria as you need, a contact must match all of the criteria to be included in the lookup results.

There's more...

You might find the **Lookup By Example** dialog window to be a bit awkward to maneuver. That's because unlike most windows the **Lookup By Example** dialog window is lacking a Maximize button. You can, however, resize the window manually by placing your mouse cursor on any of the window's edges and dragging the edge to the desired size.

You can create a query on virtually any field in your database. Don't forget to check out some of those neat fields that might be located on your various layout tabs. For example, the **Contact Info** tab contains the **Record Manager** and **Create Date** fields, which are common things to query.

Creating an Annual Event lookup/search

In ACT! there are two types of date fields: a **Date** field and an **Annual Event Date** field. A date field is year specific; for example you may need to find all contacts whose support plans expire at the end of the year 2012. An Annual Event field, however, is based on only the month; for example, you might want to find all contacts with birthdays or anniversaries in the month of January regardless of the year.

You search for a contact by date field using the basic lookup that was covered in the _Performing a basic lookup_ recipe at the beginning of this chapter. However, because searching by Annual Event means that you are searching by only part of a field, you have to use a more specific search.

Getting ready

You'll need to have created at least one Annual Event field in order to follow this recipe.

How to do it...

1. From the Contacts Detail or List views, click the **Lookup** menu and select **Annual Events...**

2. Select an annual event from the **Search for** drop-down list in the **Annual Events Search** dialog window. The following screenshot shows you an example of the **Annual Events Search** dialog window:

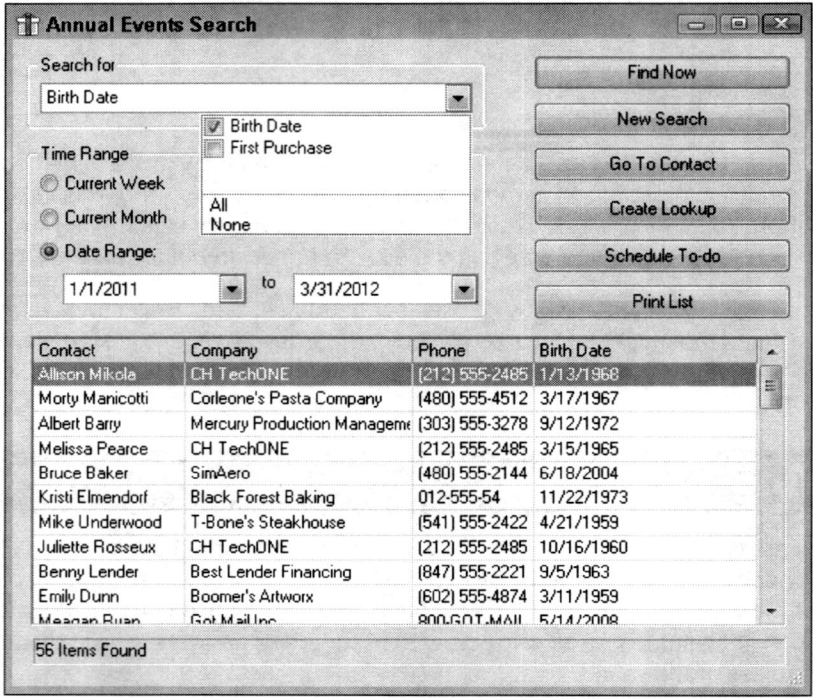

3. Choose a **Time Range** option in which you want to search.

4. Click the **Find Now** button. Your results will appear in the lower half of the **Annual Events Search** dialog box.

5. Select one of the following option buttons:

   ❑ **New Search**: This allows you to start all over again if you're not happy with the results of your search

   ❑ **Go To Contact**: Go to the contact record of the selected contact

   ❑ **Create Lookup**: Create a lookup of all the contacts

   ❑ **Schedule To-Do**: Schedule an activity for the selected contact

   ❑ **Print List**: Print a list of the contacts

How it works...

If you've added more than one annual event field to your database, you can search for more than one of them at a time by selecting each one or by selecting the **All** option in the **Search for** drop-down list. For example, you might want to find everyone who has either a birthday or an anniversary in the month of June.

Unfortunately, the **Annual Events Search** dialog window has a few limitations. You cannot select several contacts and then schedule a To-do or go to just those contacts. You can, however, create a lookup for all of the contacts in the list and then select the one you want to deal with from the Contacts List view.

Creating a lookup by Contact Activity

Research shows that 20 percent of the average database consists of long-lost contact information. That means that either many of your contacts have information that is old and outdated, or you neglected to contact those people on a timely basis.

What if you could find all the contacts that you haven't contacted in the last two years? Chances are that many of those contacts would be glad to hear from you. Maybe they lost your contact information or chose a company other than yours that they weren't happy with. Suddenly those "lost" contacts have become a virtual treasure trove. Or maybe you'd like to find those outdated contacts and either update their information or remove them entirely from your database.

You can look for the contacts that either have or have not been changed within a specified date range. You can create a lookup of contacts based on the last time that you made any changes to their record, or contacted them through a meeting, call, or To-do.

The Contact Activity lookup is extremely powerful because you can look for "touched" or "untouched" contacts. In other words, you can search for all the contacts that you contacted in a certain timeframe or for all the contacts that you haven't contacted in a certain timeframe.

How to do it...

1. From the Contacts Detail or List views click the **Lookup** menu and select **Contact Activity...**

2. Select either **Not Changed** or **Changed** in the **Look for Contacts that have:** area of the **Contact Activity** dialog window. The following screenshot shows you what the **Contact Activity** dialog window looks like:

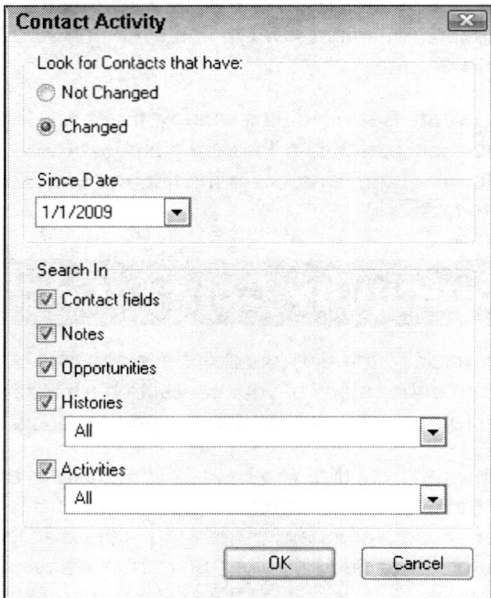

3. Select a date. The date tells ACT! to look for records that have been changed—or have not been changed—since that date.

4. Select one or more options in the **Search In** area to narrow your search. You can search in the **Contact fields**, **Notes**, **Opportunities**, **Histories**, or **Activities** areas of ACT!. If you decide to search through your History and/or Activities tabs, you can even indicate which specific types of histories or activities you want to include in your search.

5. Click **OK**.

How it works...

ACT! searches for the selected field or activity that was/was not modified within the specified date range. Because ACT! has to scour through so much data, the results of your search may take a few seconds to appear on your screen. The results of your search will appear in the Contact List.

There's more...

In order for this search to work, you have to input information in the appropriate spots. For example, you can't look for modified opportunities if you never created any in the first place, or look for histories if you don't schedule and clear activities or create histories of your various activities.

Creating a lookup using the System Date fields

If you are not happy with the results you receive in the Contact Activity lookup—or if you'd just like to find an easy alternative—you can also search on any of the system fields that update automatically as you use ACT!. These fields are easily identifiable because they're grayed out. Although you can't change the information in these fields, you can create lookups on them. For example, every time you change any of the information for a contact, ACT! automatically updates the **Edit Date** field. You can right-click the **Edit Date** field and create a lookup based solely on the contents of that field.

Creating an Advanced Query

After you use your database for a while and it slowly but surely fills up with more and more contacts, you might feel the need to add a little more power to your lookups. You also might find yourself constantly creating the same lookup and you wish to save it to use it again later. Lucky for you, ACT! has an Advanced Query option.

Many ACT! users associate the word advanced with difficult; fortunately, that's not the case here. The Advanced Query is actually a very powerful lookup that is created by following an easy to use wizard. In fact, you might even start using the term **query**, which is computer-speak for fancy lookup.

How to do it...

1. From the Contacts Detail or List views, click the **Lookup** menu and point to **Advanced** and select **Advanced Query...**You can see an example of the **Contact Criteria** dialog window that opens in the following screenshot:

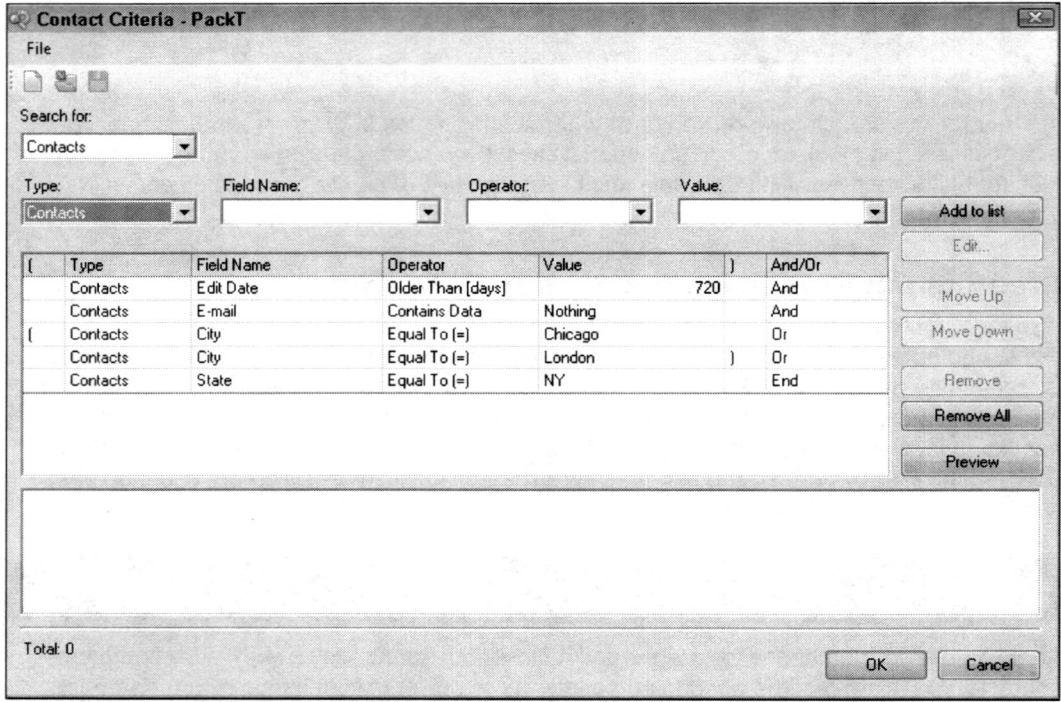

2. Select **Contacts, Companies**, **Groups**, or **Opportunities** from the **Search for** drop-down list.

3. (Optional) If you selected **Contact** in step 2, choose **Contact** or **Opportunity** from the **Type** drop-down list. You can combine **Contact** and **Opportunity** fields in the same query; however you cannot combine **Groups** or **Companies** with other database entities.

4. (Optional) If you selected **Opportunities** in step 2, choose **Opportunities** or **Opportunity Product** from the **Type** drop-down list.

5. Select one of the available fields from the **Field Name:** drop-down list.

6. Select one of the operators from the **Operator:** field.

7. Select one of the available items that corresponds to the selected **Field Name** item in the **Value** field. If the **Field** has a drop-down list, it's also available in **Value** drop-down.

8. Click the **Add to List** button. The query criteria appear in the middle part of the **Advanced Query** window.

9. To select more than one criterion, repeat steps 5 through 8.

10. (Optional) Click in the **And/Or** column at the end of a row and select **Or** if you want to indicate that only one variable is necessary in the query. For example, adding an **Or** between two city fields would indicate that the contact can reside in either city.

11. (Optional) Use the parenthesis column if necessary to group criteria together. This is a particularly important step if your query contains both "and" and "or" criteria.

12. Click **Preview** to return a list of all the contacts that match your specification and to check the query for accuracy.

13. (Optional) If the query preview did not return the expected results, modify the query using one of these options:

    ❏ **Edit**: Use this to modify a line in the query

    ❏ **Move Up/Move Down**: Use this to change the order of the lines of your query

    ❏ **Remove:** Delete a line in your query

14. Click the **File** menu, and select **Save** or **Save As** if you want to use your query later. The next time you want to run the same Advanced Query, you can return to the **File** menu, choose **Open**, and open your saved query. Contact queries have the .qry extension, group queries have the .gry extension, and company queries have the .cry extension.

15. Click **OK** when you're satisfied with the query to close the **Contact Criteria** dialog window.

16. Click **OK** at the **Run Query Options** dialog window to run the query.

How it works...

The results of the query display in the Contact List or Opportunity List.

There's more...

Although the process of opening and reusing an Advanced Query is relatively easy, you might also want to use your saved queries when you create Dynamic Groups.

If you want to really speed your way through creating an Advanced Query, you can start by entering your basic criteria into the **Lookup By Example** dialog box and then clicking the **Advanced Query** button in the lower-left corner. The dialog window that opens will contain the criteria that you had indicated in the Look By Example.

Searching on keywords

Some of us suffer from a very selective memory. For example, you might not remember a contact's name or even the name of his company, yet you remember a seemingly inconsequential detail such as the fact that his kids play soccer.

The ability to perform a simple lookup based on a single field criterion is an element common to most databases; after all, all databases contain fields. ACT!, however, provides you with the ability to create a **search on keywords**. These searches scour not only your field content but also search through your Activities, Opportunities, Histories, Notes, and Relationships looking for a match. In the above example, you could type in "soccer" and ACT! would come up with a list of contacts, all of which include soccer somewhere in their record.

How to do it...

1. From the Contacts Detail or List views click the **Lookup** menu and point to **Advanced** and select **Search on Keywords...**

2. Enter the key piece of information that you're searching for in the **Search for** area of the **Search on Keywords** dialog window. You can see an example in the following screenshot:

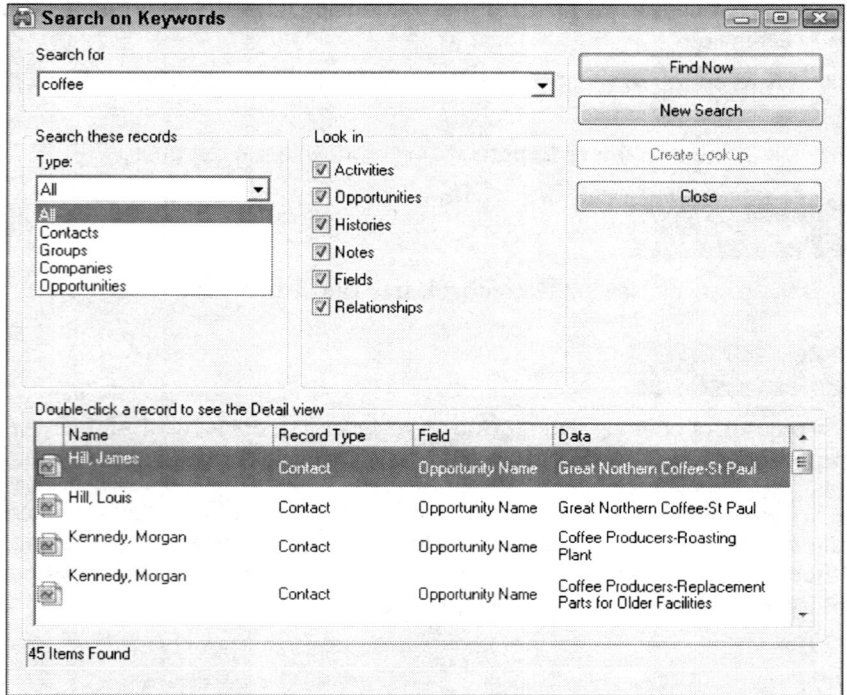

3. In the **Type** drop-down list, indicate whether you're looking for **Contact, Group, Company,** or **Opportunity** records.

4. Select all options that apply in the **Look in** area.

5. Click the **Find Now** button. The results of your search will appear in the bottom of the **Search on Keywords** dialog window.

6. (Optional) Scroll through the items to find the record you were looking for.

7. Double-click the selected record to go to that contact record.

8. Double-click the **Keyword Search** tab that now appears in the bottom-left corner of the **Contact Detail** window to return to your search.

9. Click **Close** when you are finished with the search.

How it works

ACT! responds with a list of contact records when you create a keyword search. A contact can be listed several times if the keyword appears in several places on their record. The lookup results show the contact's name, the field and record type in which ACT! finds the matching data, and the data itself.

There's more...

The keyword search is a very comprehensive searching tool, and it takes a bit longer to run than other searching methods. To speed up the process, you can limit the amount of elements to search. For example, you can limit your search to just Activities and Histories.

If you use an ACT! E-Marketing account, you've probably already noticed that a history item is created when you update the results in ACT!. These history entries contain information about whether a recipient opted out or ignored your email, or if their email address is invalid or bounces. ACT!'s **Marketing Results** tab allows you to search for these results by copying various coded information into the clipboard. At that point, you can paste the information into the **Search for** box of the **Search as Keywords** dialog window to find the results of your email.

A few commonly overlooked searches

There are several searches that an administrator of a large database may find extremely useful. These searches all pertain to databases that have multiple users and are particularly valuable if your organization limits the number of contacts that can be viewed on a user by user basis. All of these searches are accessible by going to the **Lookup** menu and choosing **Advanced**.

▶ **Users**: Creates a lookup of all the users of your database.

▸ **Contact by Access**: Creates a lookup of the contacts that can be viewed by each of your database users if you are using limited contact access. As you can see in the following screenshot, there are a number of ways to run this lookup. You might want to find all the **Public** records, or see which of the records managed by one user are accessible to another.

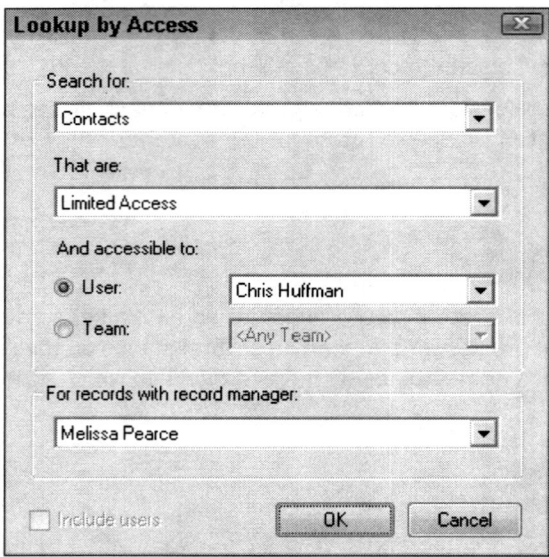

▸ **Last Synchronized**: Creates a listing of all contacts that have changed during the specified date range, including the name of the user who made the change and the changes they made.

▸ **Sync Set**: Lists the names of the contacts that are included in a sync set.

Using the universal search

With so many search options it seems like ACT! surely has all the bases covered. However, there are a few lookup limitations. Fortunately, the new ACT! 2012 universal search feature overcomes those obstacles.

The universal search differs from a traditional lookup in a number of ways:

- ▸ In addition to search through contacts, groups, companies, opportunities, notes, history, and activities, the universal search can also search your attachments.

- ▸ You can filter your search criteria by all dates, the last 24 hours, last week, or last month.

- ▸ Your results can be sorted.

- ▸ You can double-click on an item of interest to be taken to that particular linked field or attachment and then use the **Back** button to view the search results again.

- ▸ You can use special query characters to further define your search.

Let's say for example that you are looking for everyone that requested a proposal from you. You could search by keyword and have ACT! hunt through all your notes looking for the word "proposal". However, you might end up with far too many matches. By using the universal search you can sort the matching items by date, showing the most recent first. At that point, you can double-click on an item to hone in on a particular field or attachment. And, if you still haven't found what you're looking for, you can use the back button to view the search results page again or to refine your search.

How to do it...

1. Type your search term in the **Search** text box to the right of the global toolbar.

2. Click **Go** or click the *Enter* key on your keyboard.

3. (Optional) If search does not find anything, a message appears like the one in the following screenshot. Fill in a different search term, and click **Go**.

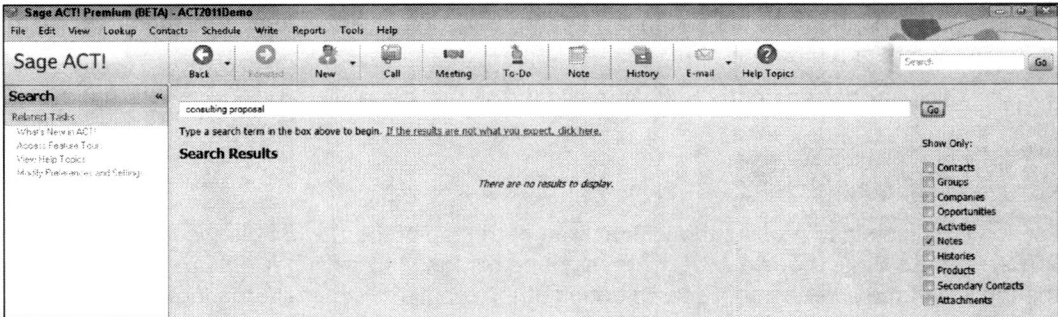

4. The universal search results appear in columns showing the record type, name, and last edited date. The following screenshot shows you a sample of a universal search results:

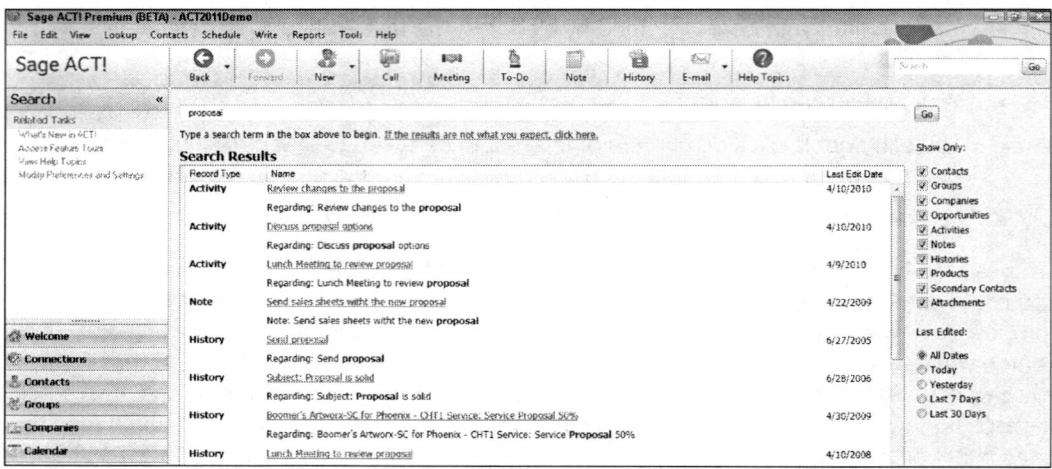

5. (Optional) If the search returned too many results you can narrow the results by removing the checkboxes in the **Show Only** area and **Last Edited** filters located to the right of the results.

6. Click an item's hyperlink to access the record.

7. (Optional) Click the **Back** button on the global toolbar if you need to return to the Search results from a contact, company, group or opportunity record, or close the Note, History, or Activity.

8. (Optional) Remove the text in the **Search** box, type in a new term, and then click **Go** to search for a different term.

9. Click any button on the Navbar to exit the search pane.

There's more...

For some unexplained reason, the lookup area at the top of the Navbar disappeared in ACT! 2012. Perhaps Sage thought ACT! users might be confused by having a lookup option on the top left of the screen and a search option at the top right. Hopefully, the lookup area will return to the Navbar in later revisions of ACT! 2012.

Using special search characters

You can use special characters and operators in your universal search. A few of the common search characters include:

- Question mark (?): Replace a single unknown character. For example, searching for "bike?" will return anything containing the word bikes.

- Asterisk (*): Replaces an unknown number of characters in your search term. For example, searching for "Tech*" will return TechONE, Tech Benders, and Technology.

- Pound (#): Searches phonetically. For example "#Brian" will return both Bryan and Brian.

4
Relating Contact Records

In this chapter, we will cover:

- ▶ Understanding Related Contacts
- ▶ Adding the Related Contacts tab
- ▶ Adding a Related Contact
- ▶ Using Related Contacts
- ▶ Adding a Secondary Contact
- ▶ Promoting a Secondary Contact

Introduction

Once upon a time—or at least during its earliest versions—ACT! was a **flat database**. Simply put, a flat database is one based on a single table. In ACT!'s case that single table was the Contact table which stored pertinent information about each of your ACT! contacts. Over the years ACT! has evolved to become more of a **relational database**. Relational databases are more powerful than flat databases because the same data can be viewed in a variety of views. The group functionality is a great example of ACT!'s relational capabilities because you can view both the contacts that belong to a group as well as the groups that a specific contact belongs to.

The **Relationships** feature arrived on the scene in ACT! version 2009. Relating one contact to another allows you to see how two or more contacts interact with one another but are not necessarily a part of the same company or contact group.

Relating contacts is a great way of cross-referencing. For example, you might be an accountant and want to track the business that is sent your way by financial planners. Or you might have trouble remembering that Client "A" is married to Client "B" because they go by different last names. In a traditional system you would have created additional fields to store this information on a contact's record. However, by using the Related Contacts feature you only need to each contact—and their pertinent information—one time to your database and then simply link the two together.

Another similar ACT! feature is the ability to add **Secondary Contacts**. A Secondary Contact is a contact that is related to the main contact but does not have its very own record. The rule of thumb is that you don't need to send mail merges to, schedule appoints with, or keep notes for a Secondary Contact.

Adding the Relationship tab

If you're a brand-new user of ACT! 2012you'll notice the Relationships tab running along the middle of the Contacts Detail View like the one you see in the figure below:

However, if you have a database that was created in a version of ACT! prior to ACT! 2009 you might find that your Relationship tab is not displayed. Not to worry, the Relationship tab is actually there but **hidden** from view. Your job is to literally **unhide** it.

How to do it...

1. Click the **Tools** menu, select **Design Layouts**, and then choose **Contact**.

2. In the **Layout Designer** click the **Edit** menu, and choose **Tabs**. If you've been following along, the **Edit Tabs** dialog box should open like the one you see in the following figure:

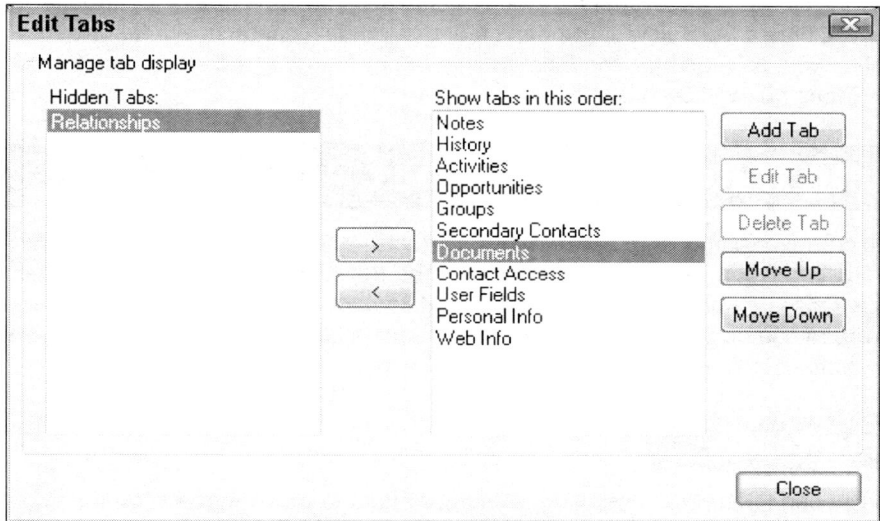

3. Select **Relationships** from the **Hidden Tabs:** area and then click the single-pointing right arrow. Relationships should now appear in the bottom position in the **Show tabs in this order:** area.

4. Optionally, you can change the tab order by selecting a tab in the **Show tabs in this order: area** and then clicking the **Move Up** button until the tab is now exactly where you want it.

5. Click **Close** to close the **Edit Tabs** dialog box.

6. Click the **File** menu and choose **Save** or **Save As** to save your changes. **Save As** is the safer option if you are using one of the "out of the box" layouts such as **Basic Contact Layout – 1024x768**, so that you'll be able to identify which layout you modified in the future.

7. Click the **File** menu and choose **Exit** to close the **Layout Designer**.

8. (Optional) Chose the name of the new layout from the Select Layout drop down box at the top of the Contact Detail view.

How it works..

Once you've modified the layout to include the Relationships tab you'll be able to start creating relationships between your various contacts. Because the Related Contacts feature links two or more contact records together you won't find the Relationship tab on the Company, Group, or Opportunity layouts.

The Relationship tab is a **system** tab, which means that you can't delete it permanently. You can, however, hide it from view. If you don't feel that relating contacts is a feature that is beneficial for you, you can hide the Relationship tab by following the steps above and clicking the left-pointing arrow in Step 3.

Adding a Related Contact

When you create a relationship between two contacts, ACT! prompts you to define the relationship. When you view a related contact in the **Relationships** tab on the **Contact Detail** screen you'll also be able to see how the two contacts are related. And, because related contacts are based on contact records you can create a Lookup for them just like you would any other contact in your database.

Getting ready

Although you can theoretically relate an existing contact to a new contact "on the fly" you might find it preferable to ensure that both contacts already exist in your ACT! database.

How to do it...

1. Click the **Relationships** tab in the **Contact Detail** screen.
2. Click **Relate Contact**. The **Relate Contact** dialog box opens like the one you see in the following figure:

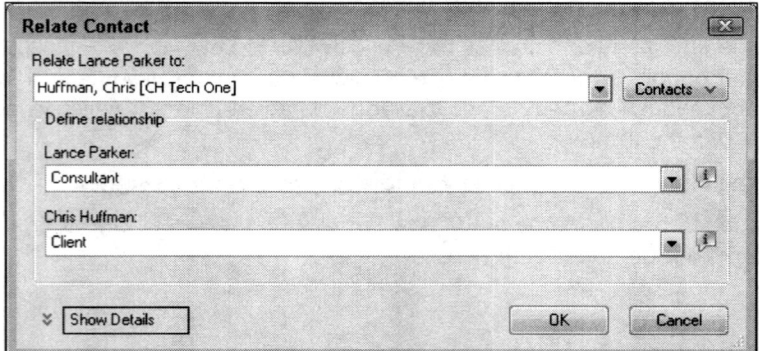

3. Start typing the last name of the person you want to relate to the existing contact in the **Relate to** field or use the Contacts button, then Select Contacts to browse for the contact if you'd prefer to pick the contact name from a list.

4. Specify the relationship of each contact in the **Define relationship** area. Optionally, click the **Show Details** button and fill in any notes that would further clarify the relationship. This information will appear in the preview pane similar to the one you see in the following figure once you've finished creating the relationship:

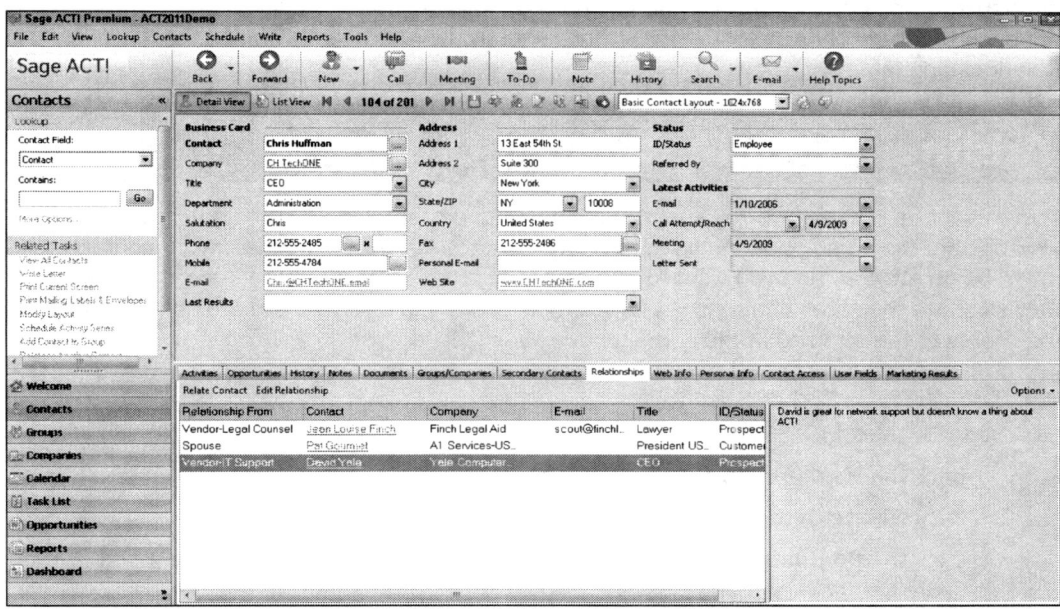

5. Click **OK** or Save.

How it works...

Any contact that you relate to a contact will appear on the Relationships tab. The Related Contact's name will appear as a hyperlink; clicking the link will immediately take you to the Related Contact's contact record and you will now see the first contact's name on the Relationships tab.

There's more...

There is no limit as to the number of Related Contacts that a contact can have. For example, an attorney in your database might be related to a dozen other contacts.

To relate a contact to additional contacts that share different relationships simply repeat the process described above. For example, you might want to relate a contact to his spouse, attorney, and accountant; each contact will appear on a separate line on the Related Contacts tab.

You have a couple of options when defining a relationship. You can select a relationship type from the drop-down list; this list is actually a duplication of the ID/Status drop-down list found on the Contact Details screen. Alternatively, you can type a relationship description if the relationship type does not exist in the list. For example, spouse or significant other might not be appropriate choices for the ID/Status field but they work really well on the Relationships tab!

Adding multiple Related Contacts

There might be times when you want to relate multiple contacts to a contact record, all of whom share the same relationship to the main contact. For example, one of your contacts might be an attorney and you want to relate several other contacts to the attorney. Because they all share the same relationship, for example client and attorney, you are able to relate all the clients to the attorney at the same time.

How to do it...

1. Click the **Relationships** tab in the **Contact Detail** screen.
2. Click **Relate Contact**. The **Relate Contact** dialog box opens.
3. Click the **Contacts** button. The **Select Contacts** dialog box that you see in the figure below:

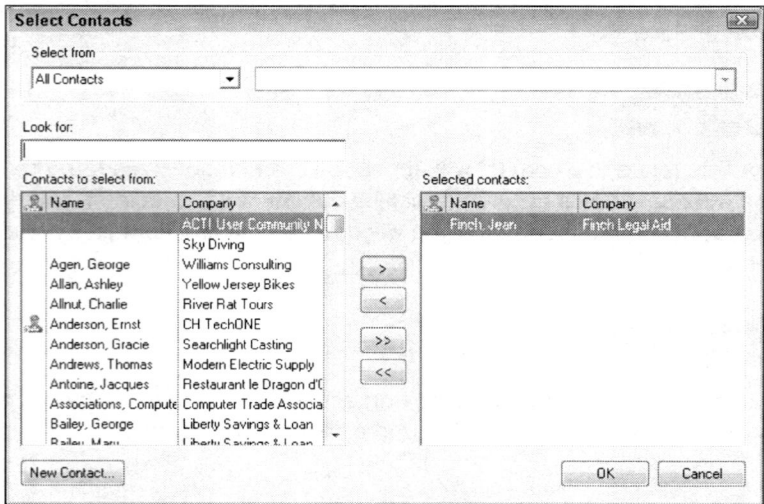

4. Select one or more contacts from Select Contacts dialog box by either scrolling through the **Contacts to select from:** area on the left or typing in the first few letters of the contact's last name in the **Look for:** field.

5. Click the right-pointing arrow to add the selected contact(s) to the **Selected contacts:** area.

6. Click **OK** to close the **Select Contacts** dialog box.

7. Specify the relationship of each contact in the **Define relationship** area.

8. Click **OK** or Save.

Changing a relationship

Once you have created a relationship it's only logical that eventually you might need to make some changes to it. You can easily modify a relationship, or get rid of it entirely.

How to do it...

1. Navigate to one of the contacts involved in the relationship and click the **Relationships** tab.

2. Right-click on the relationship you wish to modify.

3. Choose **Remove Relationship** from the contextual menu.

4. Click **Yes** in the warning dialog box to confirm that you'd like to end the relationship.

How it works...

Removing a relationship does not in any way affect the contact records themselves. Once you remove the relationship the contact records remain unchanged.

There's more...

Alternatively, you might choose the **Edit Relationship...** option from the contextual menu. This option will allow you to make changes to the existing relationship including adding more contacts to the relationship or changing the relationship definitions. Note, however, if you do add additional contacts to the relationship they will appear as separate line items on the Relationship tab.

Creating a Secondary Contact

Secondary Contacts are individuals, such as an assistant or secretary, who usually work for the main contact. Each contact's Detail view has a Secondary Contacts tab where you can access the information for all of a contact's Secondary Contacts.

Because Secondary Contacts do not have their own records, you cannot send them templated letters or e-mail messages, schedule an appointment with them, add a note to their record, or make them members of groups or companies.

How to do it...

1. Click the **Secondary Contacts** tab in the Contact Detail view.

2. Click the **New Secondary Contacts** button like the one you see in the following figure:

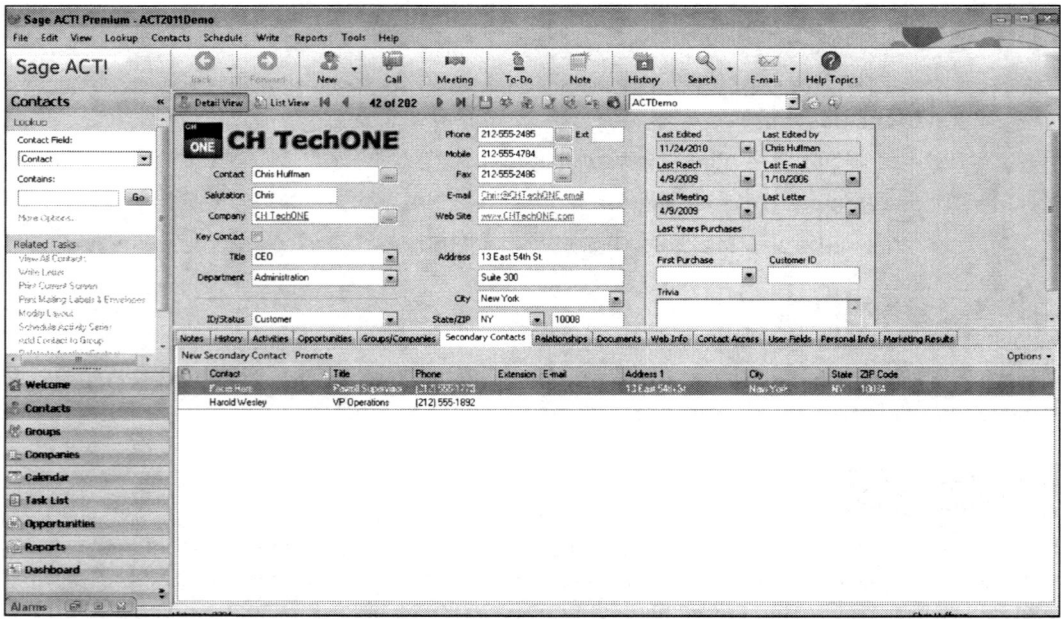

2. Fill the contact information into the New Secondary Contact dialog box. The following figure shows you what this looks like:

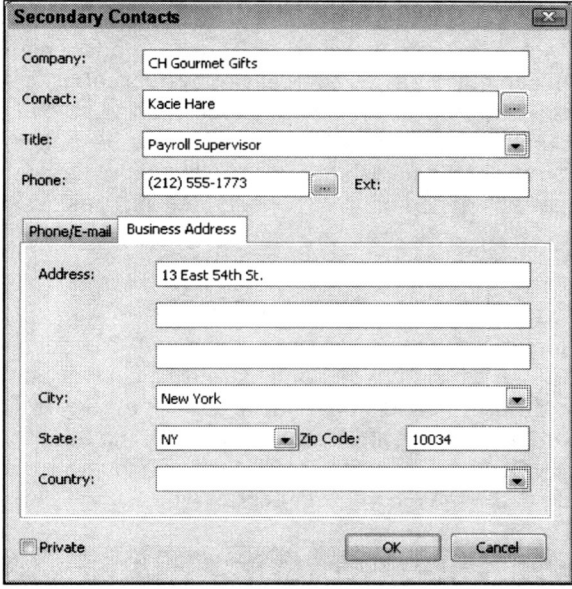

3. (Optional) Click the **Business Address tab** to fill in address information.

4. (Optional) Place a checkmark in the **Private** checkbox to make the secondary private if you don't want other ACT! users to view the Secondary Contact information.

5. Click **OK** to save the Secondary Contact record.

How it works...

The Secondary Contact will now appear on the Secondary Contacts tab. And, should the need arise to add additional Secondary Contacts, you can repeat the process and add as many as you need.

There's more...

If you need to change the information for a Secondary Contact you can simply double-click the Secondary Contact record to open it back up and make as many changes as you need. In addition, you can right-click on the Secondary Contacts tab and choose **Customize Columns...** from the contextual menu to change the columns that display on the Secondary Contacts tab.

Adding a Secondary Contact by duplicating an existing one

Adding Secondary Contacts is a snap. However, if you need to add a number of similar Secondary Contacts you can make the job even easier by duplicating an existing Secondary Contact. Select the secondary contact whose information you want to duplicate, give it a right-click, and then select Duplicate Secondary Contact. When the Secondary Contacts dialog box opens you'll notice that most of the fields are already filled in. Add the full name in the Contact field, make other changes as needed on the Phone/E-mail and Business Address tabs, click OK and you're done.

Creating a Lookup of Secondary Contacts

Occasionally, you may forget which main contact a Secondary Contact belongs to. For example, you may receive an email from an administrative assistant and need to update the main contact's record. You can find a Secondary Contact quickly by going to the **Lookup** menu and choose **Other Fields** where you'll notice that all of the Secondary Contact fields are listed. Choose Secondary Contact, fill in the name of the administrative assistant and you'll be immediately transported to the main contact's record.

Promoting a Secondary Contact

At some point, you may find that you need to start tracking interactions with a Secondary Contact. For example, you might need to add notes or schedule an appointment with the Secondary Contact. Or, the Secondary Contact may have received a promotion in his own company making him a more important contact in terms of your ACT! database.

You can promote a Secondary Contact to a Primary Contact. Once promoted, the secondary contact has its own contact record and is removed from the Secondary Contacts tab for the contact.

How to do it...

1. Navigate to the contact record and click the **Secondary Contacts** tab.
2. Right-click on the Secondary Contact you wish to promote.
3. Choose **Promote Secondary Contact...** from the contextual menu.
4. Click **Yes** to the warning dialog box to confirm that you'd like to promote the contact.

How it works...

Once promoted, the secondary contact has its own contact record and is removed from the Secondary Contacts tab for the contact.

There's more...

Over time you may no longer have a need for a Secondary Contact. To remove one simply give it a right-click and choose the **Delete Secondary Contact...** option from the contextual menu.

5
Integrating Contact Information with Websites

In this chapter, we will cover:

- ▶ Understanding the Web Info tab
- ▶ Editing an existing Web link
- ▶ Creating a new web link
- ▶ Deleting a web link
- ▶ Creating an Internet link
- ▶ Adding a website link to the history tab

Introduction

You probably open up both ACT! and your web browser first thing every morning. You're probably also used to maneuvering back and forth between the two programs. And, there are probably times when you are actually conducting a bit of research about one of your ACT! contacts using your web browser.

The Web Info tab is an internal browser that lets you display web page information on the lower portion of the Contact and Company Detail views. The cool thing about the browser is that it displays information specific to the Contact or Company record that you are currently viewing.

ACT! comes with several links to popular websites such as Google Driving Directions, LinkedIn, and Yahoo search. When you click on one of the web links the Web page displays information based on data in the various fields on a contact or company record. For example, if you select Google Driving Directions from a contact's Web Info tab, the browser opens and displays the directions from the location you use on your "My Record" to that of your contact.

You can customize what displays in the Web Info tab by adding, editing, or removing links. You can also open an external browser, copy a link to paste it into another record, and increase/ decrease the size of the tab to allow better viewing of maps and information.

In addition, you can also attach a website address to a contact or company's history. You can even add a list of your favorite sites directly to ACT!'s View menu to make it easy to get to your favorite websites without having to leave the comfort of your ACT! home.

Understanding the Web Info tab

You'll find the Web Info tab in the tabs area that runs across the Contact or Company Detail view. The Web Info tab is actually a web browser. What makes the browser unique is that rather than typing in a URL address and then filling in a web form to find information, you can simply click on one of the web links and the corresponding information from the contact record will display.

Getting ready

You'll want to start with a completed Contact or Company record, including a website address and pertinent contact information.

How to do it...

1. Click the **Web Info** tab from a Contact Detail or Company Detail record. The following figure shows you an example of the Web Info tab:

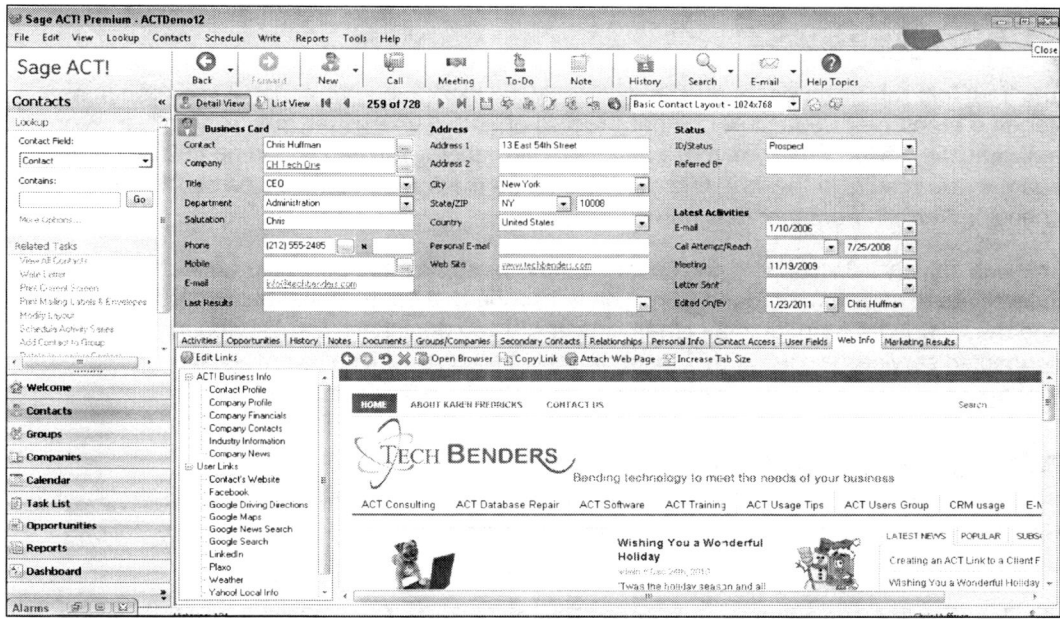

2. Select a link from the list on the left-hand side of the Web Info tab.

3. The internal browser opens and displays a web page for the selected site.

4. Navigate through the Web Info tab by using any of the following options:

   ❑ Back or Forward buttons: takes you to the previous web page

   ❑ Refresh: reloads the contents of the current page

   ❑ Stop: stops a page from loading

   ❑ Open Browser opens the web page in Internet Explorer

   ❑ Copy Link copies the Web address to the windows clipboard so you can paste it to another location

   ❑ Attach Web Page: copies the current web address into the record's history tab

   ❑ Increase Tab Size: expands the internal browser to cover the contact or company portion of the screen

How it works...

The information from the contact or company's record will automatically pour into the web form and the corresponding web page will appear before your eyes.

There's more...

The Web Info tab might not immediately display the expected information if you have just added a brand new Contact or Company record or edited an existing one. Normally a record is automatically saved when you move on to another record. You can speed up this process—and see the new results in the Web Info tab—by clicking the **Save Changes** icon on the toolbar or choosing Refresh from the **View** menu.

The web links are divided into two sections: **ACT! Business Info** and **User Links**. The Business links relate to information found when you subscribe to a Sage-connected services account and the User links connect to all other websites. If you don't have a subscription to the connected services you'll find that most of the links won't work so you might want to close up that area by clicking the minus sign that appears to the left of the section.

Adding the Web Info tab

If the Web Info tab does not appear in the middle of the Contact or Company Detail view you will need to add the tab to the Contact and/or Company layout. You can do that by following these steps:

1. Click the **Tools** menu, and choose **Design Layouts**. Open a layout and then select **Contact** or **Company**.

2. Click the Layout Designer's **Edit** menu and choose **Tabs**.

3. Select Web Info from the Hidden Tabs area of the Edit Tabs dialog window and then click the single right-pointing arrow to move it to the Show tabs in this order area. The following figure shows you what the Edit Tabs dialog window looks like:

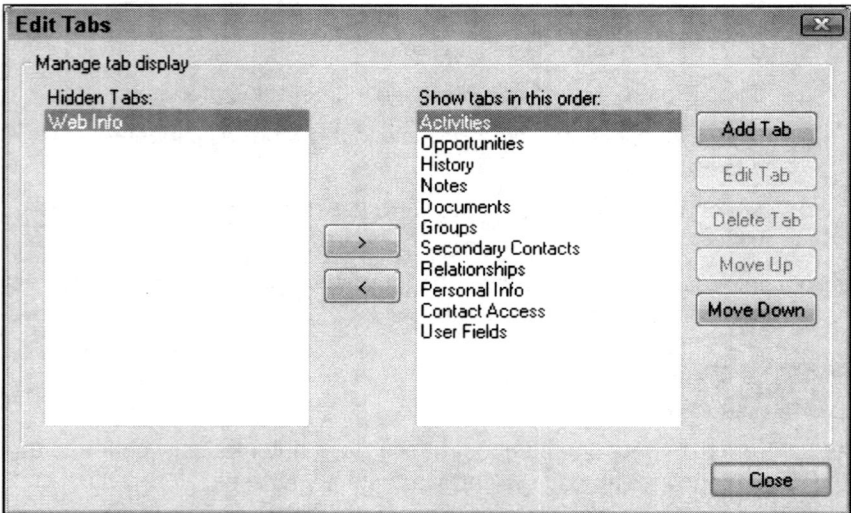

4. The tab appears in the last position of the **Show tabs in this order** list. Change the order of the tab by selecting it and clicking the **Move Up** button as needed.

5. Click **Close** to close the **Edit Tabs** dialog window.

6. Click **File**, choose **Exit**, and then click **Yes** when prompted to close the Layout Designer and save your changes.

Manually resizing the internal browser

Although clicking the Increase Tab Size icon is an easy way to increase the size of ACT!'s internal browser, there might be times when you want to increase the size of the browser and still be able to view the contents of the current record. You can do that by hovering your mouse on the line directly above the tab names and dragging it to the desired location.

Editing an existing web link

There's a very good chance that you will be content with using the web links that come with ACT!. However, it's easy to tweak the existing links a bit should you decide that you'd like to modify them. There are two areas that you can change:

▶   The link name

▶   The ACT! field that links to the website

Getting ready

Prior to changing an existing link it's a good idea to first familiarize yourself with them so that you aren't wasting your efforts by creating a new link that serves the same purpose as an existing one. As an example, the Google Search link searches for information based on the name that appears in the contact field. You might decide that you'd prefer to search Google based on the contents of the company field. In that case you might find that the Google News Search, which searches based on the company field, does the job nicely. However, if you would prefer to change the criterion used for the Google Search you can do that as well.

How to do it...

1. Click the **Web Info** tab from a Contact Detail or Company Detail view.

2. Click **Edit Links**.

3. Select a website to edit in the Edit User Links dialog box that appears.

4. Click **Advanced Edit**. The Advanced Edit dialog window opens like the one you see in the following figure:

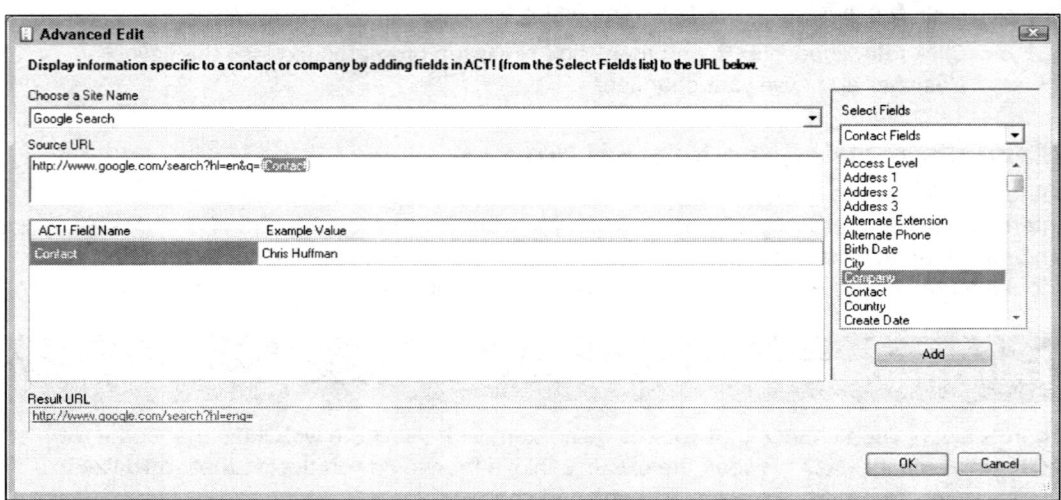

5. Type in a different **Site Name** if you'd like to change the existing one (optional).

6. Highlight the name of the field you wish to change as well as the surrounding brackets in the Source URL area.

7. Select the new field from the Select Fields area.

8. Click the **Add** button to replace the existing field name with the new one.

9. Click OK to close the Advanced Edit dialog window.

10. Click **OK** again to close the **Edit User Links** dialog window.

How it works...

The newly edited web link will now pull its information from the field you selected.

Creating a new web link

New websites are emerging on almost a daily basis and you might want to add some of your favorites to the Web Info tab. Alternatively, you might want to add a website that is specific to your business. Of course you can always go to your Internet browser and access the site manually. However, if the site is content driven and requires that you fill in a few pieces of additional information you might find that creating a new web link will be a real time saver. For example, you might need to track stock quotes for the businesses you work with; you can add a stock tracking site and associate it with the existing ACT! Ticker field. Many real estate agents create ACT! fields for listing numbers and associate those fields with real estate sites. And, when a new social networking site arrives on the scene you can use it to create a new ACT! web link.

Getting ready

The only thing you need to get ready for this recipe is a good, informational website.

How to do it...

1. Pull up the site in your Internet browser that you'd like to use as the basis for a new ACT! web link and create a search. The following figure shows you an example of a Yahoo search:

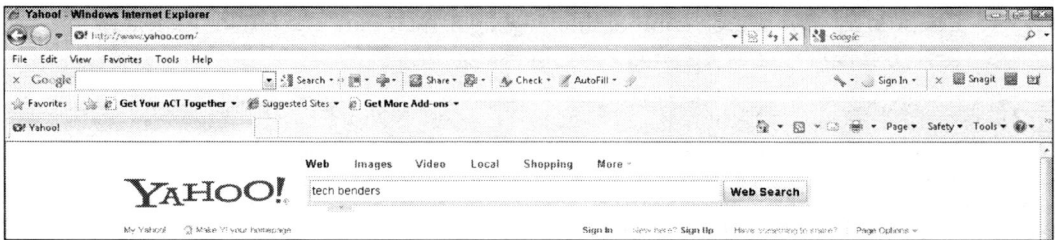

2. Run the search and right-click on the resulting URL from the address bar of your browser to copy it into the Windows clipboard.

3. In ACT! click the Web Info tab from a Contact or Company view.

4. Click the **Edit Links** icon.

5. Click **Add** in the Edit User Links dialog window. A new blank line will appear at the bottom of the list of existing web links.

6. In the **Site Name** box, type a descriptive name for the new web link.

7. In the **URL** box, paste in the address that you copied in step 2 above. You can see an example in the following figure:

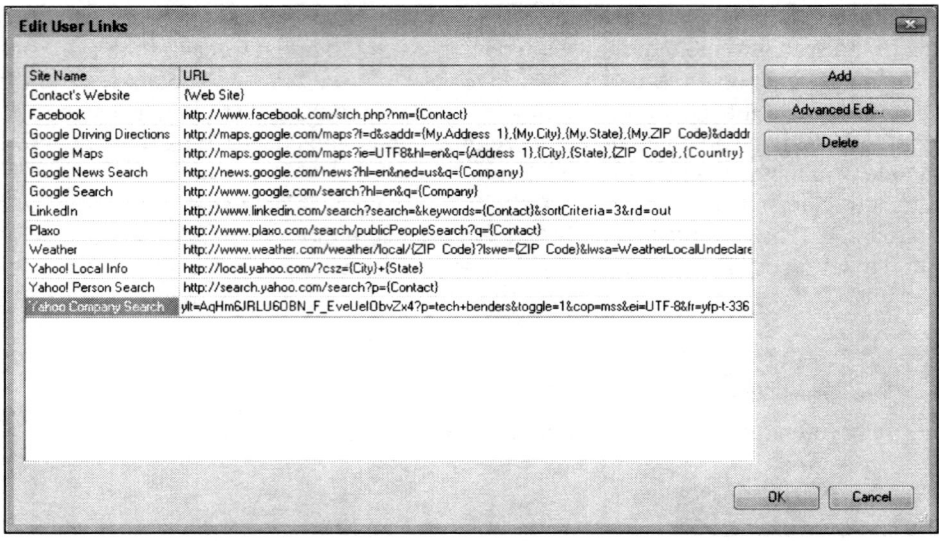

8. Click the **Advanced Edit** button.

9. Select the search criteria you had filled into the web form in step 1 above in the **Source URL** area of the Advanced Edit dialog box. For example, if you entered Tech Benders as your search criteria, then highlight Tech Benders within the text of the URL. The following figure shows you an example:

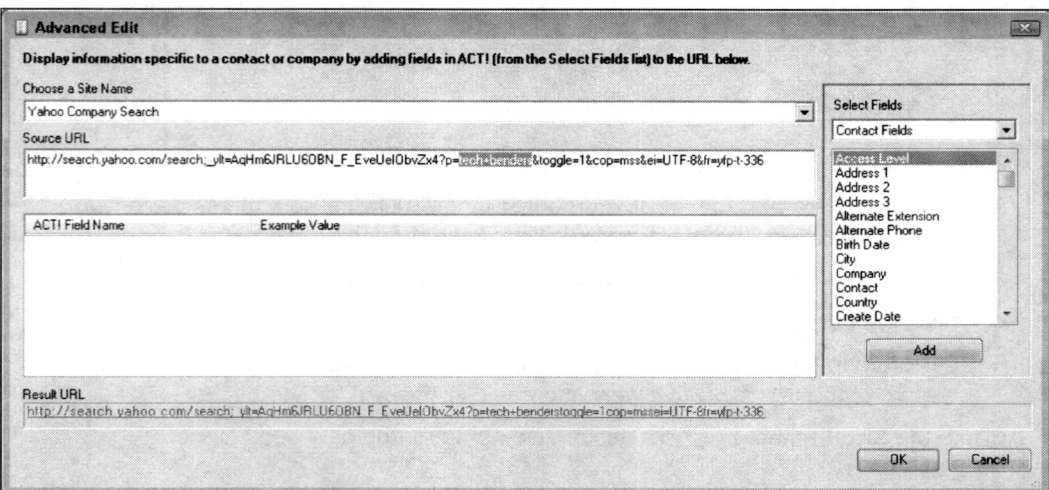

10. Under Select Field, select the ACT! field that matches the search criteria and click **Add**. Your search criteria will be replaced by the ACT! field you selected.

11. Click **OK** to close the **Advanced Edit** dialog window.

12. Click **OK** again to close the **Edit User Links** dialog window.

How it works...

Your newly created web link will now appear alphabetically in the list of web links.

There's more...

You can create as many web links as you need. However, you'll want to make sure that the websites you choose allow you to pass information into them. A good way to tell is to look in the URL for a page resulting from a search—if it contains your criteria, it will most likely work, but if not, then that page will not work.

Deleting a web link

It stands to reason that if you can add new web links to ACT! you can also remove the ones that you don't use. For example, if you work at a company that doesn't allow their employees to access social networking sites then you'll probably want to remove the links to Facebook, LinkedIn, and Plaxo.

Getting ready

Before you delete a web link you'll want to make sure that you are certain as to what each web link does. Try using each web link on a number of contact records so that you are familiar with the result of each link.

How to do it...

1. Click the **Web Info** tab on the Contact Detail or Company Detail view.

2. Click the **Edit Links** button.

3. Select the item you want to remove in the Edit User Links dialog window.

4. Click the **Delete** button.

5. Answer **Yes** to the prompt asking you if you want to delete the selected item.

6. Click **OK** to close the Edit User Links dialog window.

How it works...

The web link will no longer appear in the list of links on the **Web Info** tab.

Creating an Internet link

Previously, in this chapter, you learned how to create a web link in ACT! that pulls content from an existing contact or company record and places it into a website. However, there are lots of other websites that you might access on a regular basis that aren't necessarily associated with data. Of course, you can always create bookmarks for these sites in your Internet browser but you might like the idea of pulling them up directly from ACT!.

Getting ready

You'll need to have the URL address of the site you'd like to bookmark in ACT!.

How to do it...

1. Click the **View** menu, point to **ACT! Links**, and then click **Manage Links**. The Manage Internet Links dialog window opens similar to the following figure:

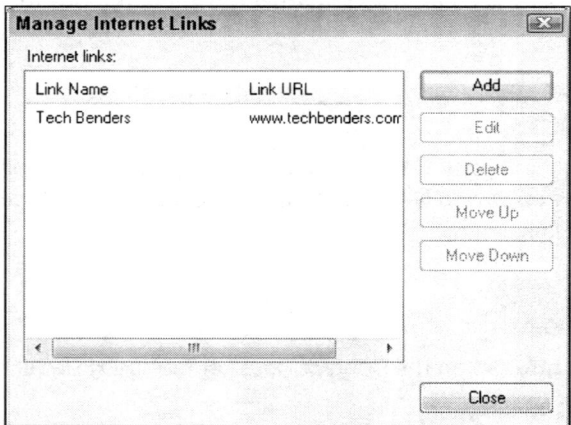

2. Click **Add**.

3. In the Add Internet Link dialog window fill in the name you'd like to assign to the web address and then fill in the website's URL. The following figure shows you an example of the Add Internet Link dialog box:

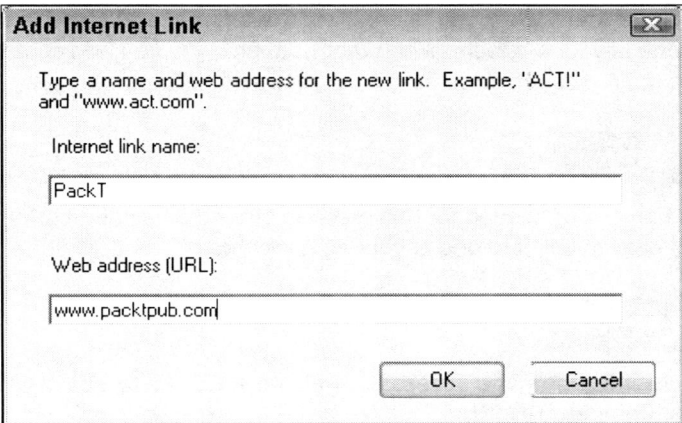

4. Click **OK** to close the Add Internet Link dialog window.
5. Click **OK** to close the Manage Internet Links dialog window.

How it works...

When you click the name of the website from the ACT! Links section of the View menu the website will open in Internet Explorer.

There's more...

Over a period of time you might want to perform a bit of housekeeping on the websites you've stored in ACT!. This can be done quite easily by clicking the View menu, pointing to ACT! Links and returning to the Manage Internet Links dialog window. Once there, select the website you'd like to change and choose one of the following options:

▶   Edit: allows you to change the link's name or the associated URL

▶   Delete: allows you to remove a website from the View menu

▶   Move Up or Move Down: changes the order of the links

Adding a website link to the History tab

So far in this chapter you've learned how to connect to the outside world from within ACT!. However, there may be times when you're browsing the Internet and stumble upon a site that has relevance to one of your contacts. When that happens, you can add content back to a contact, company, or group's record directly from your external web browser.

Getting ready

There's not much homework needed for this exercise other than remembering that if you find a relevant site, it's easy to link it to one of your ACT! records.

How to do it...

1. Open Internet Explorer and access the website you'd like to attach back to an ACT! Contact or Company record.

2. From Internet Explorer's Tools menu, click **Attach Web page to ACT! contact...** The Attach Web page to the Following Contacts dialog window appears that looks like the following figure:

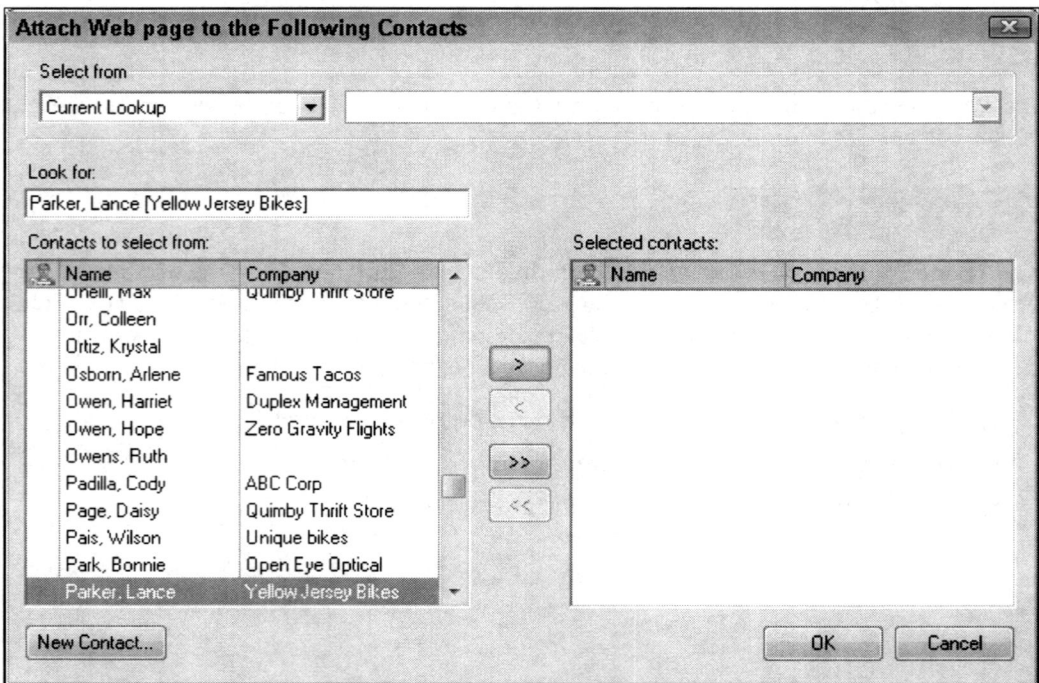

3. Choose an option from the **Select from** drop-down box to indicate whether you want to attach the website to a Contact, Company, or Group record.

4. Fill in the first several letter of the Contact's last name in the Look for: box.

5. Click the single right-pointing arrow to move the selected name to the **Selected contacts:** pane.

6. Click OK to close the dialog window and save a link on the record's history tab.

How it works...

A link to the web page now appears on the History tab. You can open the web page by clicking the link in the History tab's preview pane.

There's more...

If you are attaching the website to a Company or Group record you'll be able to select from your existing companies or groups by making a selection from the drop-down box to the right of the Select from drop-down box.

6
Grouping your Contacts

In this chapter, we will cover:

- ► Creating a Group
- ► Adding static members to a Group
- ► Removing a static member from a Group
- ► Adding dynamic members to a Group
- ► Creating a Group from a Lookup
- ► Using the Groups tab
- ► Working with the Group Detail view

Introduction

According to Webster's dictionary, a **Group** is "a number of individuals assembled together or having some unifying relationship." That definition is a fairly accurate description of an ACT! Group as well, although the "individuals" are your existing contact records. Another way to think of an ACT! Group is as a semi-permanent Lookup.

Group records work in much the same way as Contact records. The Contact Detail view helps you to keep track of all activities as they relate to an individual; the Group Detail record allows you to track activities as they relate to an entire Group of contacts. When used correctly, ACT! Groups provide you with the potential to increase the overall power and efficiency of the ACT! program. When used incorrectly they can consume your time without offering any real benefits.

All Groups share a few common elements:

- ▸ **Groups are volatile:** In general, Groups and the Contacts within them don't have to be permanent. You can change the Contacts in a Group and you can remove old Groups when they are no longer useful. Removing a Contact from a Group doesn't in turn remove the Contact from the database; alternatively, deleting a Group does not remove any Contacts from the database.

- ▸ **There is no limit to the number of Groups that you can create:** You're allowed to create as many Groups as you want; your only limitation is self-imposed.

- ▸ **There is no limit to the number of Contacts a Group can contain:** Add as many contacts to a Group as you want.

- ▸ **There is no limit to the number of Groups a Contact can belong to:** Depending on the type of Groups that you set up, you might find that a Contact belongs to more than one Group. For example, if you use Groups to help with project management, the same subcontractor might appear in several Groups.

- ▸ **Relational cross-referencing:** By creating a Group, you can easily move between the Group as a whole and the individual members within the Group. From the Group Detail window, you can see a list of all the contacts that belong to that Group; from the Contact Detail window, you can see all the Groups that a contact belongs to.

- ▸ **You can create 15 levels of subGroups:** For example, you might create a master Group of all your prospects, subdivide that Group into regions, subdivide those regional sub-Groups into sales rep Groups, and subdivide the sales rep Groups into product Groups!

- ▸ **You can't see who is not in a Group:** Although it's easy to see the members of a Group, or which Groups a specific Contact is a member of, there is no way of obtaining a list of the Contacts who are NOT in a Group.

Creating a Group

Creating a Group is the easy part. The hard part comes from deciding exactly what purpose the Group will serve.

Getting ready

You can populate a Group with contacts based on any criteria that you want. Here are a few examples of ACT! Groups that will really help you to organize your work load:

- ▶ **Project Management**: Groups work really well if you work on large projects and want to track all contacts and activities that relate to a project. For example, if you're building a home, you're probably dealing with a number of different people ranging from building inspectors and city officials to subcontractors, your own personnel, and the new homeowner.

- ▶ **Tracking real estate listings**: You might create a Group for property that you rent or are selling. Setting up a Group for each property allows you to track all clients that have visited a particular property and conversely to list all properties that you have shown to a particular client.

- ▶ **Organizing your classes and seminars**: Creating a Group for each seminar or class that you teach will allow you to see at a glance all the registrants. Conversely, you will also be able to track which classes an individual contact has taken with you.

- ▶ **Keeping in touch with your contacts**: Because Groups can be populated based on a dynamic query, they are ideal for tracking contacts that would otherwise slip through the cracks of your database. For example, you might want your Group to include customers who you haven't heard from in 90 days, or prospects that you've never contacted.

The beauty of an ACT! Group is that it can be used to track several variables. For example, your Groups might consist of customers whom you have not contacted in 90 days.

Too often ACT! users create Groups based on a single field value or use Groups as a replacement for fields. For example, you might be tempted to create one Group for the Attorneys in your database and another for all the Accountants. Unfortunately those Groups don't stand the test of time and they require too many steps on the part of the user. A better alternative would be to create one field with a drop down that contains both Attorney and Accountant that can be readily accessed from the Contact Detail view.

How to do it...

1. Click **Groups** on the ACT! Navbar. The Group Detail view opens like the one you see in the following figure. It should look vaguely familiar; in fact, it's nearly identical to the **Contact Detail** window. Just like the Contact Detail window, the **Group Detail** window features tabs along the middle of the screen. And, just like the Contact Detail window, the Group Detail window allows you to choose the layout of your choice:

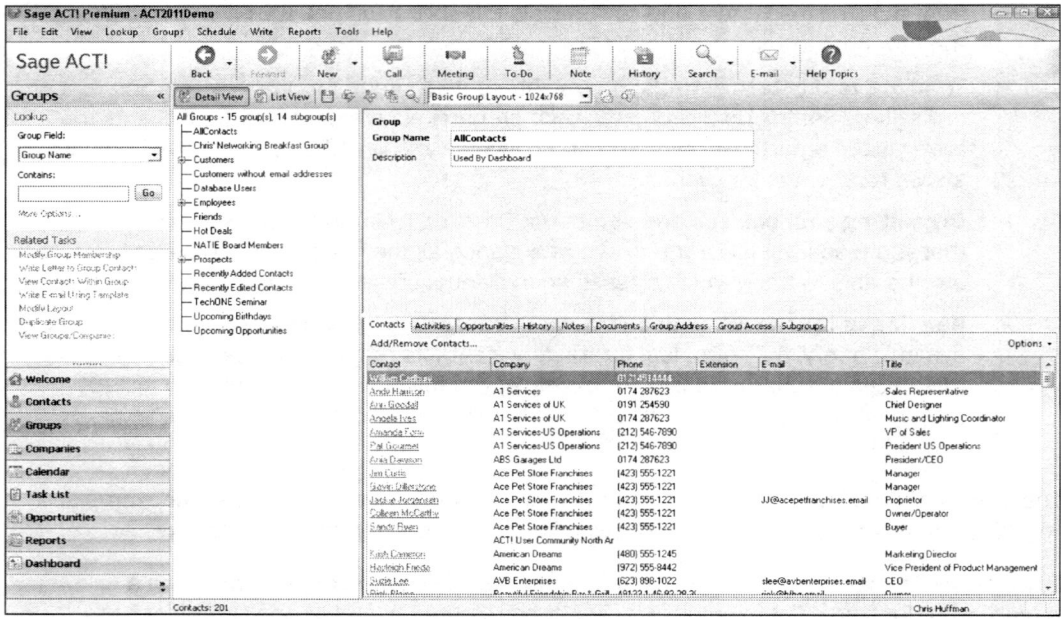

2. Create a new Group by following any of these methods:

   - Right-click in the list of Groups and choose **New Group** from the contextual menu
   - Click the **New** icon on the toolbar
   - Press the **Insert** key on your keyboard
   - Click the Groups menu and select **New Group**

3. Enter a name for the new Group in the **Group Name** field. This is the only required field.

4. Add a description in the **Description** field (optional).

How it works...

When you move to another field, the Group List tree that runs along the left side of the Group Detail view automatically updates and your Group is saved. At that juncture, you can continue to add as many new Groups as you need, or start to populate the Group you just created.

Adding Static Members to a Group

Static Group members are ones that you add to a Group manually. I sometimes refer to Static groups as **stagnant** because ACT! users often create a new Group, add a few contacts to them, and then forget about them.

Getting ready

Static groups are best used when creating a somewhat random or "hand picked" grouping of Contacts. If you're using a Group for project management you need to decide which of your Contacts will be included in the Group. If your Group represents a real estate property you'll need to decide which Contacts you'll show the property to. If your Group is to help you keep track of the RSVP's for an event you're holding, then you'll want to add specific Contacts to the Group as their responses arrive.

If possible, create a lookup of potential Group members. You can go to the Contact List and handpick the Group members using the Contact List view's **tag mode** to randomly select contact records.

How to do it...

1. Click **Groups** from ACT!'s Navbar to open the **Group Detail** view.
2. Select the Group to which you want to add the new members.
3. Open the **Add/Remove Contacts** dialog window by using one of the following methods:
   - Click the **Contacts** tab and then click the **Add/Remove Contacts** button.
   - Right-click on the name of the Group the Group tree, choose **Group Membership** from the contextual menu, and then click **Add/Remove Contacts...**
   - Click the **Groups** menu and choose **Add/Remove Contacts...**

4. In any case, the **Add/Remove Contacts** dialog window appears like the one you see in the following figure:

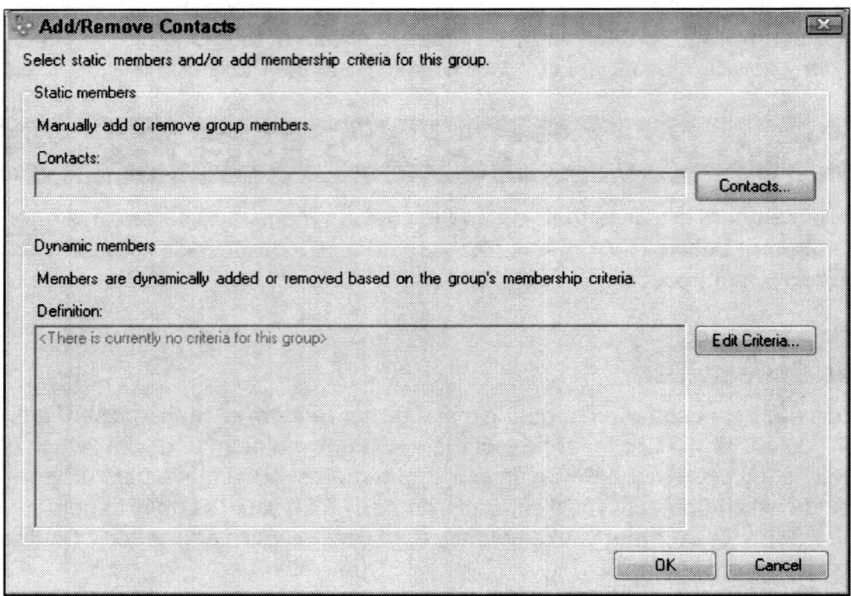

5. Click the **Contacts** button. The **Select Contacts** dialog window that you see in the following figure opens:

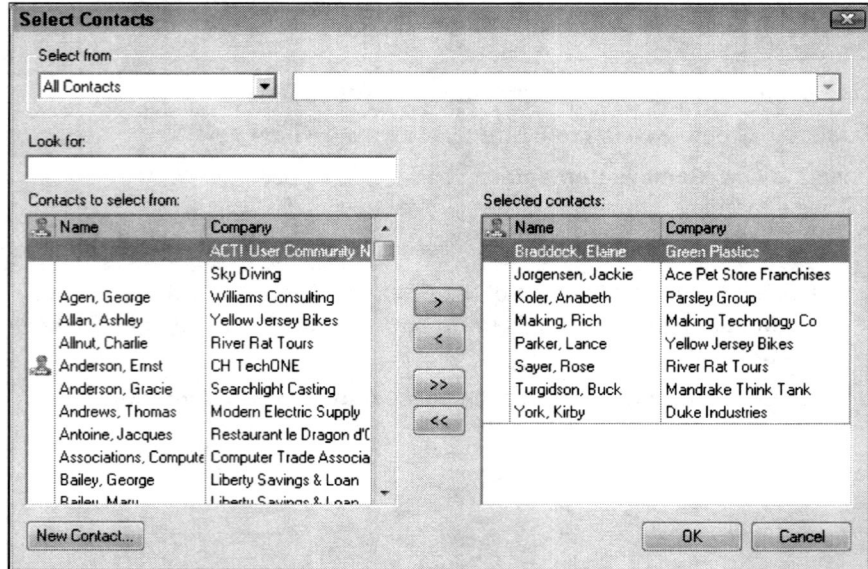

6. Select a contact from the **Contacts to select from:** area and then click the right-pointing arrows to add the contact to the **Selected contacts:** area.

7. You can select several contacts at a time by holding down the *CTRL* key on the keyboard while selecting contacts and then clicking the right-pointing arrows to add them to the **Selected Contacts** area (optional).

8. If you have already created a Lookup of the contacts you'd like to add to the Group, choose **Current Lookup** from the **Select from** drop-down box and then click the double right-pointing arrows to add the entire Lookup to the Group (optional).

9. Click **OK** to close the **Select Contacts** dialog window.

10. Click **OK** to close the **Add/Remove Contacts** dialog window.

How it works...

Once you've added Contacts to a Group they will all be listed on the Contacts tab of the Group Detail view.

There's more...

Don't feel that your additions to a Group are set in stone. Feel free to follow the directions above to manually add more contacts to a Group.

Removing Static Members from a Group

Things change and it's more than likely that you'll need to remove a Contact from a Group. Not a problem; it's just as easy to remove a Contact from a Group as it was to add it in the first place.

How to do it...

Here's all you have to do to remove existing Contacts from a Group:

1. Click **Groups** from ACT!'s Navbar to open the Group Detail view.

2. Select the Group to which you want to remove Contacts.

3. Click the **Contacts** tab and then click the **Add/Remove Contacts** button to open the **Add/Remove Contacts** dialog window.

4. Click the **Contacts** button to open the **Select Contacts** dialog window.

5. Select a contact from the **Selected contacts:** area and then click the single pointing left arrow to remove the contact from the Group.

6. Click the double left-pointing arrows to remove all Contacts from the Group (optional).

7. Click **OK** to close the **Select Contacts** dialog window.

8. Click **OK** to close the **Add/Remove Contacts** dialog window.

Adding Dynamic Members to a Group

The concept of creating static Groups is a carry-over from much older ACT! versions. However, the ability to add **dynamic** Groups didn't come along until ACT! 2005. You might think of the name dynamic as having somewhat of a double meaning when it comes to ACT! These Groups are dynamic because they are constantly updating as the information in your database itself changes, but they are also dynamic in the sense that they can really help you take charge of your database!

Getting ready

It's a good idea to identify a need that a dynamic Group can help you with before actually creating it. For example, you might find that various users are adding new contacts to your database and not bothering to include key pieces of information such as their email address, ID/Status, and mailing preference. You can create a dynamic Group to include only those contacts that are missing that information.

When you create a dynamic group you are actually combining two ACT! skills: creating a Group and combining it with an Advanced Query.

How to do it...

1. Click **Groups** on the ACT! Navbar to open the **Group Detail** view.

2. Select the Group you want to populate or create a new Group following the instructions in the *Creating a Group* section above.

3. Click the **Contacts** tab and then click the **Add/Remove Contacts...** button to open the **Add/Remove Contacts** dialog window.

4. Click the **Edit Criteria** button. Right on target the **Group Criteria** dialog window that you see opens, which looks amazingly like what you see in the following figure:

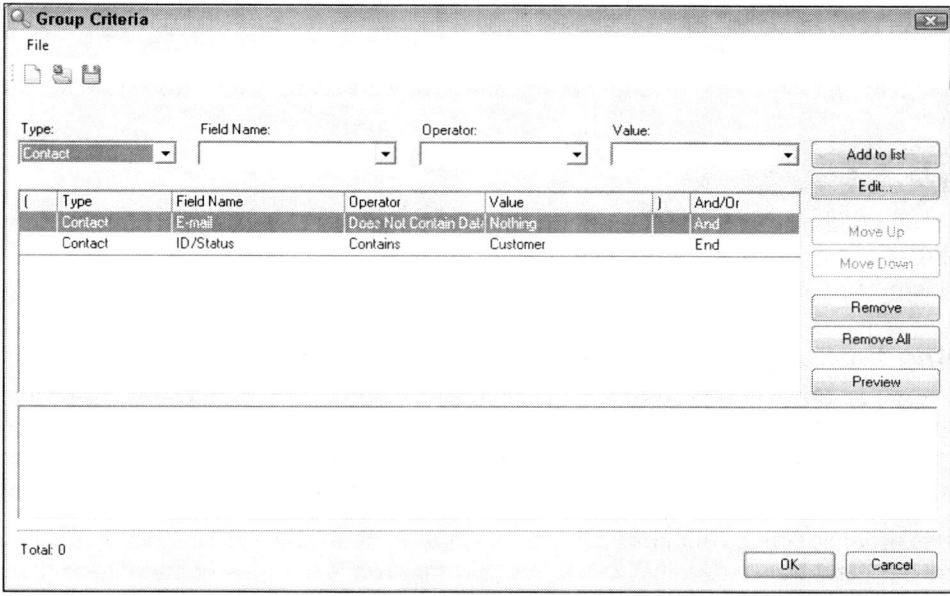

5. Fill in the criteria that you need to add a Contact to the Group:

- ❑ Type: Choose either **Contact** or **Opportunity** as the field type you are searching for.

- ❑ Field Name: Select a field from the drop-down list. If you had specified Contact as the field type you'll see a list of all your Contact fields, and if you chose Opportunity you'll see all your Opportunity fields.

- ❑ Operator: Select an operator from the drop-down list. The choices are fairly self-explanatory with options like **Equals**, **Contains**, and **Ends With**.

- ❑ Value: Type in the field value that you're looking to match. If you select the State field name, for example, the value might be "NY".

6. Click **the Add to list** button. Your entry will now appear in the bottom portion of the **Group Criteria** dialog box.

7. Add additional criteria (optional).

8. Change the **And/Or** indicator as needed (optional). The **And/Or** indicator is actually a drop-down list with two choices: **And** and **Or**. By defau t, ACT! inserts an **And** in the **And/Or** column. That means a Contact must match both criteria in order to become a member of the Group. **Or** means that a Contact need only match one of the criteria.

9. Click the **Preview** button to view a list of the contacts that match your criteria.

10. Click **OK** to close the **Group Criteria** dialog window.

11. Click **OK** to close the **Add/Remove Contacts** dialog window.

How it works...

Any contacts that match the criteria that you specified will now be listed on the Contact tab.

There's more...

If you took advantage of the Preview button in step 9 then you already had a pretty good idea of whether or not your query was going to work. However, if you're not happy with the results of the dynamic Group, feel free to go back in and change it at any time.

Adding both static and dynamic group members

There might be times when you want to add both static and dynamic members to a Group. For example, you might be planning a holiday Open House and want to invite all of your customers using a dynamic query. However, you also want to "hand pick" a select number of prospects and vendors and extend an invitation to them as well by adding them to the Group manually.

Because dynamic Groups automatically populate based on a query, you cannot manually remove a contact from a dynamic Group. You can, however, modify the query used to populate the Group so that it creates a Group that more closely matches your desired results.

Creating a Group from the current Lookup

As you delve deeper and deeper into ACT! you'll realize just how powerful—and intuitive—a program it is. And, as you master one function you'll start to see how it can be used in conjunction with other ACT! functions. A case in point is combining the power of a Group with the functionality of a Lookup. Creating a Lookup is one of the first functions that a lot of new ACT! users master. But you may not realize how easy it is to populate an existing Group with the results of a Lookup.

Getting ready

In order to take advantage of this recipe you'll need to already have a Group in mind to which you want to add additional Contact records.

How to do it...

1. Create a Lookup of Contact records.
2. Click the **Tag All** button at the top of the Contact List.
3. Right-click in the middle of the Contact List view and choose **Add Contacts to Groups**... from the contextual menu. The **Add Selected Contacts to Group** dialog window like the one you see in the following figure opens:

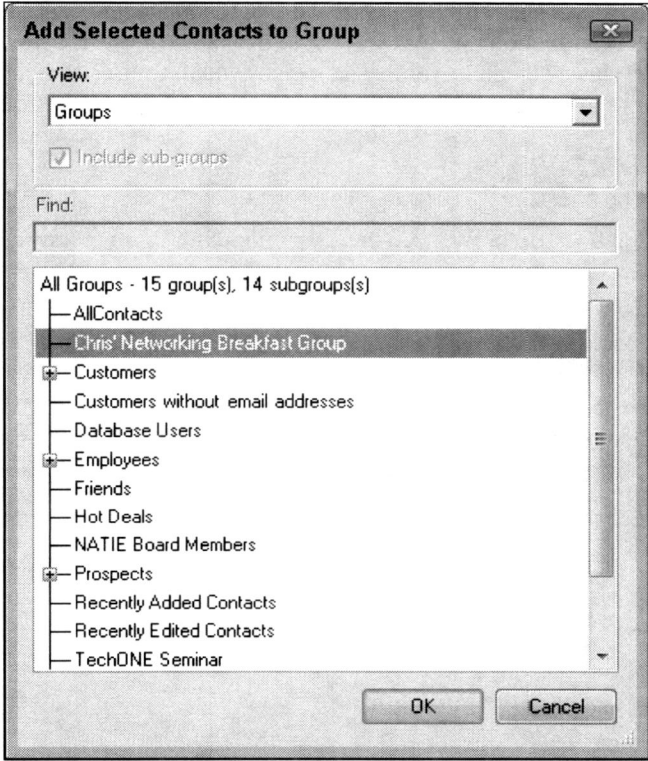

4. Select the Group(s) to which you would like to add the current Lookup from the left pane and then click the single right-pointing arrow to move it to the right pane.

5. Click **OK** to close the **Add Selected Contacts to Group** dialog window.

How it works...

All the Contacts in the current Lookup have now been added to the Group you selected in step 4.

Using the Group tab of the Contact Detail view

So far in this chapter we've been looking at several contacts as they relate to a Group. After all, by definition a Group is composed of more than one Contact record. However, there are times when you want to hone in on an individual Contact record to see which Groups he's a member of and/or add him to a Group if necessary.

As you start to become more and more familiar with ACT! you start to realize that ACT! supplies you with all the functionality that you could ever ask for. By accessing the Group tab in the Contact Detail view you can instantly see exactly which Groups the current Contact is a member of. And, more importantly, you can easily add that Contact to a Group if necessary.

Getting ready

You'll start by creating a Group or two; you can even populate them following the recipes earlier in this chapter.

How to do it...

1. Navigate to the Contact you'd like to add to a Group—or just see which Groups the Contact belongs to. As you can see in the following figure, any Groups of which the Contact is a member will be listed:

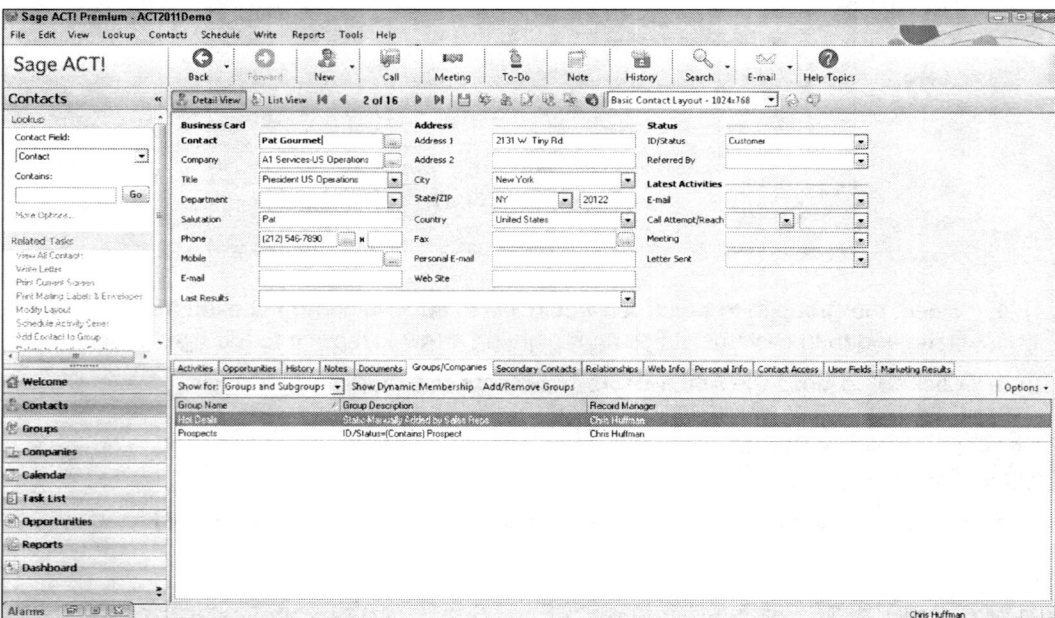

2. Click the **Groups/Company** tab and then click the **Add/Remove Groups** button. The **Add/Remove...** dialog window that you see in the following figure will appear:

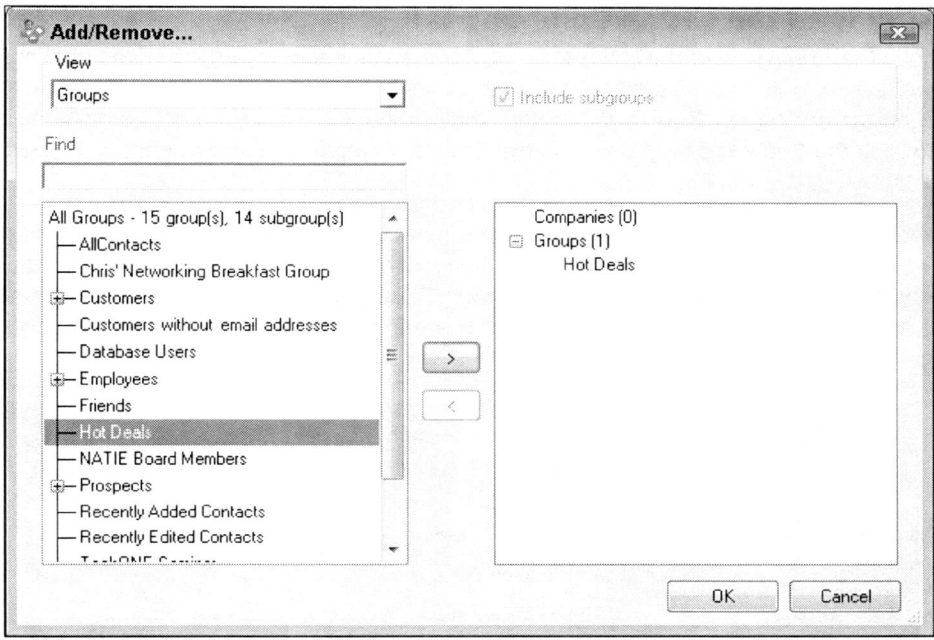

3. Select a Group name from the list in the left pane and then click the single right-pointing arrow to move it to the right pane. If you want to add a subgroup click the **+** sign to expand the main Group.

4. (Optional) Click the **View** Drop-Down and choose **Groups List**. The Groups List view provides you with two additional benefits:

   ❑ All Groups and subgroups will be listed without having to expand them

   ❑ You can type a Group name in the Find box and the cursor will automatically select the name of a Group that matches your search criterion

5. Repeat step 3 to add more Groups if necessary (optional).

6. Click **OK** to close the **Add/Remove** dialog window.

How it works...

The Group you add in step 4 will now appear on the Group tab.

There's more...

As intuitive as ACT! is at times, sometimes some of the functions are a bit quirky. This is especially true of the Groups/Company tab.

Working with the Group/Company tab

You notice that the name of the tab is Groups/Companies because, as the name implies, the tab is somewhat of a "one size fits all" tab that shows both the Groups and the Companies that a Contact belongs to. If you'd rather view the Companies that a Contact belongs to you'll need to click the **Show for:** drop-down on the Groups/Companies tab and choose **Companies and Divisions**.

Any Dynamic Groups that a Contact belongs to will not display on the Groups/Companies tab. If you want to see the Dynamic Groups listed along with the static ones, you'll have to click the **Show Dynamic Membership** button on the Groups/Companies tab. At that point the Dynamic Groups Membership will appear like the one you see in the figure below. However, as soon as you click **Close** the information will disappear.

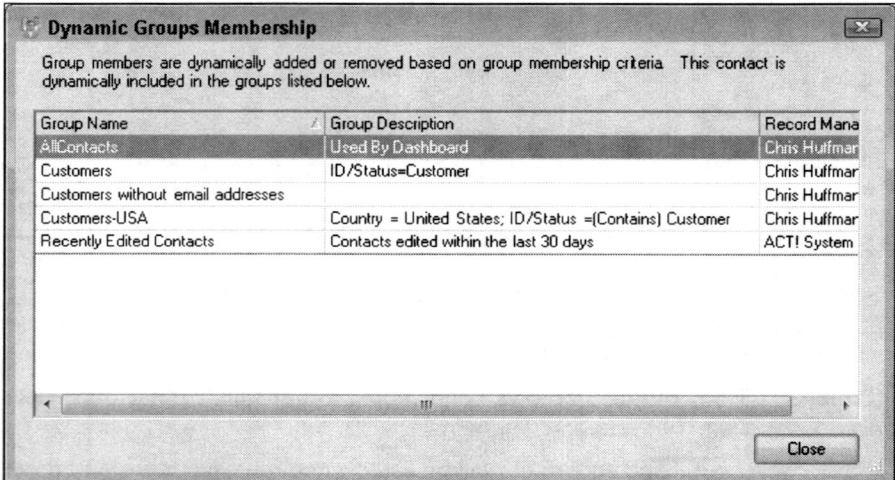

Working with Groups

Working with individual Contact records is fine if you only have a very limited number of Contacts in your ACT! database. But if you're like the typical ACT! user you probably have closer to 5,000-10,000 Contacts in your database, and I can almost hear the sound of dead Contacts falling through the cracks.

After you create a Group and stick a few Contacts into it, you can begin to take ACT! to the "next level.". You can start viewing your Contacts not as unrelated entities, but as the moving parts of your business machine.

You can customize the Group Detail view layout in the same way you can customize the Contact Detail layout. You can move or remove existing fields, add new fields, and modify the tabs. You can even do a special Group lookup to search for a Group based on the information in any one of the Group fields that you create.

I like to think of the Groups functionality as a program within a program. Group functionality is pretty much identical to Contact functionality with one big difference: notes, histories, activities, and opportunities you create while in the Group Detail window affect the entire Group and not just a single Contact. You can create Group notes, histories, activities, and opportunities in exactly the same way you set them up for a Contact. You can even attach a Group-specific file to the Group Documents tab. The information that you input belongs to the Group and doesn't have to be duplicated on the contact level. Best of all, you won't have to wrack your brain trying to remember which contact in your Group you attached a note to.

Getting ready

Since you're working with Group functionality it makes sense to have already created a Group or two, and filled them with at least a few Contact records. At this point the sky's the limit and you can perform any of the actions you normally associate with a Group.

How to do it...

1. Click **Groups** on ACT!'s Navbar.
2. Select the name of the Group to which you want to add additional information.
3. You can perform any of the following actions exactly as if you were working with a Contact record:
   - Create a History: Hold down the *Ctrl* key on your keyboard and tap the letter *H*.
   - Add a Note: Click the **Notes** tab and then click the **Insert New Note** icon.
   - Add a Document: Click the **Documents** tab and then click the **Add Document** icon.
4. Click the **Activities** tab and then click the **Call**, **Meeting**, or **To-Do** icon on the Groups Detail view icon bar to create a new Group activity.
5. Click the **Opportunities** tab and then click the **Add/Remove Opportunities** button to associate the Group with an existing Opportunity. The **Add Remove...** dialog window will open like the one you see in the following figure.

6. Select an Opportunity name from the left pane, click the single pointing right arrow to move it to the right pane, and then click **OK** to close the **Add Remove...** dialog window.

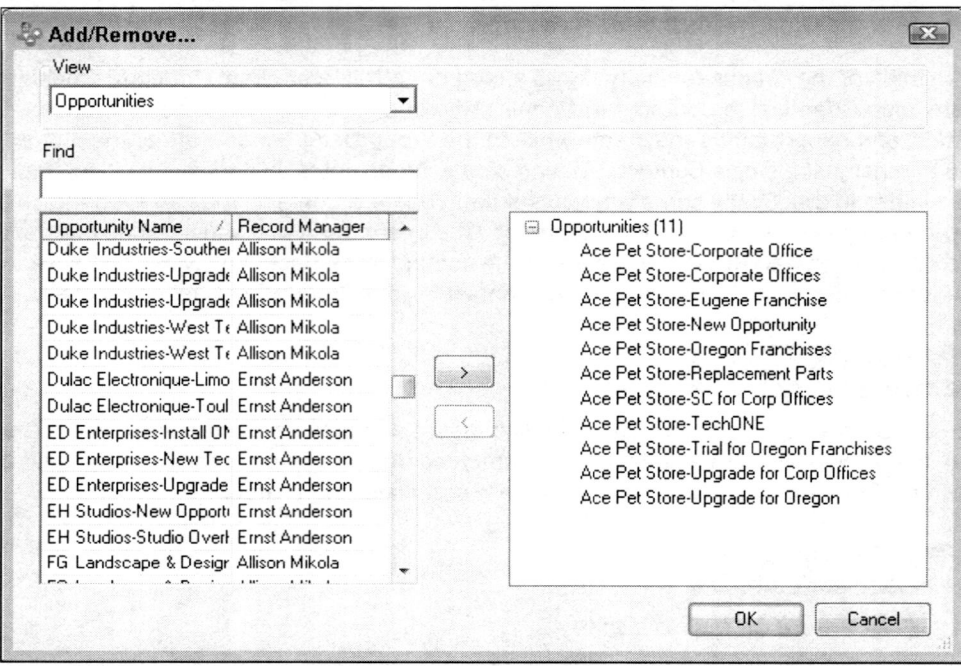

7. Click the **Contacts** tab and then double click the name of the Contact to open the Contact Detail view of one of the Group members.

How it works...

Any actions that you've scheduled with a Group can now be viewed on the appropriate Group tab.

There's more...

Activities, Opportunities, Histories, and Notes can be associated with both Contact and Group records. Consequently, the list of items in any one of these tabs can get really long if the Group contains a lot of Contact records. ACT!, being the intuitive product that we've come to love, includes the **Show For:** drop-down box to help filter out some of the unnecessary items.

The **Show For:** drop-down contains three choices:

▶   **All**: shows items associated with both the Group notes and with specific Contact records

- ▸ **Group**: shows only items that are associated with the current Group
- ▸ **Group Contacts**: shows only items associated with the members of the Group

ACT! started as a Contact manager and is still basically a very contact-centric software program. Although you can schedule a Group activity, it must also include at least one Contact name. Unfortunately if you don't specify a Contact when scheduing a Group activity, ACT! will automatically insert the name of the last Contact that you accessed even if that Contact is not a member of the Group. Go figure!

You can't create a new Opportunity from a Group record; again all Opportunities must be associated with at least one Contact record. However, you can associate a Group with an existing Opportunity as shown in step 5 above, or you can associate a Group with the Opportunity when you originally create the Opportunity.

7
Working with Companies

In this chapter, we will cover:

- ▶ Learning about Company Views
- ▶ Creating Companies
- ▶ Creating a Company from a Contact Record
- ▶ Adding a Division
- ▶ Deleting a Company
- ▶ Linking Contact and Company Records
- ▶ Adding a Contact to a Company
- ▶ Working with a Company
- ▶ Linking Company and Contact Fields
- ▶ Creating a Lookup of Company Contacts

Introduction

The more you work with ACT! the more you'll begin to discover the true power of the program. And, as you delve into some of the more advanced features, you'll be pleasantly surprised at how easy and versatile those features are. A case in point is the Companies feature.

For years ACT! considered itself to be a **contact** centric program, which means that the individual or contact was the main focus of the program. However, some CRM programs are **account** centric, which means the focus is on company or account information.

In ACT! you can have the best of both worlds. You can create a number of Contacts and optionally attach related ones to a Company record. Conversely, you can create a Company record and attach as many Contact records to it as you need.

Learning about Company views

If you've mastered the Contact functionality, mastering the Company functionality becomes a snap. The main difference lies in the fact that the Contact record includes a hyperlink to the associated Company records whereas the Company record contains a tab of Contacts that hyperlink back to the actual Contact records.

How to do it...

1. Click the **Companies** icon on the **Navigation** bar to access the Company Detail view. The Company Detail view will appear like the one you see in the following screenshot:

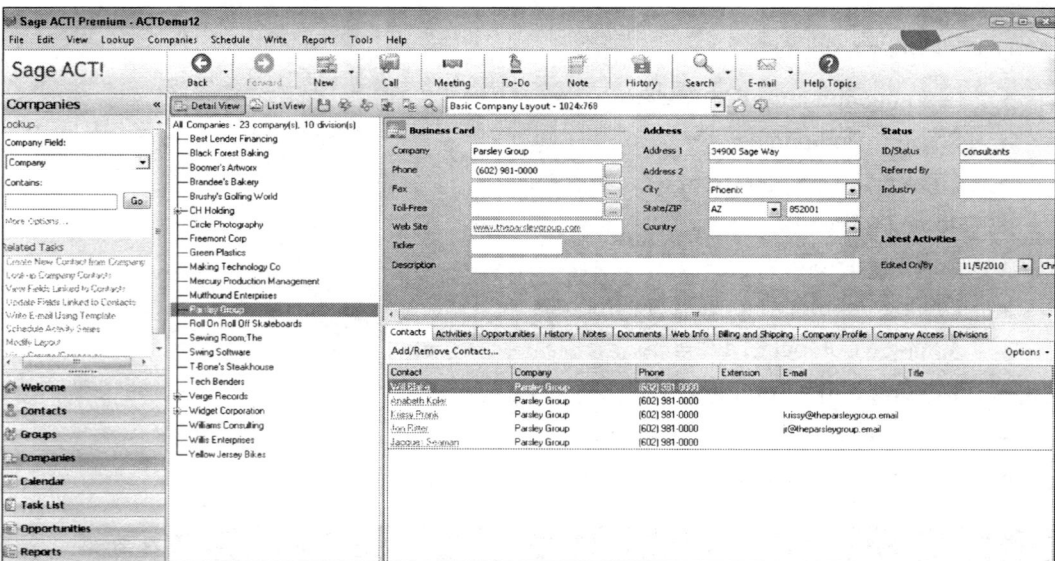

2. Click the various tabs that run along the middle of the Company Detail view to familiarize yourself with the Company Detail view.

3. If you prefer to work in the Company List view click the **List View** icon on the Company Detail icon bar.

4. Click the **Contacts** button on the Navigation bar to return to the Contacts area of ACT!.

How it works...

You follow the exact same steps to add new fields, design layouts, track notes, histories and appointments, and create Opportunities for both Contact and Company records. For example, if you click the Notes tab you'll notice the familiar Insert New Note icon.

Creating Companies from the Companies Detail view

Adding a new Company record works in the same way as adding a new Contact record. The main difference, however, is that you can create a new Company record from either the Company view or directly from an existing Contact record.

You'll probably create a new Company record from the Company view if you have not already created a Contact record from someone at the company. For example, you might want to start doing business with a company but don't as yet know the names of any of the company's personnel.

Getting ready

Obviously, before you create a new Company record you'll at the very least need to know the name of the company you are creating. In addition, knowing other pertinent information including the address or website will prove to be useful.

How to do it...

1. Click the **Companies** icon on the **Navigation** bar to access the Company Detail view.
2. Click the **Companies** menu and choose **New Company.** A new blank Company record will open.
3. Fill the necessary information into the various company fields. The only mandatory field is the name of the Company.
4. Click the **Contacts** button on the Navigation bar to return to the Contacts area of ACT!.

How it works...

When you leave the new Company record the name of the new company will now appear alphabetically in the list of companies that appears on the left-hand side of the Company Detail view.

There's more...

The directions above assume that you like to access features using the Menu bar. However, some of you might prefer to use the icon bar. If that's the case you can click the New icon bar. Alternatively, if you prefer using a keyboard you can also tap the Insert key and a new, blank Company record will magically appear.

Entering new Companies from the Company List view

Some people are more comfortable working in the Company List view. For example, you might want to see a list of all the companies you do business with and don't want to be distracted by any erroneous information. If that's the case, you can add a new Company record directly from the Company List view following the directions above. However, you will be automatically transported to the Company Detail view the moment you select New Company from the Companies menu.

Every new Company must have a name

Occasionally you might start to create a new Company record but never finish the process. For example, you might inadvertently tap the Insert key or you might get interrupted before you have a chance to finish adding the new Company record to your ACT! database. If that's the case, a friendly warning like the one you see in the Figure below will appear if you try to move away from the new, blank Company record.

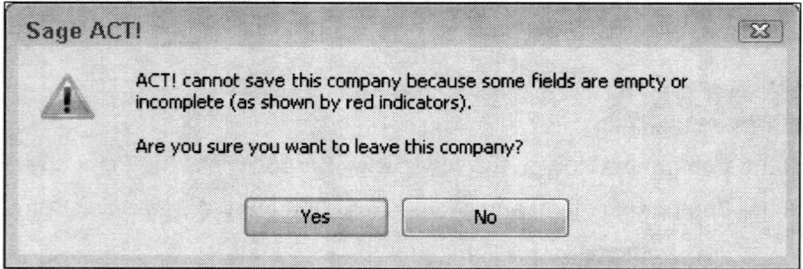

If you click **Yes** you can navigate away from the blank record and no record will be created. If you click **No** you will remain at the blank Company record until you fill in at least a company name.

Creating a Company from a Contact record

Sometimes in life—and in ACT!—it becomes a matter of "which comes first." In the recipe above we assumed that you wanted to create a new Company record and that you didn't necessarily have any existing Contact records that worked in that Company.

When you create a Company record from an existing Contact record all of the pertinent contact information automatically copies into the new Company record. This is a nice time-saver because you alleviate the need to type in boring address information into the Company record when you've already entered it into a Contact record.

You can create a Company record based on the contents of a single Contact record. Generally, you'll want to create a Company record to help you organize several contacts in your database that all work for the same Company. A good rule of thumb to follow is to create a new Company record any time you have more than one contact in your database that works for the same company.

Getting ready

A good starting point is to sort your Contact List by Company to see if you have multiple contacts working at the same company. At that point you can create a Lookup by a specific company to zoom in on all the contacts that work for a specific company.

How to do it...

1. Navigate to the Contact record on which you want to base the new Company record.
2. Click **Contacts** on the menu bar and then choose **Create Company from Contact**.
3. Click on the Company List running along the left-hand side of the Company Detail view or navigate to another area in ACT! to save your changes.

How it works...

Your new Company record will now appear and will contain the address information, main phone number, and website as they appeared in the Contact records.

There's more...

Normally, you'll want to create a new Company record from the Contact Detail view where you'll be able to double-check that all your information is accurate before you create the new Company record. However, if you prefer, you can also create the new Company record from the Contact List view.

Adding a Division to a Company

Companies come in all shapes and sizes. You might work with a tiny company whose owner runs the business from a backyard tree house or you might work with a mega-corporation with locations all around the world. You might even find yourself working with the government and its multitude of agencies.

ACT! allows you to create 15 Division levels so that you can have Divisions of a Company as well as Divisions of your Divisions. For example you might be working with "Megasoft Corporation" and want to divide the main Company record into several Divisions reflecting the seven continents. From there you might further divide the Company Divisions into countries, the country Divisions into cities, and the city Divisions into territories.

Getting ready

You can only create a Division from an existing Company or Division so you'll need to make sure that one exists in your ACT! database.

How to do it...

1. Click the **Companies** icon on the **Navigation** bar to access the Company Detail view.
2. Right-click anywhere on the Company layout and choose **New Division** from the shortcut menu. A blank Company Detail window appears.
3. Enter the pertinent info for the Division that you're creating.
4. Click on the Company List running along the left side of the Company Detail View or navigate to another area in ACT! to save your changes.

How it works...

The new Division will now appear in the list of companies running along the left side of the Company Detail view directly under the name of the parent company. If you don't see it at first you might need to click the plus side next to the parent company to expand the list of Divisions:

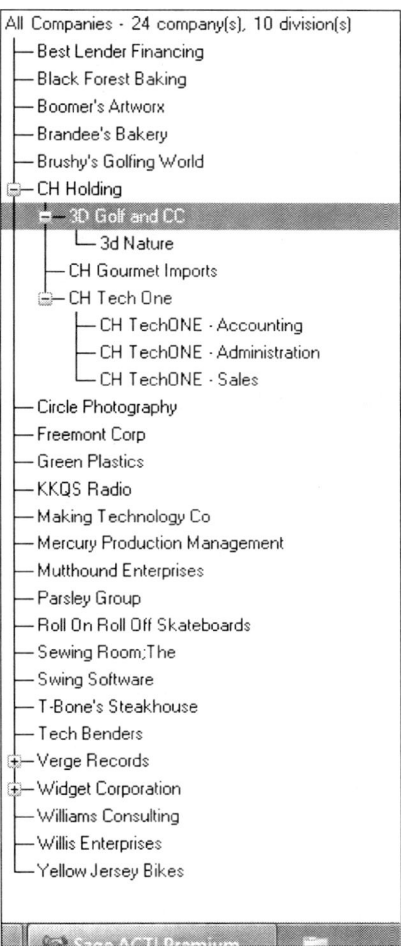

There's more...

You can also create new Divisions from the menu bar. Select the name of the Company from the list of companies, click the Companies menu, and choose New Division.

Viewing Divisions from the Company List view

Theoretically you can also view a list of all your Companies and Divisions from the Company List view. You'll notice the **Include Divisions** option at the top of the Company List View. As the name implies, clicking it shows you all the Divisions and subdivisions. However, the list appears in alphabetical order, so you'll find it pretty impossible to figure out which Divisions belong to what company. Although you can create Divisions from the Company List, chances are pretty good that you'll find the Company Detail view a much easier area to work with.

Moving Divisions

There might be an occasion when you have two Company records and realize that one is actually a Division of another. Or you might create a Division and later decide that it would be more appropriate to be listed as a Company. ACT! allows you to "drag and drop" any of the Companies or Divisions that appear in the list of companies that runs along the left-hand side of the Company List View:

- ▶ To create a Division from an existing Company, drag the Company to the new parent company

- ▶ To create a Company from an existing Division, drag the Division to the top of the list of companies

Deleting a Company

It is very easy to delete a Company record. However, although all the information from the Company record's fields will be lost forever when you delete a Company record, the Contact records associated with the company are not deleted.

Getting ready

Before diving in headfirst and deleting a Company record, you might want to check it out a bit first by determining if there are any Contact records associated with the Company record. If there are a number of Contact records associated with a Company record you'll probably want to leave the Company record intact.

How to do it...

1. Click the **Companies** icon on the **Navigation** bar to access the Company Detail view.
2. Select the Company you want to delete from the Company Detail view.
3. Right-click the Company and then choose **Delete** from the contextual menu.
4. Click **Yes** to confirm that you want to delete the selected Company.

How it works...

The Company will no longer appear in the Company List view.

There's more...

If you delete a company that contains Divisions, the Divisions don't get deleted; instead, they get promoted to their very own companies. If your intention is to delete a Company and all its Divisions, you need to delete the various Divisions prior to deleting the Company itself.

Linking Contact and Company Records

One of the key benefits of the company feature is the ability to link Company and Contact records so that you can easily find all the Contacts that belong to a Company. In addition to seeing the Contacts that are associated with a Company on the Contacts tab in the Company Detail view, the name of the Company will appear as a hyperlink on the Contact Detail view.

Getting ready

In order to link a Contact record to a Company record you'll want to make sure that both of them already exist in your ACT! database.

How to do it...

1. Create a lookup of the Contact that you want to link to a Company.

2. Click the **Ellipsis** (three dots) that appears at the end of the Company field. The Link to Company dialog window appears similar to the one you see in the following figure:

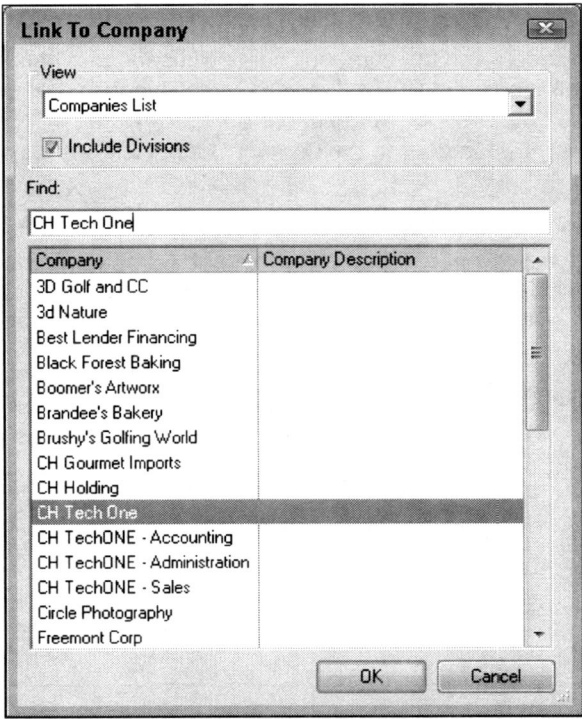

3. Select the Company to which you want to link the contact and then click **OK**.

How it works...

When you link a Contact record to a Company record, the company name turns to blue in the Contact Detail view, indicating that they are now linked together. You can click on the company hyperlink on the Contact Detail view to go directly to the Company Detail view. Conversely, you can click the Contacts tab in the Company Detail view and go directly to a contact record.

There's more...

If the name of a Company record is an exact match the company field on the Contact Detail view then the name will be automatically selected in the Link To Company dialog window. However if there is a slight discrepancy between the two names, you can type the first few letters of the company name in the Look for field so that ACT! automatically scrolls down the list of companies and finds it for you. For example, you might have created a Company record with the name **Smith & Sons** and entered the name **Smith and Sons** on the Contact record. When you manually link the two together the Contact Detail view will change to reflect the name of the Company record.

Moving between Contact and Company records

Any Contact records that are associated with a Company record are automatically hyperlinked on the Contact Detail window and the company name will appear in blue. Click the hyperlink and the Company Detail window will open. Conversely, you'll notice that the name of all the contacts appear in blue on the Contacts tab of the Company Detail view; click a contact name and you'll be immediately transported to the Contact Detail View of the contact you clicked.

Removing the Company hyperlink

If you find that you no longer want to link the Contact and Company records click the ellipsis on the Contact Detail view. A dialog box like the one in the following figure appears, asking you whether it's okay to disable the link. Click OK, and the link is history:

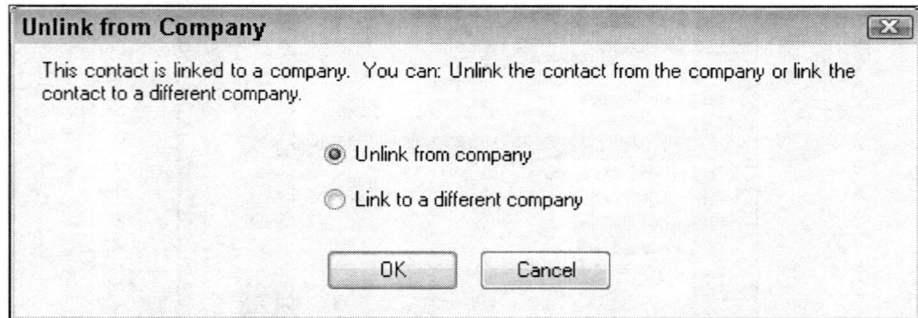

Adding a Contact to a Company

Once you've created a Company record, it's easy to create a new Contact record based on the existing company information. By starting from the Company record you'll be able to accomplish two time-saving tasks:

- The new Contact record will automatically contain the basic contact information based on the information of the existing Company record
- The new Contact record will be automatically hyperlinked to the existing Company record

Getting ready

It might seem a bit obvious to mention this but you'll need to have a Company record with the appropriate address information filled in.

How to do it...

1. Click the **Companies** icon on the **Navigation** bar to access the Company Detail view.
2. Select the company for which you want to add a new employee.
3. Click **Companies** from the Menu bar and then select **Create Contact from Company**.
4. The Contact Detail window opens filled in with all the pertinent company information.
5. Fill in the contact name and any other information specific to the contact.

How it works...

When you create a new Contact record from an existing Company record, the two records will be automatically linked together. In addition, ACT! intuitively copies generic information from the Company record such as the company's website and address information. You'll only need to fill in information that is specific to the contact such as the contact's name, e-mail address, and extension number.

Working with a Company Record

You might think of a company as a mini database within a database. The Company Detail window includes the same tabs as other views including Notes, History, Act vities, Opportunities, and Documents. However, there is one major difference: you can filter the Notes, History, Activities, and Opportunities tabs to show just the information that pertains directly to a company. For example, your Company record might be linked to several contacts; you can view all the notes for all of those contacts on the Notes tab of the Company record. Or, should you be confused by all those notes, you can filter the notes to just those notes that were created for the company itself.

Getting ready

In order to see this feature at work you'll want to make sure you have a Company record that contains several linked Contact records. You'll also want to make sure that you've created notes for most of those Contact records.

How to do it...

1. Click the **Companies** icon on the **Navigation** bar to access the Company Detail view.
2. Select the company for which you want to add a few notes.
3. Click the **Notes** tab in the Company Detail window.
4. Click the **Insert Note** icon at the top of the **Notes** tab.
5. Fill in the details of the note. As you can see in the following figure, no contact name is associated with the note but the company name appears automatically in the Share with field:

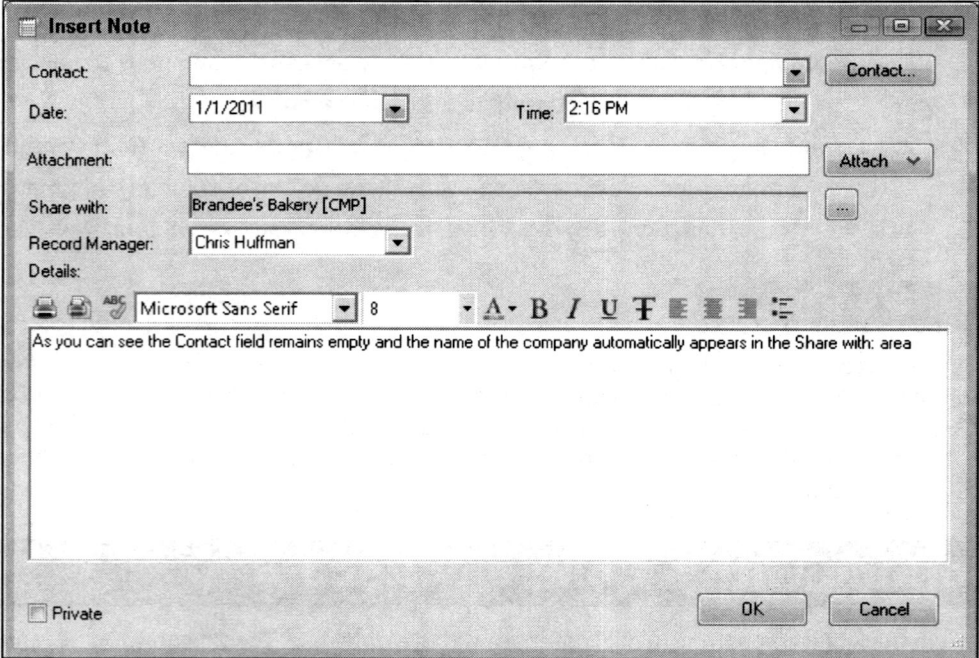

6. Click **OK** to save the note.

7. Make a selection from the **Show For** drop-down list to filter the contents on the Notes tab:

- ❏ All: Shows both company-specific and contact-specific notes
- ❏ Company: Shows only company-specific notes
- ❏ Company Contact: Shows only contact-specific notes

How it works...

By default, the Notes tab is set to show all notes relating to the Company record. By changing the filters you can focus on just those notes that are company specific, or only those notes that pertain to specific contacts.

There's more...

When you enter a note from the Company Detail window, you can only access it from the Company Detail window. However, if you enter a note from the Contact Detail window of a company member, you can view the note from both the Contact Detail and Company Detail windows.

Adding the contact's name to the Notes tab

Optionally, you can fill in the name of the contact in the Contact field of the note if the note pertains to a specific individual as well as to the company. And, you have associated many of the company notes with specific contacts you can include that information on the **Notes** tab. You can do that by right-clicking on the **Notes** tab, selecting **Customize Columns...** from the contextual menu and then adding the Contact field. The following figure shows how you can customize the **Notes** tab to include all the pertinent data:

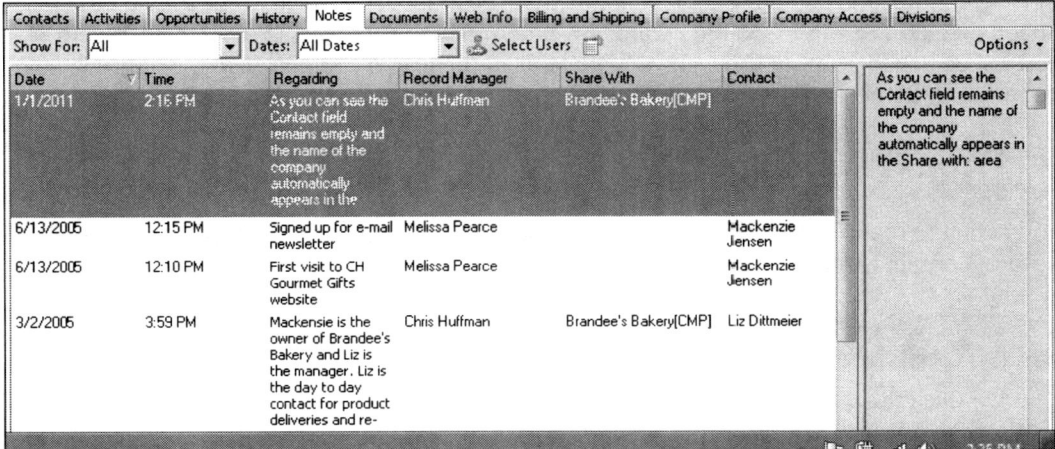

Working with the History and Document tabs

Most of the other company tabs work exactly like the Company Note tab. For example, you can create a company-specific history or attach a specific document directly to the Company record.

Working with the Company Activity tab

When scheduling an activity you must include the name of one of your ACT! contacts. Optionally, you can also attach a Company record to an activity. You can then filter the Activity tab of the Company Detail view in the same way you filter the Notes tab.

Working with the Company Opportunities tab

An Opportunity record is the only ACT! record that you can create without having it attached to either a Company or Contact record. Ironically, you can't create a company-specific opportunity from the Opportunity tab of the Company Detail view. However, you can use the tab to attach the current Company record to an existing Company record.

Linking Company and Contact Fields

In ACT! Company records and Contact records each have their own set of unique fields. And, if there is an overlap between the two sets of fields, you can link them together. For example, you may have a Company record for the MiniSoft Corporation as well as individual Contact records for the 50 employees who you regularly deal with. By linking the address fields of the Company record to the corresponding address fields for the Contact records you'll save yourself a whole lot of time should MiniSoft decide to relocate the company's headquarters. By linking the appropriate fields together, you can update the Company record and have all the individual records update automatically based on that information.

Linking contact and company fields requires that you first define which fields should be linked together. From that point forward, any time you make changes to a company record you will be asked whether you'd like to update all of the linked contacts with the current company information.

Getting ready

You'll want to make sure that you have created a Company record and that you have linked several Contact records to it.

How to do it...

1. Click the **Companies** icon on the **Navigation** bar to access the Company Detail view.

2. Click the Companies menu and select **View Linked Fields...** You can see an example of the View Linked Fields dialog window which shows you the contact and company fields that are already linked together in the following figure:

3. If you're happy with the links that already exists, click **Close** to close the open dialog window.

4. If you'd like to link more fields make sure that all other users have exited out of the database and then click the **Define Fields....** button (optional). You can see the first screen of the Define Fields wizard in the following figure:

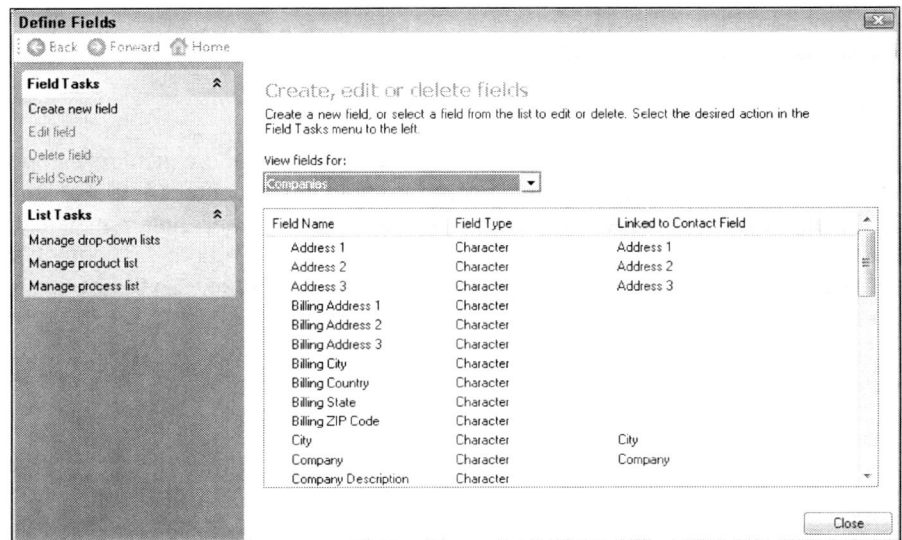

5. Double-click the name of the company field that you want to link to a contact field and then click **Next** to advance to the next window in the Define Fields wizard.

6. Click **Next** to advance to the Customize Field and List Behavior wizard window and then click **Next**.

7. Place a check mark next to the Link to contact field and then select the contact field from the dropdown that you want to link to the company field you selected in step 4 above.

8. Click **Finish** to close the Define Fields wizard and then click **Close** to return to the Company Detail View.

How it works...

The next time you change any of the information in the Company Detail screen the dialog box you see in the following figure will appear:

Click **Yes** if you'd like to update the related Contact records with the latest and greatest information.

There's more...

Although this feature is commonly used as an easy way to update address information for multiple contacts you can theoretically link a company field to any contact field. For example, you might link the ID/Status fields to reflect the status of the company. Just realize that this feature will update all of the linked contacts so proceed with caution; if a contact is at a different address than the company his information will be replaced with the company information and the old information will be lost forever.

Creating a Lookup of Company Contacts

The Company Detail window includes the Contacts tab which is an easy way to view all the Contacts that belong to a Company. And, as is the case with all of ACT!'s lists and tabs, you can change the sort order, add or remove columns, filter the information, and print the list. However, there might be times when you want to view your Company Contacts in full detail. If that's the case, it's easy to create a Lookup of the Company Contacts.

How to do it...

1. Click the **Companies** icon on the **Navigation** bar to access the Dashboard view.
2. Right-click the name of the Company from the Company List.
3. Chose **Create Lookup** from the contextual menu.

How it works...

The Contact List will open, displaying a list of all of the Company Contacts. If the Company only contains a single Contact then the Contact Detail window will open.

There's more...

Whether you work in the Contact Detail or List view is purely a matter of preference. If you prefer examining your Contacts in full detail you can do so by simply clicking the Detail View button on the left side of the Contact List's icon bar.

Creating a Lookup from the Company List view

Whether you work in the Company Detail or List view is also a matter of preference. Most ACT! users prefer the Company Detail view because it allows you to see all the pertinent information about a Company in one place. However, if you prefer working in the Company List view you can still follow the steps above to create a Lookup of your Company Contacts.

8
Creating Golden Opportunities

In this chapter, we will cover:

- ▶ Working with the Opportunity view
- ▶ Adding processes and stages
- ▶ Adding Products and Services
- ▶ Working with Opportunity fields and layouts
- ▶ Creating an opportunity
- ▶ Editing an opportunity
- ▶ Working with the Opportunity List
- ▶ Creating an opportunity graph

Introduction

In ACT!, an **opportunity** is a potential sale, normally to a contact or a company. Any opportunities that you have connected to either a Contact or Company record will appear on the Opportunities tab of that record. In addition ACT! provides you with both the Opportunity Detail and List views where you can view the pertinent details about a specific opportunity or work with a list of all your opportunities.

When you create an opportunity, you can include the names of specific products or services, specify a sales stage and forecasted close date, and make use of customizable opportunity fields. You can even schedule a follow-up activity or create notes for the opportunity in the same way you do for a Contact or Company record. As if that weren't enough, you can choose from a dozen opportunity reports so that you can analyze the progress of your sales.

By using ACT! to track the sales process, you have a better chance of closing more sales. First of all, you have significantly fewer contacts falling through the cracks of your database when you can find all of your pending sales in one location. Secondly, you can analyze opportunities as they move through the sales stages to make sure that your follow-up activity is done on a timely basis. You can generate reports that focus on the deals that you think have the best chance of closing or on the performance of specific sales staff. In addition you can see all the sales you've previously had with any of your contacts.

ACT! allows you to customize and create multiple sales processes. For example, your sales process might be very long and complicated, or might be used to track simple orders. And, a sales process doesn't necessarily have to be used to track sales. For example, some companies use ACT! for project management as well as sales and create separate processes for each of those aspects of their business. Other companies use the opportunities area solely for project management.

Working with the Opportunity View

ACT!'s opportunity functionality is arguably the most powerful of the ACT! features. Fortunately, even though it's capable of handling very complex processes an Opportunity record works in much the same way as the Contact, Company, and Group records do. And, if you feel comfortable with those record types you're bound to feel right at home once you start working with Opportunity records.

Getting ready

It would probably help if some nice person had already added a number of opportunities to your ACT! database. However, if you find yourself diving into a database that is devoid of opportunities you might want to open the ACT! demo database that automatically installed when you installed ACT!. The demo database has already been populated with a number of opportunities.

How to do it...

1. Click the **Opportunities** icon on the **Navigation** bar to access the Opportunity List view. The Opportunity List view will appear like the one you see in the following figure:

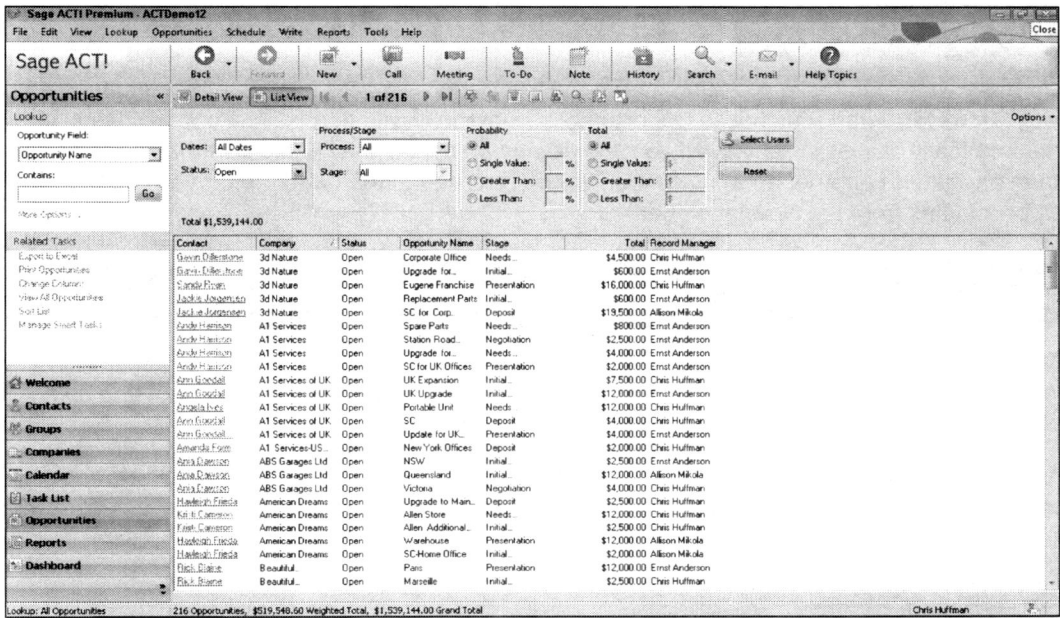

2. Click the **Detail View** icon on the icon bar to access the Opportunity Detail view similar to the one you see in the following figure:

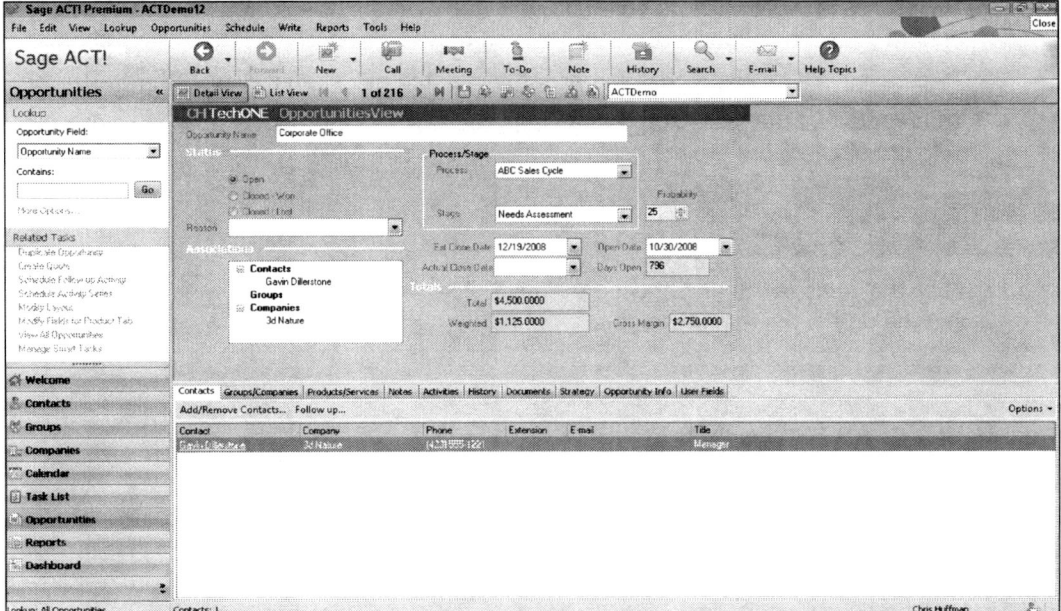

How it works...

Normally when you make a selection from the Navigation bar ACT! opens up the detail view. However, when you choose Opportunities from the Navigation bar the opportunities automatically display in list view. If you are viewing an opportunity in the detail view and then navigate to another area in ACT! you will be returned to the detail view if you choose Opportunities from the Navigation bar.

Adding processes and stages

Once you've become familiar with the overall opportunity process you'll want to customize whatever process you intend to work with and the corresponding stages. You'll need to be a manager or administrator of your database in order to do this.

ACT! comes with two process lists right out of the box. You can either delete them and replace them with a brand-new process, or you can modify one of the processes and make it your own.

Getting ready

You'll save yourself a great deal of time and aggravation if you think about your overall sales process before heading over to ACT!. You might consider a few rules of thumb as you begin to flesh out your sales process:

  ▸ The stages of a process are generally milestones. It might take you several smaller, behind the scenes activities before you can move an opportunity to the next stage.

  ▸ The stages in a sales process represent completed milestones.

  ▸ The purpose of the sales stages is to help you track your progress until you close the sale or complete the project.

How to do it...

  1. Click the **Tools** menu and choose **Define Fields**. The Define Fields window will open like the one in the following figure:

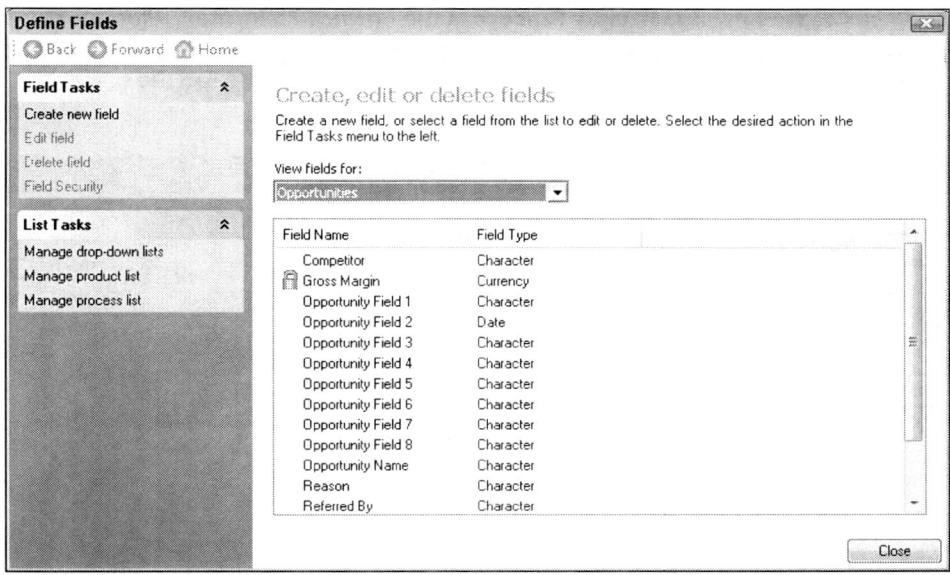

2. Click **Manage process list** from the **List Tasks** area. The Manage Process Lists window will open like the one you see in the following figure:

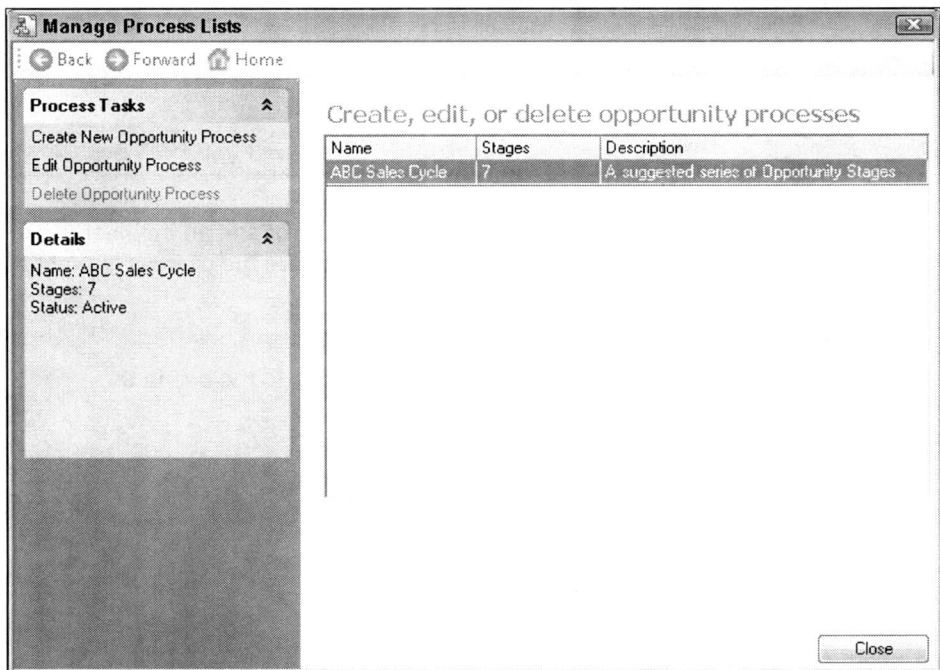

3. Click **Create New Opportunity Process** in the Process Tasks area. Alternatively, you can select an existing process and click **Edit Opportunity Process** if you want to edit an existing process. The **Manage Process Lists** wizard opens like the one in the following figure:

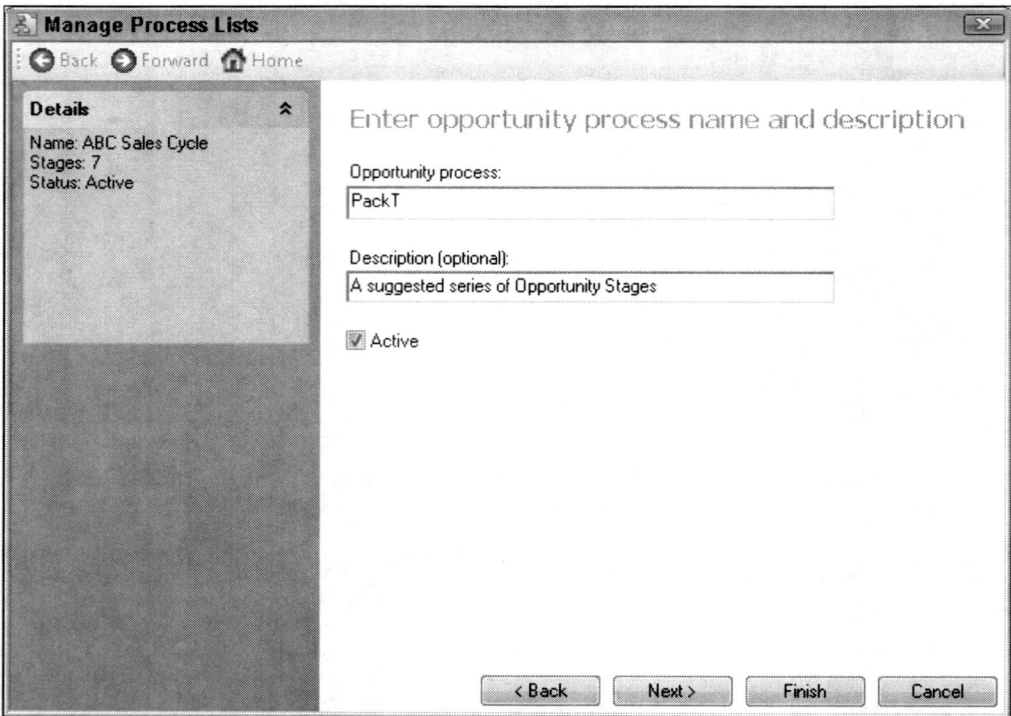

4. Add the process name or edit the existing one and add or edit an optional description. Click the **Active** checkmark box to make sure the process is available when creating a new opportunity.

5. Click **Next** to continue.

6. The **Customize stages** step of the wizard opens similar to the one in the following figure:

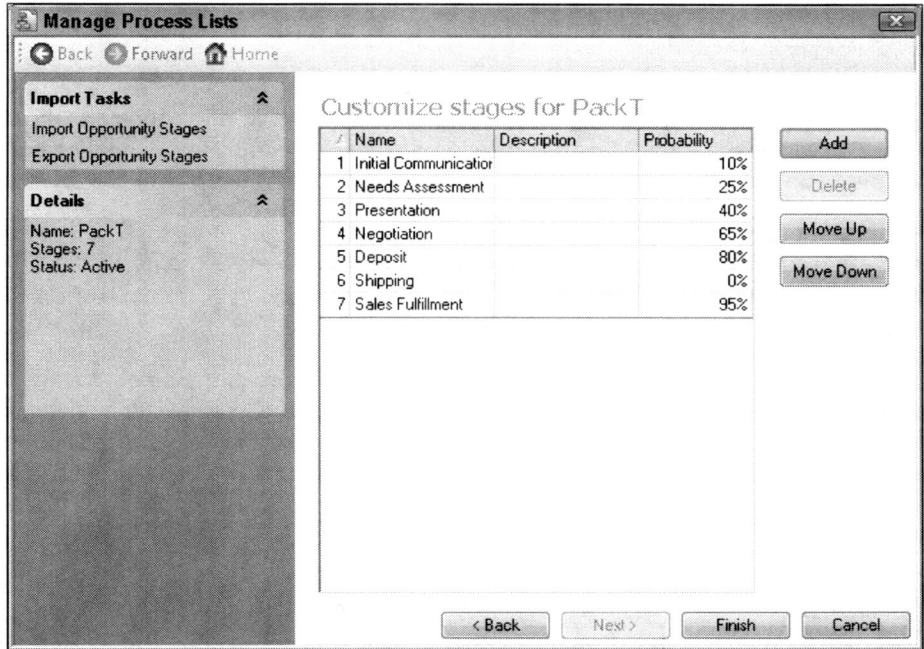

7. Click the **Add** button. An additional stage will appear at the bottom of the list of stages.

8. Type the name of the stage in the **Name** field.

9. Type a description of the stage in the **Description** field (optional). Normally if you supply the stage with a good name you don't need a description as well.

10. Type the estimated percentage for closing the opportunity at this stage in the **Probability** field. This is simply your best guess estimate of how likely opportunities are to close at this stage of the sales cycle.

11. To add more stages to the process, click **Add**, and repeat steps 8-10.

12. Select a stage and then click **Move Up** or **Move Down** to change the order of the stages in the process (optional). The stages will renumber automatically.

13. Click **Finish** when you're finished adding all the stages to the process and then **Close** to close the **Manage Process Lists** dialog window.

How it works...

Your new process list will now appear in the **Process:** drop-down list when you create new opportunities. You'll also be able to select the process list from the Opportunity List's **Process:** drop-down list. And, when you select your new process, all of your stages will automatically appear in the **Stage:** drop-down list.

There's more...

Although it's always a good idea to plan in advance, you can also edit a process directly from the Opportunity Detail view by clicking the Process drop-down arrow and choosing **Edit List Values...** which will open up the Manage Process Lists dialog window. This is also a handy way to tweak an existing process list as you start adding new opportunities to your database.

You might have noticed that ACT! automatically numbers the stages of a process. If you add a new stage you can use the **Move Up** or **Move Down** buttons to move the new stage into the desired order; all of the other stages will renumber automatically. If you delete a stage the remaining stages will renumber in the same manner.

You might want to delete either an existing process or one of more of the process stages. However, you cannot delete a process or a stage if it is being used in an existing opportunity. You'll need to either delete any associated opportunities first, or associate the opportunities to other processes or stages. From time to time you might notice that the Delete option is grayed out; that's because ACT! requires that you have at least one process and that each process contains at least one stage.

Creating a process for project management

One of the things you're bound to love about ACT! is its flexibility. The opportunities feature is a prime example of way that ACT! can be moulded to fit any industry. For example, you might work at a construction company that uses other software to create estimates and track outstanding quotes. Or you might be using ACT! for customer service tracking. In any event, you can create a process with stages that reflect other important milestones in your business such as "ordered blue prints" or "waiting for final payment."

Adding products and services

Lack of uniformity is the kiss of death for a database. Whenever possible you'll want to use drop-down lists to make sure that you use the same naming conventions throughout your database. Creating a list of products and services helps to keep your database consistent and has the added benefit of allowing you to determine which of your products are selling the best.

Some companies struggle with developing a product list because of the nature of their work. For example, each project that a builder works on might be unique, or the sales people in an organization don't want to add hundreds of products to each new opportunity. In those cases you might consider simply adding your major profit centres as your products so that you can still determine which areas of your business are producing the most revenue.

Getting ready

Normally you'll want to add your products to ACT! prior to creating your first opportunity. To make the job easier you'll want to have a copy of your company's price list or have a list of its profit centres.

How to do it...

1. Click the **Tools** menu and choose **Define Fields**.

2. Click **Manage product list** from the **List Tasks** area. Alternatively you can click the Manage Product List icon that appears in the icon bar in both the Opportunity Detail and List views. The Manage Product List dialog window shown in the following figure appears:

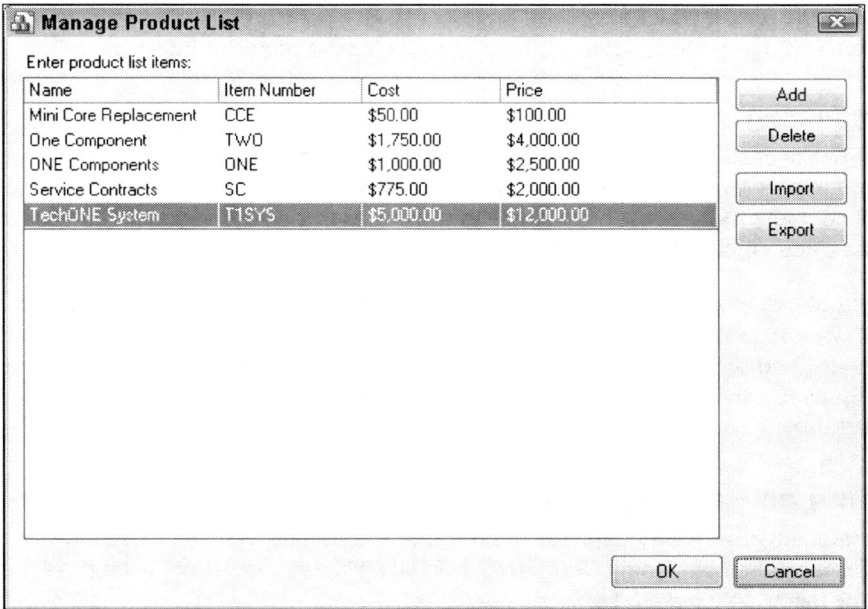

3. Click the **Add** button. A new line appears at the bottom of the list of products.

4. Type the name of the product in the **Name** field.

5. Type an item number in the **Item Number** field (optional).

6. Type the cost of the product In the **Cost** field if you want to track gross margins (optional).

7. Type the price of the product in the **Price** field if your prices remain fairly constant (optional).

8. To add more stages to the process, click **Add**, and repeat steps 3-7.
9. Click **OK** to close the **Manage Product List** dialog window.

How it works...

Your product list will now be available on the Products tab in the Opportunity Detail view where you can add products to new or existing opportunities. The products will be arranged alphabetically by product name.

There's more...

Adding products to your ACT! database has an additional advantage for the math-challenged readers in the crowd. When you select products to include in an opportunity, ACT! will allow you to add a quantity. This quantity will be multiplied by the pricing of the product to create a line item total. And, if you add several products to an opportunity all the product lines will automatically add together to create a total amount for the opportunity.

Product Pricing

There are two occasions in which ACT! users are hesitant to add specific pricing to their products. Sometimes there is a huge variance in the pricing. For example, a cabinet maker might sell cabinets that have a huge range in pricing. In this scenario you might consider leaving the price amount blank and filling in the correct price for each new opportunity.

In other situations your pricing might vary according to the circumstance. For example, you might want to extend a 25% discount to your best clients, or the pricing may vary based on a number of other variables. In those situations you might want to set a default price knowing that you can adjust it accordingly on an as needed basis each time you create a new opportunity.

Importing an existing price list

Some companies have a very large list of products and adding them all manually might prove to be extremely time consuming. Thankfully ACT! will allow you to import a list of your current products by following these steps:

1. Create an import file in `.csv` or `.txt` format for your existing products. The file must contain these column headers in exactly this order: Name, Item Number, Cost, and Price.
2. Make sure that data appears in all rows of your import file. If you don't use item numbers consider placing an X in that row and if you don't track cost use a 0.
3. Click the **Import** button on the Manage Product List dialog window. The Import Products dialog box will open like the one in the following figure:

4. Click the **Browse** button to navigate to the import file and make sure that a checkmark appears in the **Source file has column headers** field.

Working with opportunity fields and layouts

In ACT!, an opportunity is an **entity** or a cluster of related data that works in the same way as the other entities in ACT! including contacts, companies, and groups. This means that you can create new opportunity fields and modify the opportunity layout to best suit the needs of your company.

There are many situations that may warrant the addition of new opportunity fields. For example, you might want to include a shipping method and tracking number with your opportunity, or perhaps you need to add a Purchase Order field.

The basic opportunity layouts include a User Field tab which includes eight generic opportunity fields. Rather than creating new opportunity fields you might consider making use of those fields first by simply renaming them and perhaps moving them to a more visible location on your layout.

The purpose of this recipe is not to make you an expert in creating fields and designing layouts but to simply familiarize you with the overall process.

Getting ready

Adding new opportunity fields to your database is a very powerful feature. However, before you start adding new opportunity fields you'll first want to make sure that you are very familiar with the existing ones.

How to do it...

1. Click the **Tools** menu and choose **Define Fields**. The Define Fields dialog window opens like the one in the following figure:

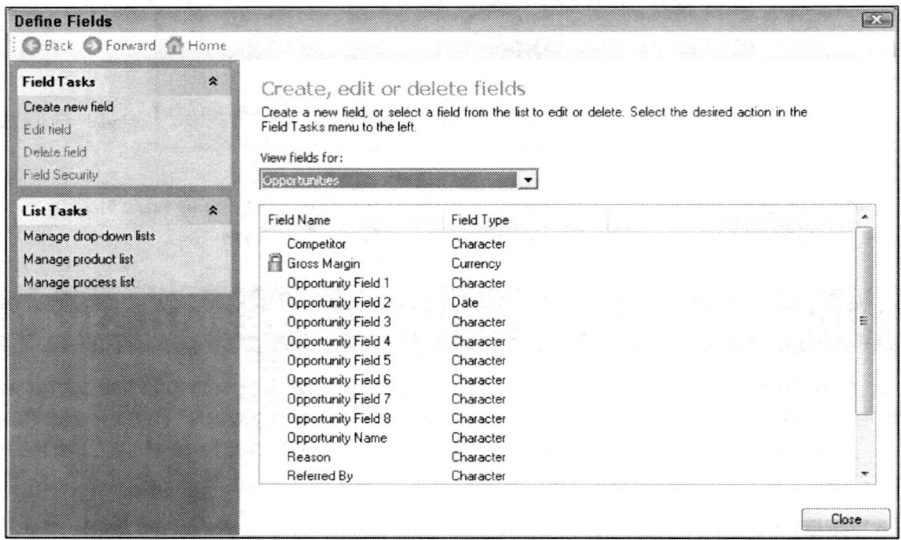

2. Select **Opportunities** from the **View fields for:** drop-down list.
3. Click **Create new field** in the **Field Tasks** area to start the Define Fields wizard. The following figure shows you an example of the first screen of the wizard:

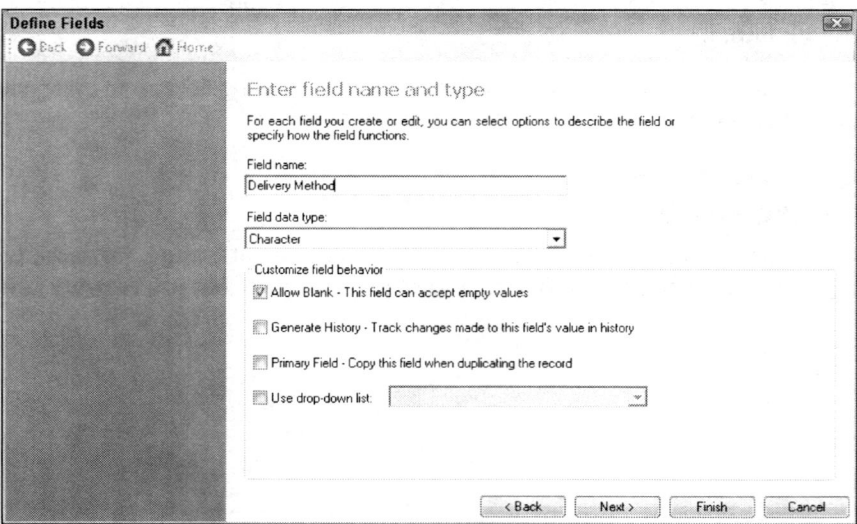

4. Add a field name, a data type, and then click **Next** to continue through the wizard exactly as you would if you were creating a contact field.

5. Click **Finish** when you are finished creating the field and then **Close** to close the Define Fields dialog window.

6. Click **Yes** to the prompt to modify your existing layout. The Layout Designer opens.

7. Click the **Field** icon in the **Field** area of the **Layout Designer Toolbox** of the Layout Designer.

8. Position the pointer on the layout where you want to add the field, drag to define the proper sizing, and then release the button.

9. The **Select Field** dialog box appears similar to the one you see in the following figure:

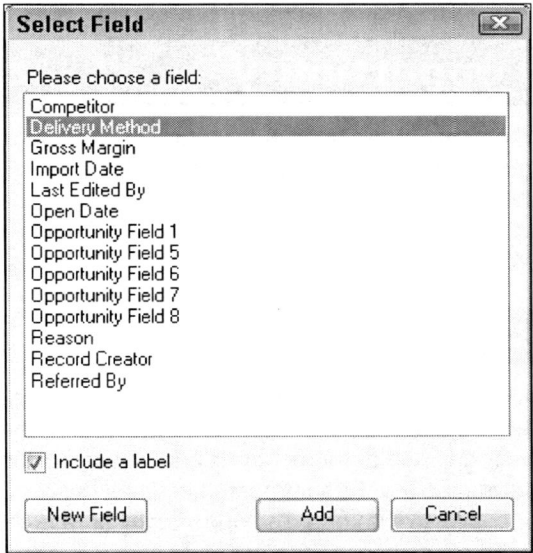

10. Select the new field from the **Select Field** dialog box and then click **Add** to add it to your layout.

11. Close the **Layout Designer** and then click **Yes** when prompted to save the layout.

How it works...

Your new field will now appear on the layout of the Opportunity Detail view and you are now free to start entering data into it. It will also appear on the Opportunity List if you customize the columns that are shown to include it.

There's more...

If you are familiar with the various ACT! features you can start applying your knowledge to the various areas in ACT!. For example, you might want to save the opportunity layout using the name of your company, making it easier to identify. You might also want to go back and edit your new opportunity field to include a drop-down list or to make the field a required one.

Creating an opportunity

By now you're probably chomping at the bit in anticipation of creating a new opportunity. If you've already followed the previous recipes in this chapter you have all the tools you need to start adding an opportunity. You've created your process and the corresponding stages, added in your products and possibly even included a new field or two. There's only one thing missing: you need to try to sell someone something!

Getting ready

Many ACT! users get a bit confused as to when they should begin to add new opportunities to their database and start to create opportunities for any and all of their prospects. If that's the case you might consider this rule of thumb: don't add new opportunities until you have **qualified** a prospect to determine that he's interested in doing business with you and that you're interested in doing business with him. The opportunity area is the only area of ACT! that performs calculations so there's no sense creating an opportunity until you have some idea of the value of an opportunity unless you're using opportunities to track projects.

How to do it...

1. Perform a lookup to find the contact for whom you're creating an opportunity.

2. Create a new opportunity by clicking the **Opportunities** tab and then clicking the **New Opportunity** icon on the Opportunities tab icon bar. The Opportunity Detail view will open like the one you see in the following figure:

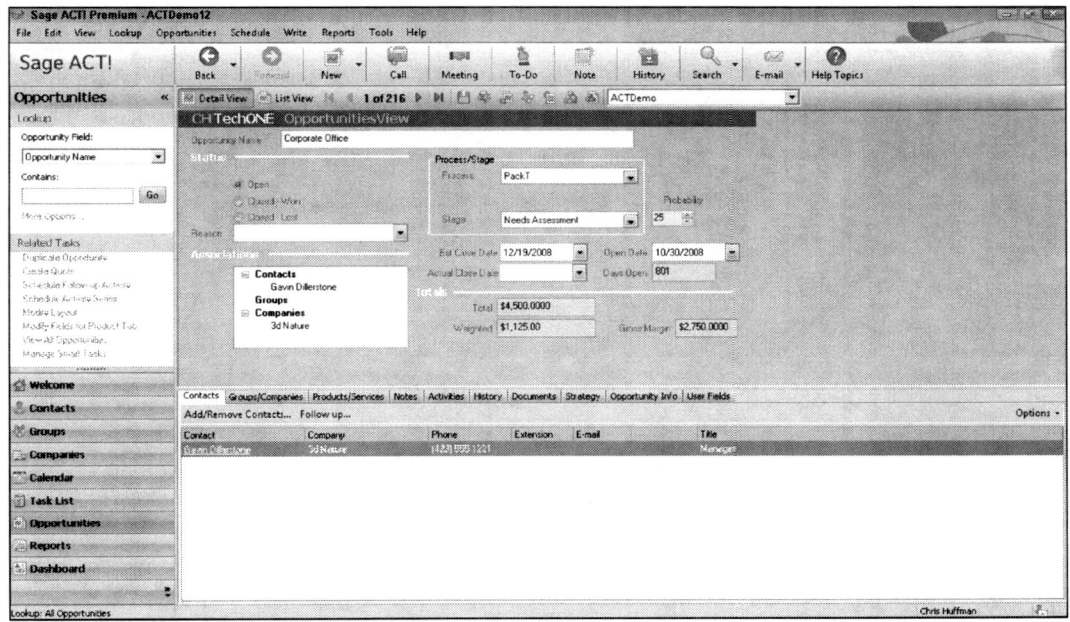

3. Give the opportunity a name. If you don't give the opportunity a name, ACT! automatically assigns one: New Opportunity.

4. Select a process from the **Process** drop-down list.

5. Select a stage from the **Stage** drop-down list. If you don't select one, ACT! will default to the first stage of the process.

6. Change the probability of closing (optional). By default, the probability you assigned to the sales stage when you set up the sales process already appears.

7. Enter the estimated close date. By default, today's date appears but you should change it to your best guess as to when you'll actually be able to close the opportunity.

8. Click the **Contacts** tab and click the **Add/Remove Contacts...** button on the Contacts tab to associate additional contacts with the opportunity (optional).

9. Click the **Products/Services** tab and click the **Add...** button. The **Add/Edit Product** dialog window will open like the following figure:

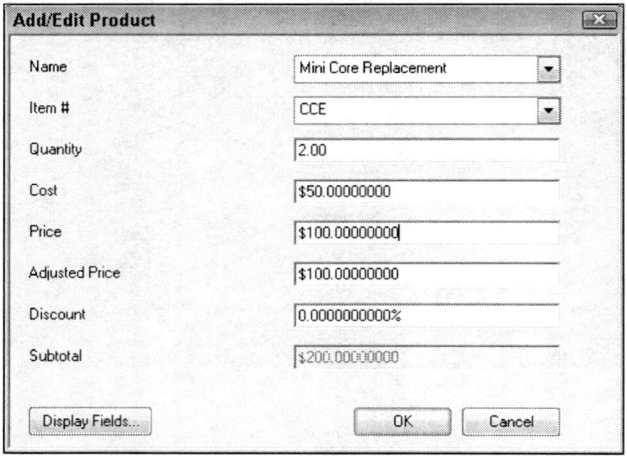

10. Choose a product or service name from the Name drop-down list and then fill in the quantity if you are adding more than one of the product to the opportunity. Optionally, you can change the price if necessary.

11. Click **OK** to close the **Add/Edit Product** dialog window.

12. Repeat Steps 9, 10, and 11 above to add more products to the opportunity (optional).

13. Fill in any additional opportunity fields that are pertinent to the opportunity (optional).

How it works...

Your new opportunity will now appear on the opportunity tab of the contact's record and in the Opportunity List view. You'll also notice that ACT! automatically filled in several fields including the creation date and the name of the person who created the opportunity. The person who created the opportunity is automatically listed as the Record Manager of the opportunity; they can reassign the opportunity to another Record Manager if needed, or wait until a Manager or Administrator changes it. The Days Open counter starts running so that you'll know exactly how long the opportunity has been open.

There's more...

Because an opportunity is a separate entity you can work with it in much the same way that you work with other records types. You can head to the Notes tab and add a note, schedule a follow-up activity, and even associate the opportunity with existing groups and companies. You'll also want to check out the opportunity's history tab where you'll find a running list of all the changes that you've made to the opportunity.

Working with probabilities

New ACT! users are often confused about the probabilities that are associated with the sales stages. By using probabilities you'll be able to have a better idea of the amount of revenue you can expect to see in the coming months. Probabilities are based on the assumption that even the best sales person can't close 100% of their projected sales. For example, the first stage in your process might be Initial Communication and you might give this stage a 10% probability of closing. Of course you can change that probability on an individual opportunity basis if you want to.

The weighted total gives you a more realistic idea of the amount of future earnings. When you create a new opportunity the probability percentage is multiplied by the total value of the opportunity to give you a **weighted** total. The status bar at the bottom of a contact's Opportunities tab and the one that runs along the bottom of the Opportunity List shows the weighted total as well as a grand total of all the opportunities that are listed.

Give 'em a discount

Feel free to overwrite the default price of a product as you create the opportunity. You can |also lower (or raise!) a price if you're extending special pricing to a customer by using one of these methods:

- ▶ Enter a new price in the Adjusted Price field of the Add/Edit Product dialog window. ACT! will automatically calculates the discount percentage.

- ▶ Enter a discount percentage in the Discount field of the Add/Edit Product dialog window. ACT! automatically calculates the adjusted price.

Editing an opportunity

Many people refer to their sales opportunities as their sales **funnel** or pipeline. If you visualize what a traditional funnel looks like and how it works you'll start to see the similarities. You pour something into the top of a funnel and ideally everything flows out again through the bottom. The funnel can become "clogged" and have to be shaken up a bit, and at times some of the items that enter into the top of the funnel never make it all the way out through the bottom.

The whole concept behind a sales pipeline is that you probably won't be able to close 100% of your deals but that the rate of success increases as the opportunity progresses through your pipeline. Additionally, you'll probably want to track the progress of an opportunity as it travels through the pipeline and use that information to find out what's working well for you and what's not.

Getting ready

If one of your opportunities changes it is necessary to edit the opportunity in ACT! to reflect those changes. This information appears in your various reports and dashboards so updating your opportunities is vitally important.

How to do it...

1. Click Opportunities in the Navigation bar.
2. If you are not there already click the List View button on the icon bar (optional).
3. Double-click the opportunity that you want to update to open it. Do not click the contact's name on the Opportunity List or you will end up on the contact's record instead.
4. Change the information in the Stage field as necessary.
5. Update the Estimated Close Date (optional).
6. Change the opportunity's status (optional).

How it works...

All reports and dashboards that you access will automatically reflect the updated information. In addition, ACT! will automatically change the information in the Last Edited and Last Edited By fields to reflect the current date and the name of the user who implemented the change.

There's more...

There are a number of ways that you can access an opportunity in order to change it. In addition to double-clicking the opportunity from the Opportunity List you can also:

▶ Create a lookup for the contact associated with the opportunity and then click the contact's Opportunities tab. On the Opportunities tab, double-click the opportunity.

▶ Search for an opportunity by clicking the Lookup menu, choosing Opportunities, and then selecting one of the field choices. You can search by opportunity name, product, or status. If more than one opportunity meets your search criteria the Opportunity List will open and you can double-click the opportunity you want to modify.

Closing the deal

All new opportunities are assigned the Open status. When you close a sale, you can record the outcome by changing the status to either Closed—Won or Closed—Lost to reflect the outcome. ACT! will automatically fill in the Actual Closing prompting you to choose an option from the Reason field drop-down list. In addition ACT! records a history on the contact's History tab; if you associated the opportunity with a group or company, ACT! records a history on the History tab for the group or company as well.

There is also an Inactive status. However, rather than making an opportunity inactive and potentially forgetting about it, you might consider simply changing the Estimated Close Date to a much later date.

Working with the Opportunity List

The Opportunity List provides you with a way to view all your opportunities for all your contacts in one place. You can filter the Opportunity List to display only those opportunities that match your specifications. You can print the Opportunity List or you can export the Opportunity List to Excel. The Opportunity List even contains a status bar that runs across the bottom and displays the total number of opportunities as well as weighted and grand totals of all the opportunities. You'll also notice that the Opportunity List has its own toolbar containing icons pertaining specifically to the Opportunity List.

Getting ready

If you haven't created any opportunities you won't find the Opportunity List to be very helpful because it won't contain any data. Therefore, you'll want to create as many opportunities as possible prior to taking a look at the Opportunity List.

How to do it...

1. Click Opportunities in the Navigation bar.
2. If you are not there already click the List View button on the icon bar (optional).
3. Configure the Opportunity List in any of the following ways:
    - **Sort**: Click on a column heading to sort your data.
    - **Dates:** Limits the opportunities to those matching the estimated closing date that you indicate.
    - **Status:** Indicates whether you want to view Open, Closed-Won, Closed-Lost, Inactive, or all opportunities. You can also choose None, which frankly doesn't make a whole lot of sense because then you don't see any of your opportunities!
    - **Process:** Allows you to select one or all of the processes that you set up.

- ❑ **Stage:** If you are viewing a single process then you can indicate which stages within that process that you want to view.

- ❑ **Probability:** Select one of the parameters and then type the percent you want to use; you can find opportunities that match a specific percentage or those that are greater than or less than a percentage.

- ❑ **Total:** Select one of the parameters and then type the amount of the opportunity you want to use; you can find opportunities that match a specific amount or those that are greater than or less than a given amount.

- ❑ **Select Users:** Select the names of the Record Managers associated with the opportunities you want to view.

There's more...

When you change the filter options, the Opportunity List changes to include the options you selected. In addition to the basic filtering options mentioned above, there are a number of other ways that you can make the Opportunity List your own.

Hitting the Reset button

After you diligently work to set all your filters, you'll probably want to reset them again sooner or later. Of course, you can always go into each of the drop-down boxes and set them back to **All**. Or you can accomplish that task by clicking the Reset button at the top of the Opportunity List which will set back all the filters to All.

Customizing the columns

Each column that appears in the Opportunity List shows you the data from a single opportunity field. You can determine exactly which columns you want displayed by right-clicking in the middle of the Opportunity List and selecting **Customize Columns...** from the contextual menu. A Customize Columns dialog window similar to the one you see in the following figure opens:

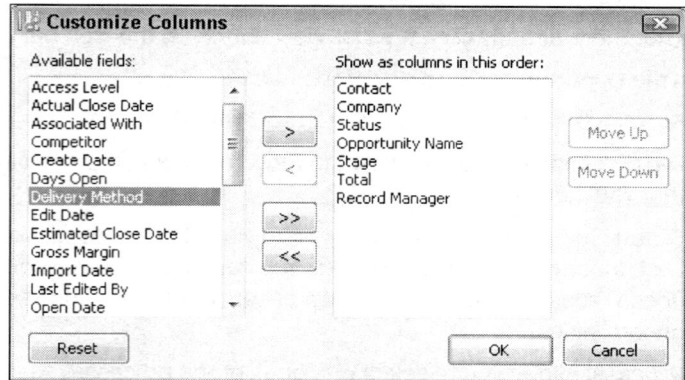

You can choose the columns you wish to display from the pane on the left, click the single right-pointing arrow, and then click **OK**. The column(s) you selected will now appear in the Opportunity List.

Once you've added new columns to the Opportunity List you can change the order of the columns by dragging the column headings to the left or right. And, should you want to widen or narrow a column you can do so by hovering your mouse on the right edge of a column heading and then dragging the column's edge to the right or left.

Exporting to Excel

As hard as it may be to believe, there may be times when you want to get a bit more functionality out of the Opportunity List than what it has to offer. For example, you may want to display sub-totals or calculate commissions. Or there might be times when you need to share your pipeline with non-ACT! users. You can solve those dilemmas in a heartbeat by following these steps:

1. Filter the Opportunity List to display just the data you need
2. Add or remove column and place them in the order you'd like
3. Click the Excel icon on the Opportunity List's icon bar

Your Opportunity List will open up in a brand new spreadsheet—provided, of course, that Excel is installed on your computer. And, as an added bonus, the spreadsheet will also include pivot tables displaying your information in graphical form.

Quick printing the Opportunity List

ACT! comes with a myriad of opportunity reports and chances are very good that one of them will display exactly the information you need. And, if you've read the Dashboards and Reports Cookbook by Packt you know how to customize them. However, should you need a simple list you might want to just create a print-out of the Opportunity List. This task is easy if you follow these steps:

▸ Filter the Opportunity List to display just the data you need

▸ Add or remove column and place them in the order you'd like:

  ❑ Click the **File** menu and choose **Quick Print Current Window** to print the entirety of the Opportunity List

  ❑ Select specific Opportunity List items by holding down the *CTRL* key and clicking on them and then Click the **File** menu and choose **Quick Print Selected** to print only the highlighted selections

Creating an Opportunity Graph

Most ACT! users have discovered the ACT! reports and dashboards along the way and use them to display their data. However, not all users have discovered the pipelines and graphs that can be easily created from the ACT! opportunity data.

Getting ready

To get the full effect of the pipelines and graphs you'll want to make sure that your database is loaded with opportunities.

How to do it...

1. Create a lookup of opportunities (optional).
2. Click the Opportunity Graph icon on the Opportunities List's toolbar. Alternatively, you can click the Reports menu, select Opportunity Reports, and then choose Opportunity Graph. A Graph Options dialog window will open like the one in the following figure:

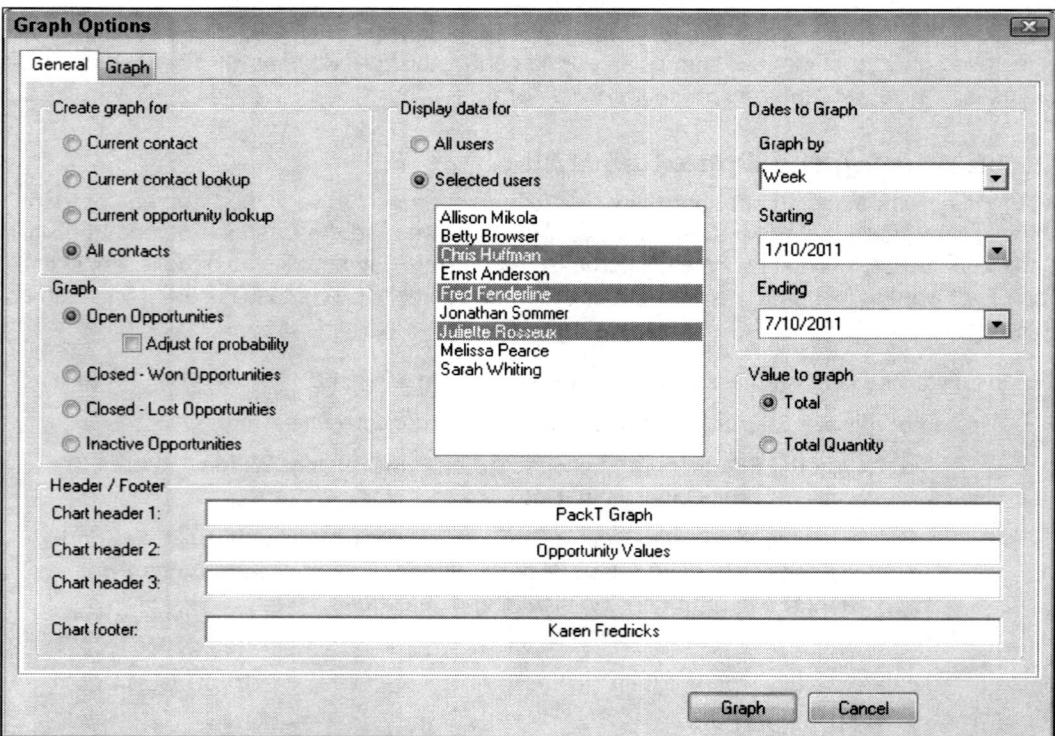

3. Specify the data you'd like to graph by changing the fields on the **General** tab to:

    ❑ **Create graph for:** specify what contacts will be displayed

    ❑ **Graph:** select the status of the opportunities you want to graph

    ❑ **Display data for:** select the names of the Record Manager

    ❑ **Dates to Graph:** select the date increments to be displayed on the graph and the starting and ending dates of the opportunities

    ❑ **Value to graph:** indicate whether you want to graph the total value of the opportunities or the total quantity of products

    ❑ **Header/Footer:** fill in the appropriate information that will appear at the top and the bottom of the graph (optional)

4. Click on the **Graph** tab and specify your changes. This is where you can specify whether you want a bar or line graph and the colors that will be used on the graph.

5. Click the **Graph** button. You can see a sample graph in the following figure:

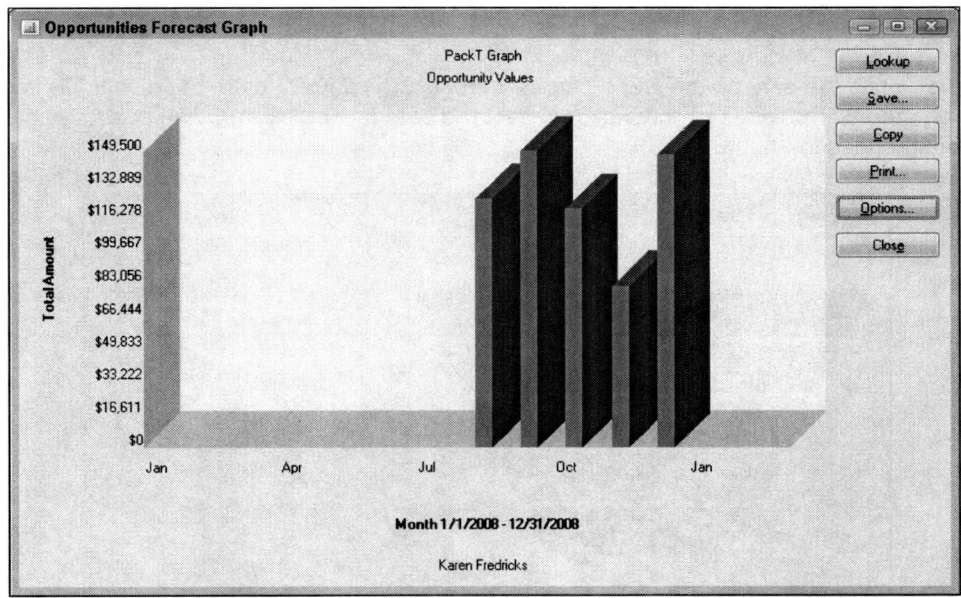

How it works...

Once the graph opens you can use the graph in a number of additional ways:

    ❑ **Lookup:** creates a lookup of all the opportunities listed in the graph

    ❑ **Save:** saves the graph as a .bmp or .jpg file

    ❑ **Copy:** copies the graph to the clipboard

- ❏ **Print:** creates a hard copy of the graph
- ❏ **Options**: returns you to the Graph Options dialog window
- ❏ **Close:** closes the Graph Options dialog window
- ❏ Click a bar on the graph to view a lookup of the opportunities represented by that bar

There's more...

You can also create an opportunity pipeline following basically the same steps as those you follow to create a graph.

- ▶ Create a lookup of opportunities.
- ▶ Click the Opportunity Pipeline icon on the Opportunities List's toolbar or select Opportunity Reports, and then choose Opportunity Pipeline.
- ▶ Specify the data you'd like to have displayed on the pipeline.
- ▶ Click the **Graph** button.

However, while the bars on the graph change to reflect the current data, the pipeline is based on a set graphic that does not change to reflect the data it contains. You can see a sample pipeline in the follow figure:

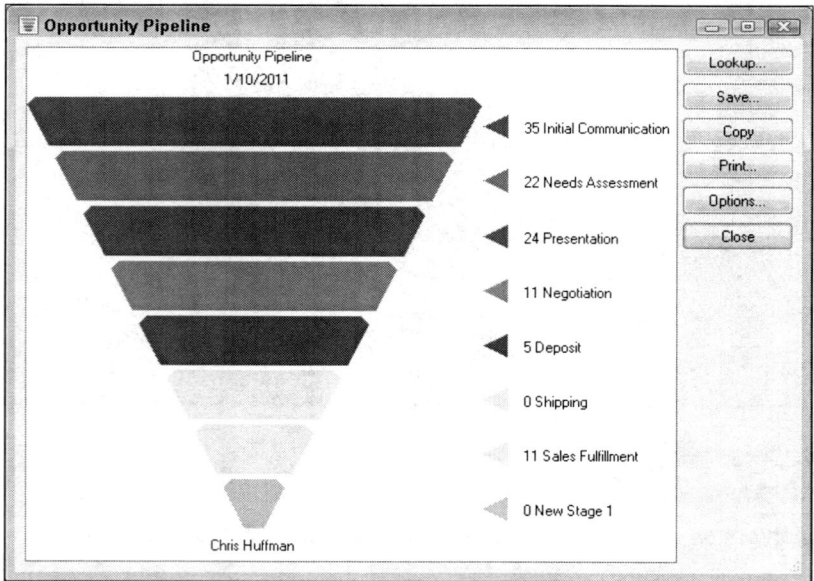

9
Integrating with Microsoft Outlook

In this chapter, we will cover:

- ▸ Setting up Outlook as your ACT! email client
- ▸ Sending an Outlook message from ACT! to a single contact
- ▸ Sending an Outlook message from ACT! to multiple contacts
- ▸ Sending an email to an ACT! contact in Outlook
- ▸ Associating incoming Outlook email to ACT!
- ▸ Creating a new ACT! Contact from Outlook
- ▸ Synchronizing your calendar information
- ▸ Synchronizing your Contact information

Introduction

Most ACT! users want to send email. Chapter 12 explains how to send bulk emailings through ACT!. In this chapter you'll learn how to send ACT! email by linking your ACT! database to Microsoft Outlook.

If you choose to link ACT! to Outlook, you can choose to use either Outlook or ACT! E-Mail as your email editor. If you use the ACT! E-mail editor you manage, view, and send email messages using the ACT! E-mail system; however, Outlook will still be responsible for the actual email transmission. If you use Outlook as your email client you manage, view, and send email messages directly from within Outlook. However, both scenarios will result in a record of the email being created on ACT!'s History tab.

Because Outlook is a much more robust email client than ACT! E-Mail, I recommend that you use Outlook as your email client.

ACT! 2012 can integrate with Outlook versions 2003, 2007, and 2010. However, in order for ACT! and Outlook to properly integrate, you must install Outlook prior to installing ACT! and make sure that you have installed all the available Microsoft Office service packs. If you install or upgrade Outlook after you install ACT!, you will need to uninstall and reinstall ACT! in order to integrate it with Outlook.

Setting up Outlook as your ACT! e-mail client

Before you can start sending email in ACT! you'll need to set up your email preferences. Fortunately ACT! makes the task extremely easy by providing you with an 8 step E-Mail Setup Wizard. Best of all, each step includes recommended options to make progressing your way through the wizard a snap.

Getting ready

You'll need to make sure that Outlook is fully functional prior to installing ACT!. If Outlook is not working properly, or hasn't yet been activated, you'll need to correct the problem and then uninstall and reinstall ACT!.

How to do it...

1. Click the **Tools** menu, and then choose **Preferences**. The Preferences dialog box opens.

2. Select the **E-mail & Outlook Sync** tab and then click the **E-mail System Setup...** button to start the E-mail Setup Wizard.

3. Click **Next** at the Welcome screen.

4. Select Microsoft Outlook and then click **Next**. The following figure shows you the second screen of the wizard:

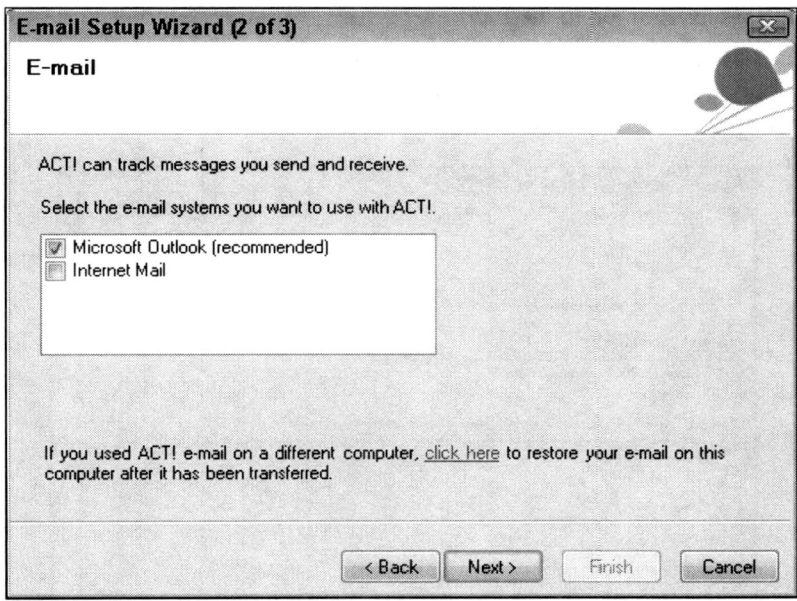

5. The **E-mail - Outlook Address Books** dialog box appears. Click **Add** to fill in your password credentials and then click **OK** to return to the E-mail-Outlook Address Books dialog box. You can see what this looks like in the following image:

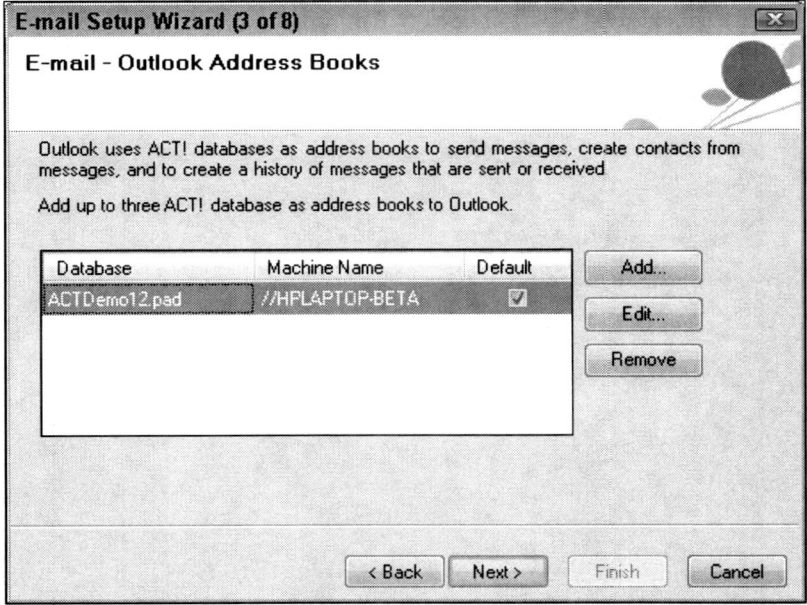

6. Click **Next** to continue to the fourth screen of the E-mail Setup Wizard.

7. Choose **Microsoft Outlook (recommended)** from the drop-down list as your email editor and then click **Next** to continue. The following screenshot shows you the fourth step of the E-mail Setup Wizard:

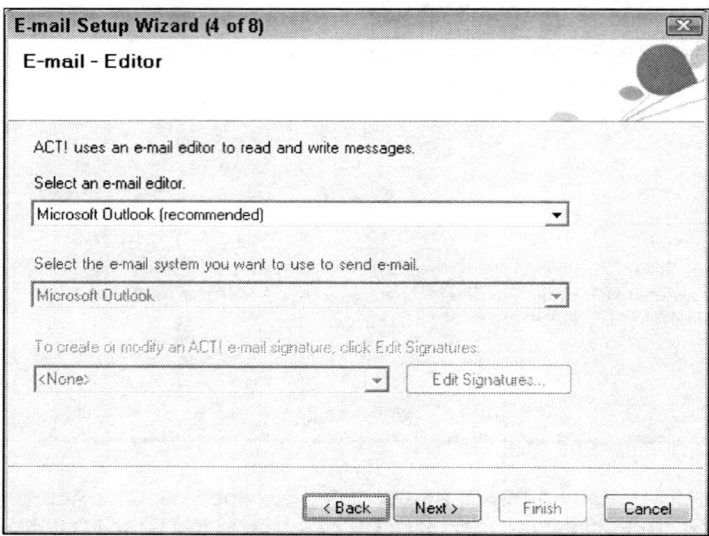

8. Select the **E-mail subject and message (recommended)** option from the drop-down list and then click **Next** to continue. The following image shows you what the fifth step of the E-mail Setup Wizard looks like:

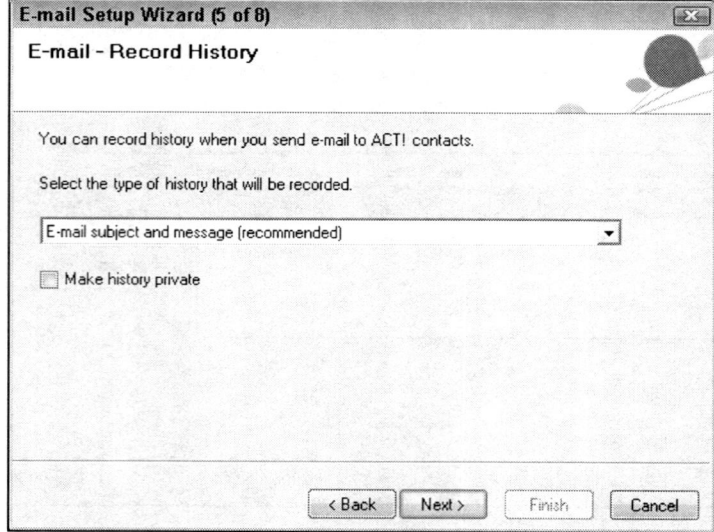

9. This page of the wizard allows you to select how ACT! should handle incoming messages. Choose the **E-mail subject and message (recommended)** option from the first drop-down list and then "From" contact only (recommended) from the second. The following image shows you an example of the sixth step of the E-mail Setup Wizard:

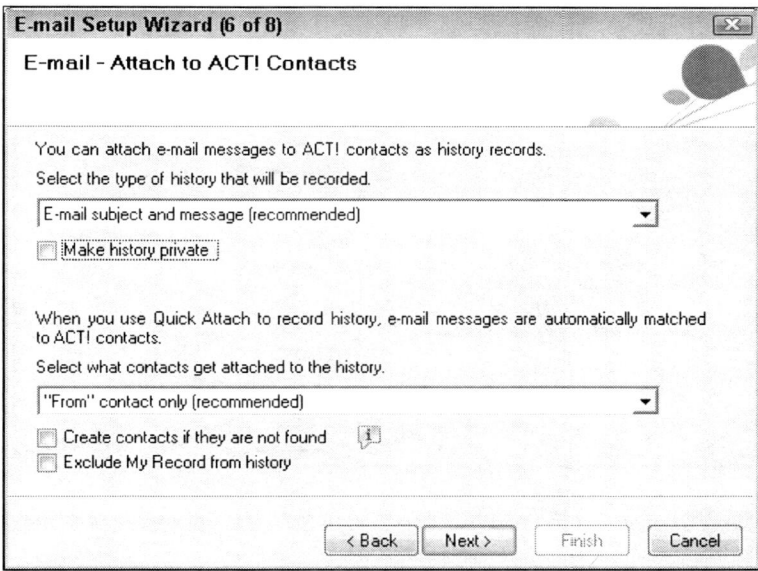

10. Click **Next** to continue to the seventh step of the wizard to select the activity invitation options:

   □ **Select the application that displays the activity alarm:** select **ACT!, Outlook**, or **ACT! and Outlook** to indicate which program will display an alarm when synchronizing your ACT! activities with Outlook calendar items.

   □ **You can create an ACT! activity when you accept a meeting invitation in Outlook:** select whether or not you want the ACT! activity to automatically open when you receive iCalendar invitations.

   □ **Create contacts if they are not found:** select this option if you want ACT! to create a new contact record when it cannot match an incoming invitation to an existing contact record.

11. The following image shows you the **E-mail – Activity Invitation** dialog window:

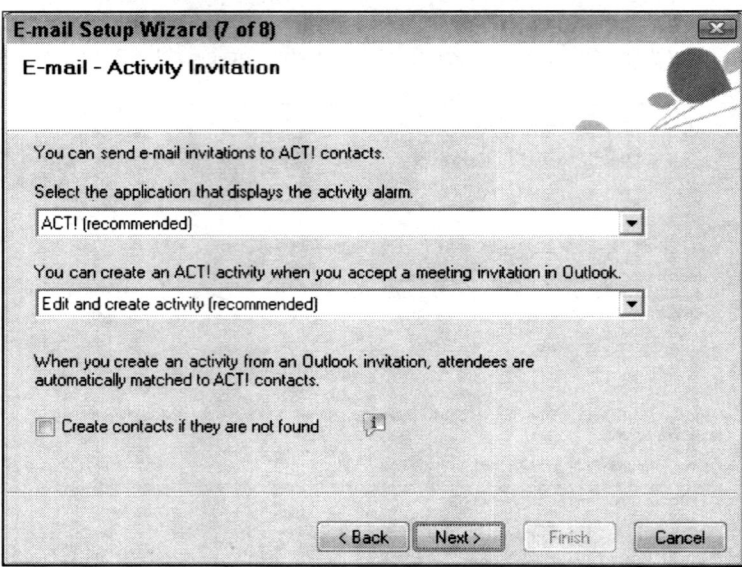

12. Click **Next** to proceed to finishing the E-mail Setup and then click **Finish** to close the wizard.

How it works...

Once you integrate Microsoft Outlook to ACT! and choose it as your email editor the two will begin to work seamlessly together. A new Outlook email message will automatically open when you send an email message to one of your ACT! contacts. You'll also notice that several ACT! icons now appear in Outlook.

You'll find that this process will work much faster if Outlook is already open and ready to go prior to sending ACT! email. Once the new Outlook message opens you'll be able to work with it exactly as you do for any other outgoing Outlook email message.

There's more...

For those of you who are working with multiple ACT! databases, the wizard allows you to add up to three ACT! databases as address books to Outlook so that you can move back and forth between your databases and still continue to send email.

Once you choose the Microsoft Outlook option you will not be allowed to add any other email programs to the ACT! E-mail client such as Outlook Express or Lotus Notes. If you would like to set up more than one email client in ACT!, you're better off choosing ACT! as your email client.

Deciding on the email - record history options

In step 8 you are asked to select the default history option for the email messages that you send. Basically, you can select which part of the message you want to record to history, if at all. Or, you can choose to attach a copy of the message to history. To make email history private so other ACT! users cannot see it, select **Make history private**.

Your options include the following:

- ▶ **None:** no history of the message will be recorded.
- ▶ **E-mail Subject Only:** records only the subject line of the message.
- ▶ **E-mail Subject and Message (Recommended)**: records both the subject line and the contents of the outgoing email message.
- ▶ **E-mail Subject, Message and all Attachments**: creates a file of the outgoing email. This is the only option that will retain the attachments sent with an email. When you compose messages, you can change these settings on an individual basis. For example, you might not want to include the body of the email on messages you send that are based on a template, or you might decide that you don't need to record any history at all for personal email messages.

Many ACT! users love the idea of creating an attachment file for **all** their outgoing messages. However, this is not a good option to select as the default option. If you're typical of most ACT! users, over a period of time you will have created thousands of files and placed unnecessary pressure on your computer's resources.

Sending an Outlook message to a single contact

When you configure Outlook to integrate with ACT! and choose to use Outlook as your email client each product has separate duties. If you look at the overall process you see that it begins and ends with ACT! but that Outlook does all the actual work.

A breakdown of the process looks something like this:

- ▶ The email originates in ACT! where you have the option to either send a blank or a template email message
- ▶ At that point Outlook takes over; you can add finishing touches to your message and then Outlook sends the message on its way
- ▶ Outlook performs the actual sending of the email message; the message will remain in the Outbox until Outlook performs a Send/Receive
- ▶ Once the message is sent ACT! creates a history of the email on the contact's History tab

Getting ready

There are two things necessary in order to send an ACT! email message with the help of Outlook:

▶ Outlook must be open and fully functional. You've completed the E-mail Setup in ACT! and indicated your preference to use Outlook

▶ There is an email address in one of the email fields of the current contact record.

How to do it...

1. Create a new email message using one of the following four methods:
   - Click on the contact's E-Mail field
   - Choose Write@@-->E-Mail Message
   - Click the Write E-Mail Message icon on the icon bar

   These methods all result in the opening of a new message Outlook message.

2. Fill in the Subject field and create your message.
3. If you're using Outlook 2007 or 2010, click the **Add-Ins** tab to change the default history option or to mark the history as private (optional). In Outlook 2003 you'll find this option on the main email toolbar.
4. Click **Send**.

How it works...

You'll notice that when the new Outlook email message opens, the contact's name already appears in the To field. If the ACT! contact record only contains an email address then only the contact's email address appears.

There's more...

In a situation where your Outlook email is stored on a local computer, Outlook must perform a Send/Receive before the message is sent; the message will remain in the Outlook Outbox until that happens. You can configure Outlook to perform a Send/Receive on a regular basis if it is open. If Outlook is not open, the email will not be sent.

If you have configured Outlook to access a Microsoft Exchange Server and your Outbox is actually located on the server, the server will send the email message automatically even if Outlook is not open on the local computer.

Sending an email template

You're probably using ACT! because you know it will save you lots of time. One of the great ACT! timesavers is its ability to merge the contents of a contact record directly into a previously created template. This is a great way to cut down on the time it takes to send routine emails.

You can take advantage of those templates by clicking on the Write menu, choosing email message (from template), and then selecting your previously created template. When the Outlook message opens it will contain not only the contact's name in the To line but the body of the message will already be filled in.

Sending an Outlook message to multiple contacts

There are probably times when you'd like to send an email message to all the members of a Group or all the associates in a Company. Fortunately in ACT! you can do it pretty much with a click of a button.

Getting ready

You can send an email message only to those contacts that have an email address. To help you along, ACT! will only include those Group or Company members having email addresses; those without email addresses will not be included. Although you may be grateful that ACT! is taking such a proactive role in determining who is to receive your message, you might not be so happy to realize that several of your contacts might not be receiving your message.

Prior to sending out your message you might create a lookup of the Group or Company contacts by right-clicking the Group or Company name and selecting and then choosing Create Lookup from the contextual menu. At that juncture you can narrow your lookup to include only those contacts without an email address to make sure that all Group or Company members have an email address prior to proceeding.

How to do it...

1. Click **Group** or **Company** on the Navigation Bar to open the Group or Company Detail view.

2. Select the Group or Company that you'd like to email.

3. Click the **Write E-mail** icon on the toolbar. The Outlook message window appears with the recipients' names in the To field.

4. Fill in the Subject field.

5. Click the Add-Ins tab to change the Record history option **ACT! History** and indicate whether the message is public or private (optional).

6. Type your message in the text box.

7. Making any necessary formatting changes, check the spelling and/or attach a file (optional).

8. Click **Send**.

There's more...

If you think there are endless ways that you can use ACT! to save you time—you're right. In addition to sending your messages to the members of a Group or Company you can also easily send a message to your current lookup by following these steps:

1. Create a lookup of contacts.

2. Click **Tag All** on the Contact List toolbar.

3. Click the **Write E-mail** icon.

Sending an e-mail to an ACT! contact in Outlook

As an ACT! user, you probably spend the majority of your day in your ACT! database. And, should you want to send an email to one of their contacts, you know that you can do it by simply clicking the contact's email address. Once in a while, however, you might want to send an email to an ACT! contact while you are in Outlook without having to return to your ACT! database. It will probably come as no surprise to learn that ACT! allows you to do that as well.

Getting ready

You'll need to make sure that you have already set the ACT! email preference to Outlook before you get started.

How to do it...

1. Create a new email message in Outlook.

2. Click either the **To**, **Cc**, or **Bcc** button.

3. Select the name of your ACT! database from the Address Book drop-down list. The following figure shows you an example of the Select Names: Contacts dialog box:

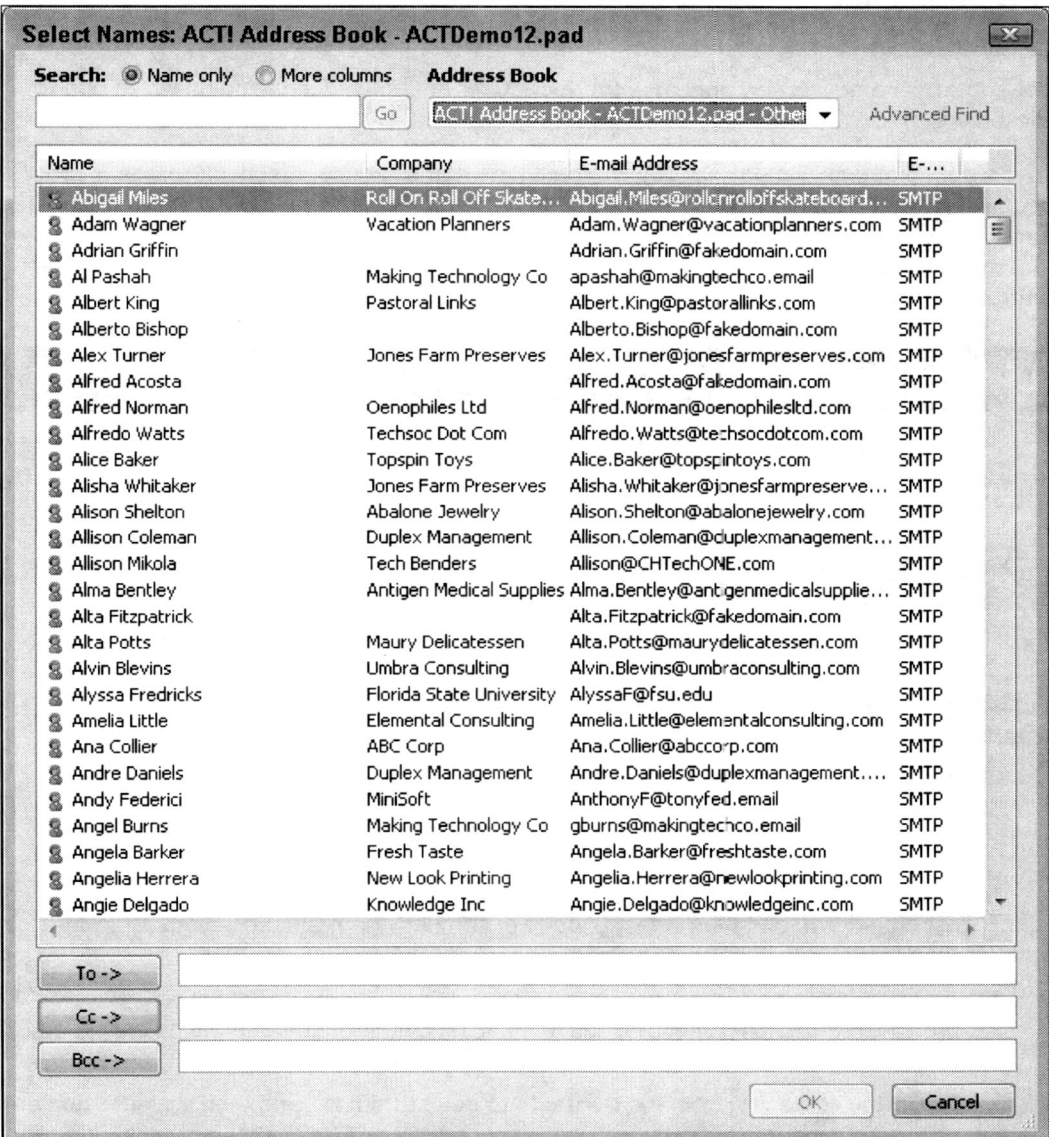

4. Type the first several letters of the contact's first name (optional).

5. Select the name(s) from the list on the left.

6. Click **To**, **Cc**, or **Bcc** to add the names.

7. Click **OK** to return to the Outlook email message.

How it works...

The contact's name will now appear in the Too, CC, or BCC field, depending on which one you clicked in step 6.

Over a period of time Outlook will begin to recall the names and/or email addresses of the people you have previously communicated with. When you begin typing the first few letters of a name or email address, Outlook automatically begins to display the first alphabetical record that matches. If a correct match is found, select it and it will appear in the To field, saving you a trip to the address book.

Linking incoming Outlook e-mail to ACT!

So far in this chapter we've been discussing ways to handle outbound mail but you might want to attach inbound mail to a contact record and create a history item. Fortunately for you, ACT! is already one step ahead of you and has included that functionality.

Getting ready

You'll want to make sure that you've probably configured Outlook as ACT!'s email client.

How to do it...

1. In Outlook, select or open a message that you want to attach to an ACT! contact record.
2. Click the **Attach to ACT! Contacts** icon on Outlook's toolbar.
3. To select contacts for certain groups or companies, select an option from the Filter list drop-down, and then select a group or company from the drop-down list to the right (optional).
4. Type the first letters of the contact's last name in the **Look for** field. If you have previously attached a similar email to an ACT! contact their name will be greyed out and already appear in the **Attach to these contacts:** pane.
5. Select the contact(s) from the **Contacts to select from** list and then click the single right-pointing arrow button to move the contact to the **Attach these contacts** list. The following figure shows you what the **Attach E-mail to Contacts** dialog box looks like:

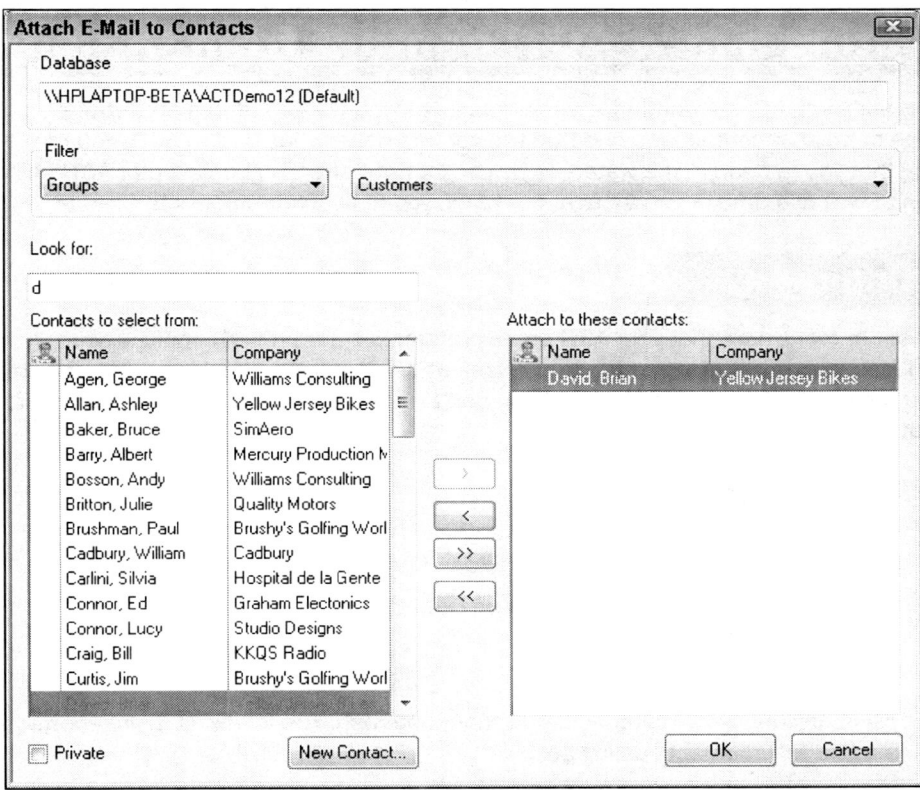

6. Click **OK**.

How it works...

A history of the incoming email message will now appear on the contact's History tab. Future messages arriving from the same contact will automatically attach to the contact record.

There's more...

You might have noticed the Quick Attach icon on Outlook's toolbar. Theoretically, when you click Quick Attach the incoming email automatically attaches to the corresponding ACT! record. Unfortunately, this is not always the case. ACT! makes the connection by matching the email address of the incoming email to the email address of the ACT! contact record. If the appropriate ACT! contact record is not found the message won't attach—and you will not receive a notification that the attachment did not take place!

Creating a new ACT! contact from Outlook

At this point you might be wondering what happens if you want to attach an Outlook email message to an ACT! contact and find that the contact doesn't yet exist in ACT!. You might be thinking that you're dead in the water—or you might have already guessed that ACT! has a solution to that dilemma. If you thought the latter, you're absolutely correct!

Getting ready

You'll want to make sure that your ACT! email preferences are properly configured to work with Outlook. You might also want to take a look at the Duplicate Checking preference that you had previously set up in ACT! so that you don't inadvertently add duplicate records to your ACT! database.

How to do it...

1. Select a message from an Outlook folder.
2. Click the **Create ACT! contact** icon on Outlook's toolbar.
3. The New Contact dialog box opens with the sender's name and email address already filled in.
4. Fill in any additional contact information (optional). The following figure shows you a sample New Contacts dialog box:

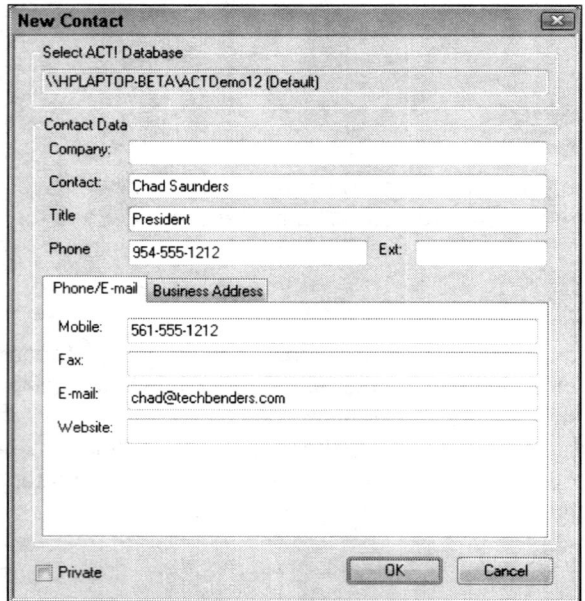

5. Select or clear the **Private** checkbox (optional).

6. Click **OK**.

How it works...

You'll receive a confirmation if the contact was successfully added to your ACT! database. If you have enabled duplicate checking enabled and the contact matches an existing record in your database, a message appears telling you that the new contact was not created. However, because not all ACT! fields are available when adding the new contact you might want to find the new contact in your ACT! database and fill in the remaining fields.

There's more...

At this point you might be wondering what happens if you receive an email that was addressed to several contacts, none of which exist in your ACT! database. As you've probably guessed, ACT! can handle this situation as well.

If the message contains multiple senders' names or addresses, the **Select Contacts** dialog window will open, listing the contacts included in the email message in the **Outlook contacts** pane. Use the single right-pointing arrow to move the contact to the **Save to ACT!** pane. The following figure shows you what the **Select Contacts** dialog window looks like:

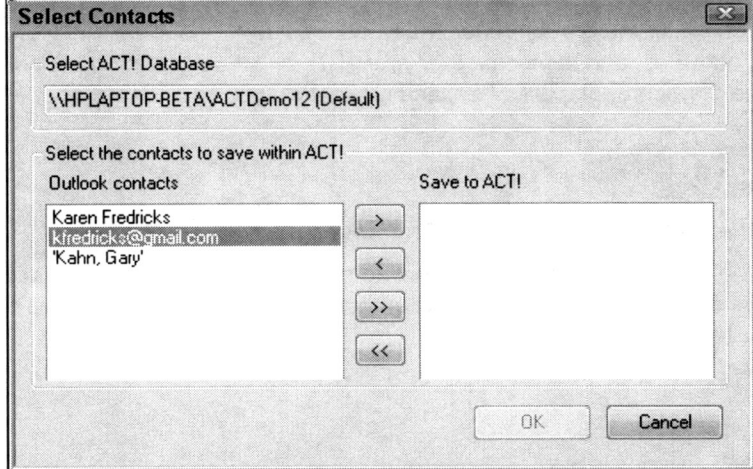

Scheduling a task from an Outlook email Message

ACT! has so many neat tricks up its sleeve that it's hard to keep track of them all. If you like the idea that "one piece of software does it all" then you'll undoubtedly love ACT!'s ability to schedule an appointment directly from incoming Outlook messages in one of two ways:

▶ If you had set your ACT! email preferences to include incoming meeting invitations, Outlook automatically adds an activity to your ACT! calendar when you accept a meeting request

▶ Click the **Create ACT! Activity** icon in the Outlook toolbar to open ACT!'s Schedule Activity dialog box and schedule a new activity with the sender of an incoming Outlook email message

Synchronizing your ACT! calendar to Outlook

Although most ACT! users love the ACT! calendar, there are times when you need to use the Outlook calendar as well. For example, you might work for a company that keeps a company calendar in Outlook yet all the sales people rely on the ACT! calendars. Or maybe you use the Outlook calendar to keep track of your personal activities. The bottom line is that if you use two sets of calendars, ACT! will allow you to synchronize your activities between the two products.

ACT!'s Outlook calendar integration functionality allows you to schedule and view appointments, activities, and tasks in either your ACT! or Outlook calendar. In addition, you can synchronize appointments, activities, and tasks from one calendar to another.

How to do it...

1. Click the **Tools** menu and choose **Preferences**.
2. Click the **E-mail & Outlook Sync** tab and then click the **Outlook Synchronization Preferences...** button. The Outlook Synchronization Preferences dialog box appears similar to the following figure:

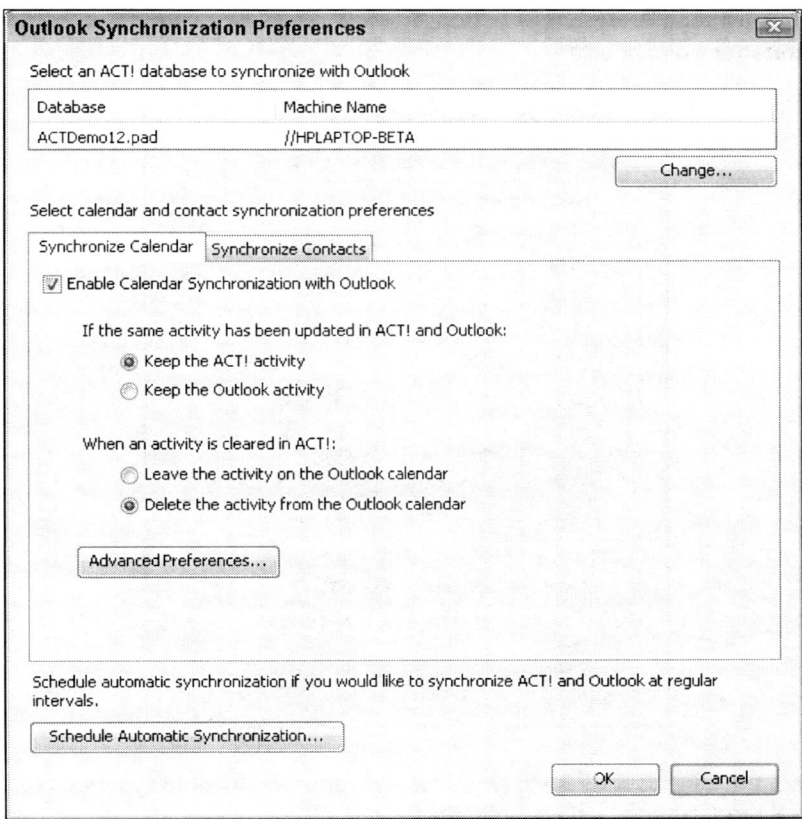

3. The name of your database should appear at the top of the dialog window (optional). To select a different ACT! database, click **Change** to navigate to and select a different database.

4. Click the **Synchronize Calendar** tab and select the **Enable Calendar Synchronization with Outlook** checkbox.

5. Select the following calendar synchronization options from this tab:

   ❑ **If the same activity has been updated in both ACT! and Outlook**: Select **Keep the ACT! activity** if you want to save the changes made in ACT! when there is a conflict or **Keep the Outlook activity** if you want to save the changes made in Outlook.

   ❑ **When an activity is cleared in ACT!**: Select **Leave the activity on the Outlook calendar** if you want the activity to remain on your Outlook calendar or **Delete the activity from the calendar** if you also want the activity removed from your Outlook calendar.

6. Click **Advanced Preferences** button. The following figure shows you the **Advanced Preferences** dialog box:

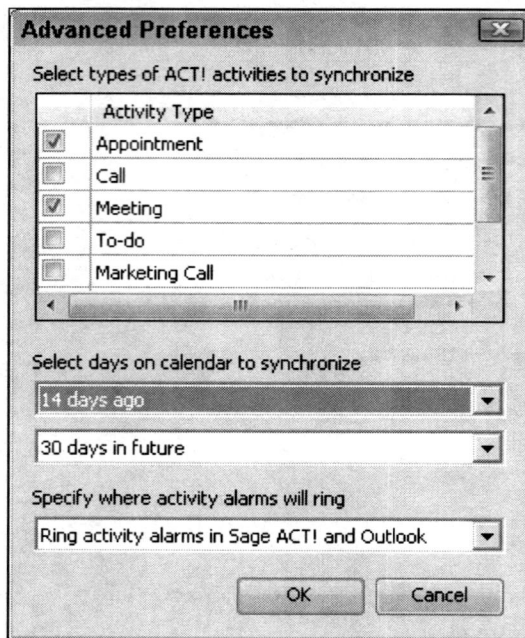

7. Select the checkbox for each type of activity that you want to synchronize between your Sage ACT! and Outlook calendars.

8. Select a date range from the **Select days on calendar to synchronize** drop-downs to determine the date range of the activities that will be synchronized between your Sage ACT! and Outlook calendars.

9. Use the **Specify where activity alarms will ring** dropdown to determine whether alarms will appear in Outlook, ACT!, or in both programs.

10. Click **OK** to close the Advanced Preferences dialog window.

11. Click the **Schedule Automatic Synchronization...** button to set your synchronization scheduling preferences. The figure below illustrates the Synchronization Schedule dialog window:

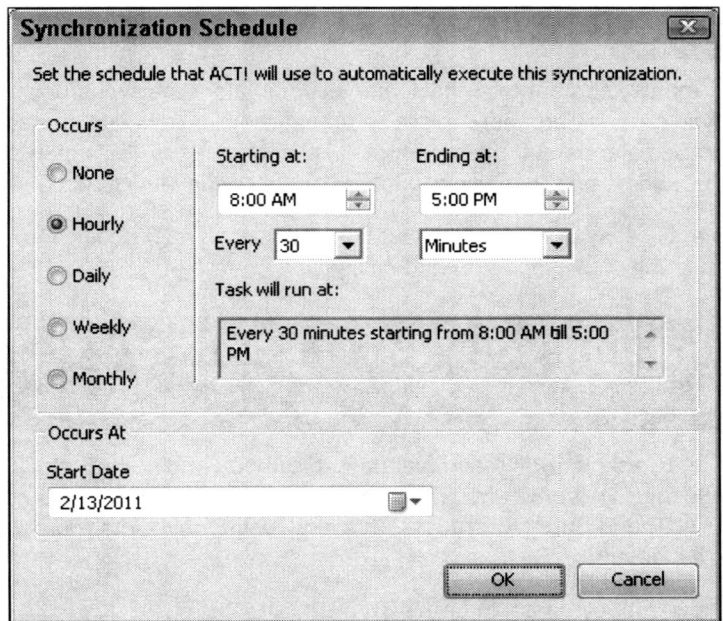

12. Select how often the calendar synchronization should occur in the **Occurs** area. Depending on the option you select, you will be able to change the start date, start time, day, or month.

13. Click **OK** to save your synchronization preferences.

14. Click **OK** to close the **Outlook Synchronization Preferences** dialog window. You will be prompted to synchronize; click **Yes** if you'd like to proceed.

15. Click **OK** to close the Preferences dialog window.

How it works...

Your ACT! and Outlook calendars will now synchronize according to the schedule you created. Once you've started synchronizing the ACT! and Outlook calendars you can view your Outlook activities in the ACT! Task List as well as in any of the ACT! calendars. Conversely you'll be able to see your ACT! activities in your Outlook calendar. Best of all you can make changes to either calendar and know that the changes will be passed to the other calendar the next time you sync.

There's more...

Although you're probably content to sit back and let your calendars synchronize according to the schedule you determined, there might be times when you'd like to immediately synchronize your two calendars. If the urge strikes, simply click the Tools menu, point to Synchronize with Outlook, and then click Synchronize Calendar with Outlook.

You'll also find that it's easy to identify the Outlook activities in ACT! because they include a gold clock icon, making them Appointment activity types.

Synchronizing your ACT! contacts to Outlook

ACT! users have been able to sync their calendars to Outlook and send Outlook email to their ACT! contacts for quite some time. However, until ACT! 2012, ACT! users could not synchronize their ACT! and Outlook contacts. This new functionality lets you perform a number of tasks including:

- ▶ Create new Outlook contacts from ACT!
- ▶ Create new ACT! contacts from Outlook
- ▶ Control which ACT! contacts are synced to Outlook
- ▶ Keep both sets of contacts up to date regardless of where they were created or changed

As part of the synchronization setup process you'll want to create a **sync set** or a set of rules that determine which of your ACT! contacts will synchronize over to Outlook.

Getting ready

If there are contacts that exist in both ACT! and Outlook, there is potential for duplicated contact records. Ideally, you'll start without any contacts in your Outlook address book to avoid possible duplication.

Contact syncing requires that ACT!'s email preferences be configured to work with Outlook. In addition, until you are comfortable that the preference settings you select for synchronizing contacts will work correctly you'll want to create backups of your Outlook and ACT! programs. You'll also need to have Manager or Administrator access rights to create and manage sync sets.

How to do it...

1. Click the **Tools** menu, select **Preferences**, and then click the **E-mail & Outlook sync** tab.

2. Click the **Outlook Synchronization Preferences...** button.

3. Click the **Synchronize Contacts** tab and select the **Enable Contact Synchronization with Outlook** checkbox. The following figure shows you the Outlook Synchronization Preferences dialog box:

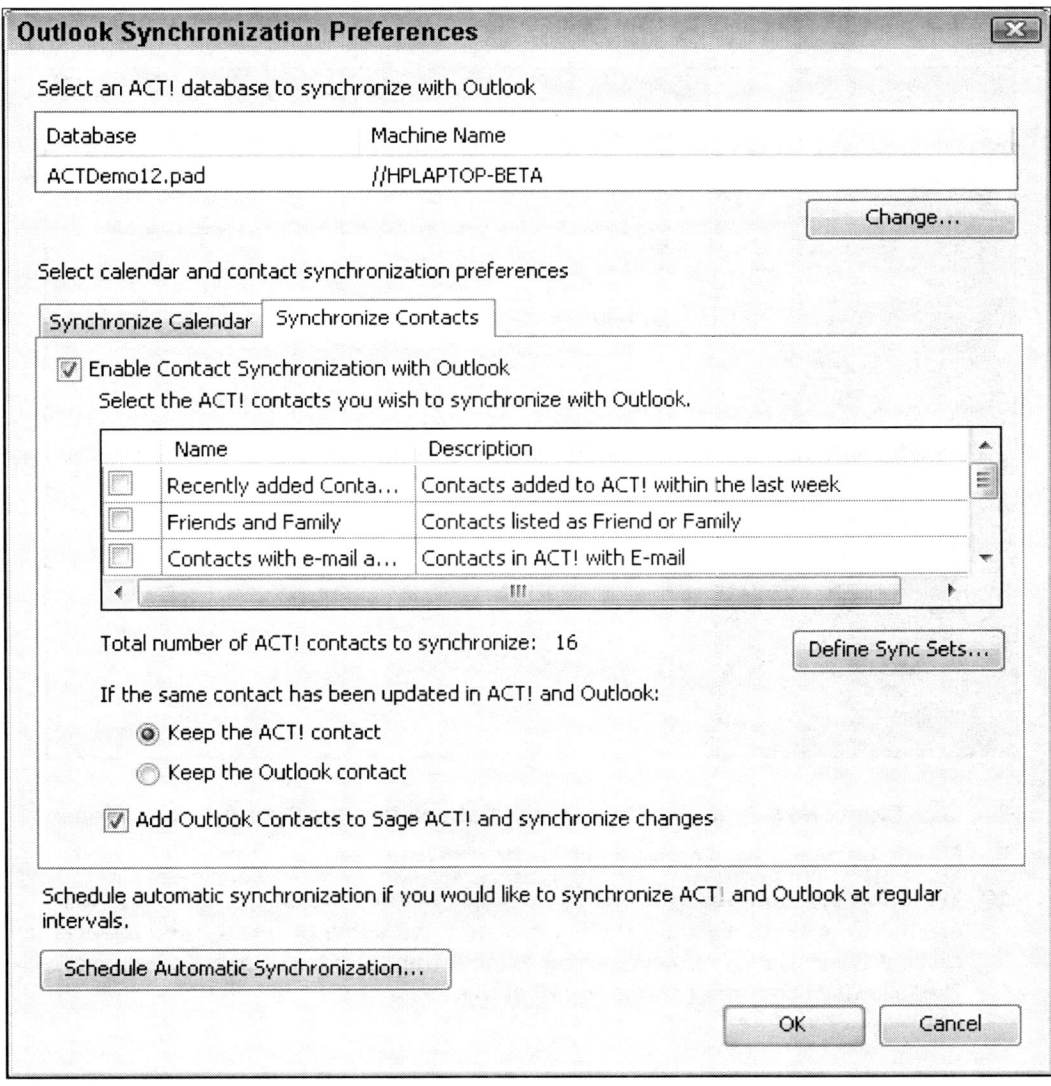

4. The name of your database should appear at the top of the dialog window. To select a different ACT! database click **Change** to navigate to and select a different database (optional).

5. Click the **Add Outlook Contacts to Sage ACT! and synchronize changes** checkbox if you want to be able to add new contacts in Outlook and have them appear in ACT! (optional).

6. Click the **Schedule Automatic Synchronization...** button to set your synchronization scheduling preferences (optional).

7. Click the **Define Sync Sets** button. The **Manage Outlook Contact Sync Sets** dialog box appears like the one in the figure below:

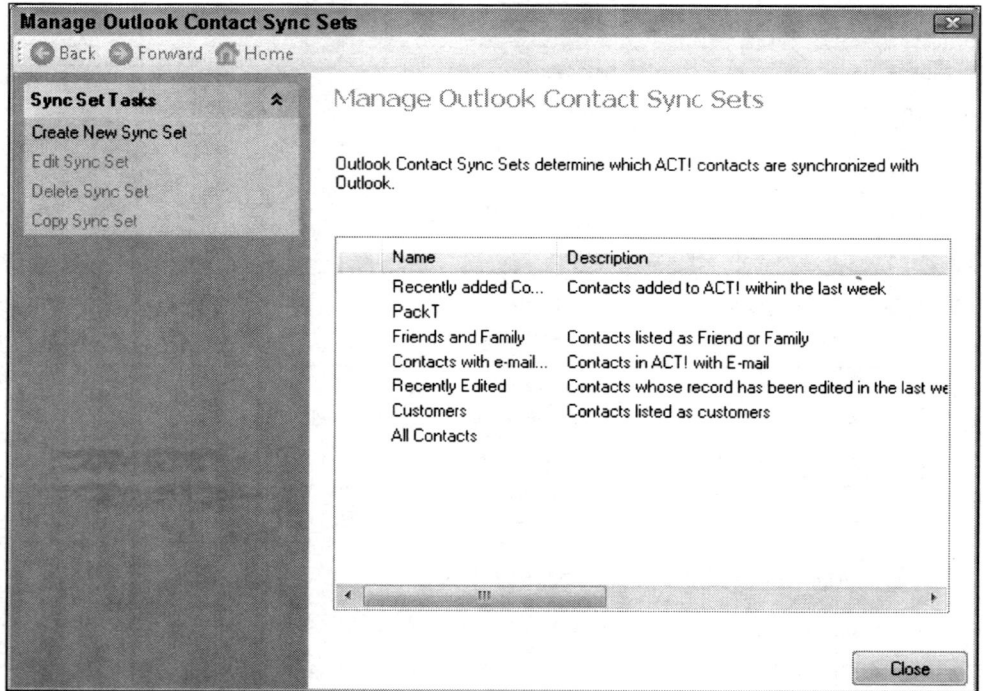

8. Click **Create New Sync Set**. The **Manage Outlook Contact Sync Sets** wizard opens.

9. Enter a name for the sync set and click **Next** to continue.

10. In the **Outlook Contact Sync Set Users** dialog window choose the users who will use this sync set by selecting their names from the **Users to select from:** panel and clicking the single right-pointing arrow to move the name to the panel on the right. The following screenshot shows you what this looks like:

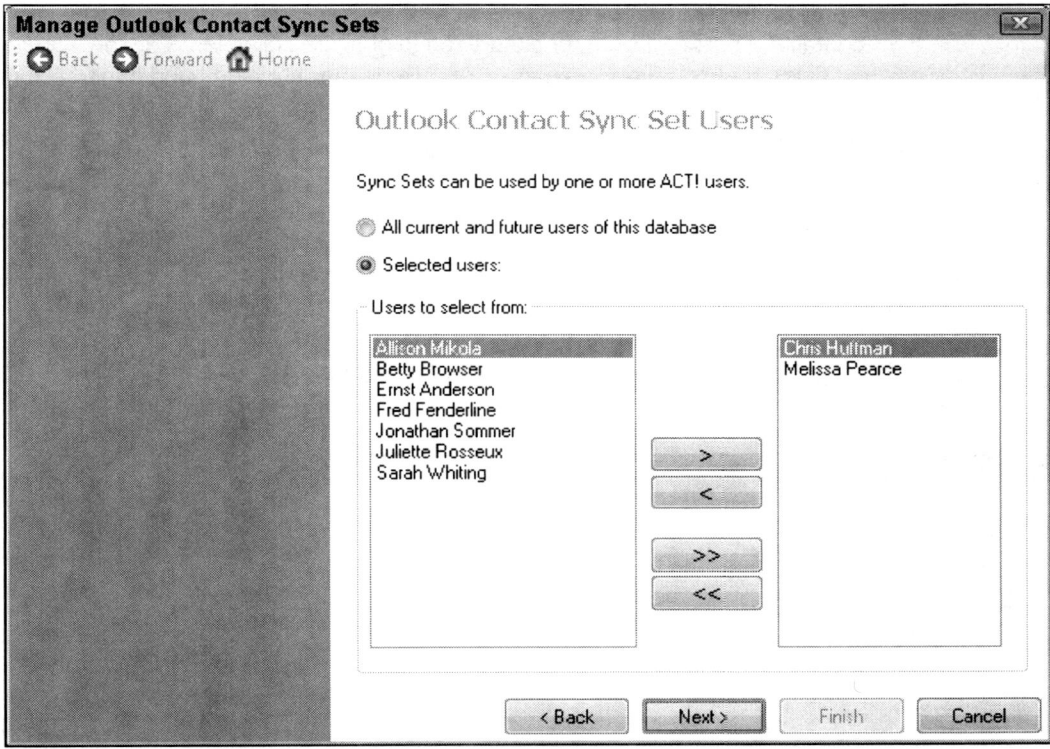

11. Click **Next** to continue.

12. Indicate the number of contacts you will be synchronizing and click **Next** to continue:

    ❑ **Synchronize all available contacts**: synchronizes all of your contacts. Skip to step 16.

    ❑ **Define Sync Set criteria**: allows you to create a query to determine which contact records will synchronize with Outlook.

13. Click **Create Criteria** in the Outlook Contact Sync Set Criteria dialog window to open the Sync Set Criteria window.

14. Define the contact records that will be included in the sync set by selecting the following criteria:

    ❑ **Type**: Your only choice here is to choose Contact.

    ❑ **Field Name**: Select one of the contact fields from the **Field Name** drop-down list.

    ❑ **Operator**: Indicate whether you're looking for a specific word, a field that contains a part of a word, or even a range of figures or dates. You can search for fields that contain some data, or for fields that are blank and don't contain any data.

    ❑ **Value**: Select one of the available items that corresponds to the selected Field Name item.

15. Click **Add to list** to include the criterion.

16. Click the **Preview** button to see the number of contacts that match your query criteria (optional).

17. Click **OK** to add the query to the Sync Set and to close the Sync Set Criteria dialog window. The following figure gives you an example of a completed Sync Set Criteria window:

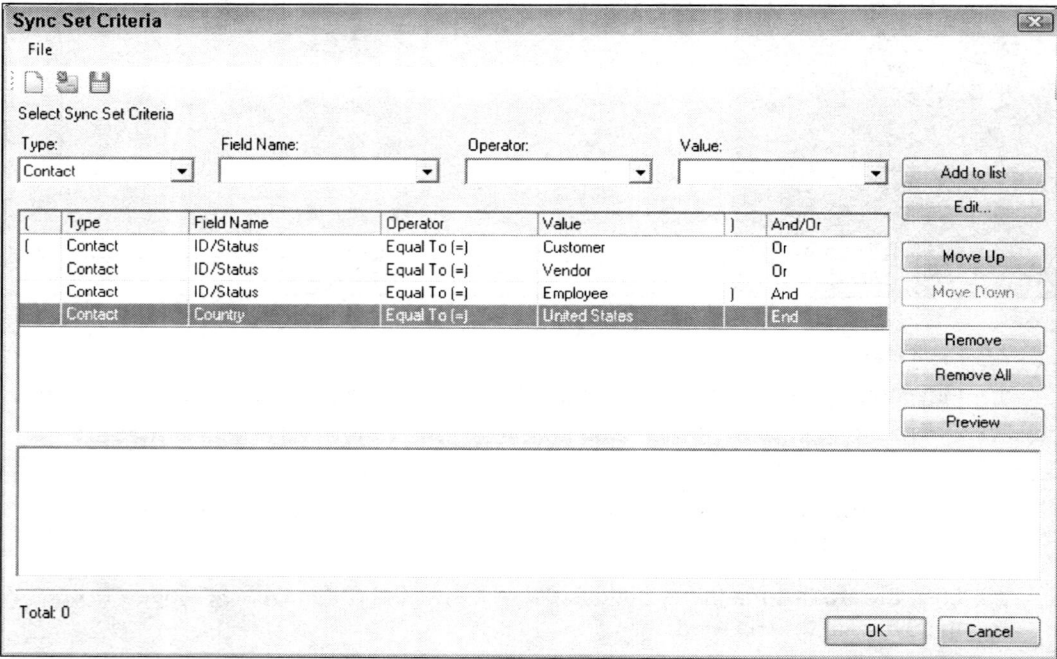

18. Click **Finish** to close the Manage Outlook Contact Sync Sets wizard and then **Close** to close the Manage Outlook Contact Sync Sets dialog window.

19. Place a checkmark next to the sync sets that you want to include in your ACT!/Outlook synchronization.

20. Click **OK** to close the Outlook Synchronization Preferences dialog window.

21. Click **Yes** in the Sage ACT! Outlook Sync dialog window to synchronize your ACT! contacts to Outlook (optional). An indicator will appear measuring your progress and a confirmation screen will appear when your contacts have finished synching.

22. Click **OK** to close the Preferences dialog window.

How it works...

Don't be alarmed if you don't see your changes immediately—you might need to **refresh** ACT! by clicking ACT! View menu and choosing Refresh.

Your ACT! and Outlook contacts will now synchronize according to the criteria you selected. You'll want to take a moment to peruse both your ACT! and Outlook databases to make sure you got the expected results. If something doesn't look correct restore your backup and tweak the above instructions until your contacts are synchronizing correctly.

There's more...

In addition to creating new sync sets, the Manage Outlook Contact Sync Set dialog box allows you to edit and/or delete existing sync sets. You'll also notice that ACT! comes with several "out of the box" sync sets that you can use "as is" or modify to better suit your needs. Keep in mind, however, that the sync sets only apply to ACT! contacts and not to your Outlook contacts.

When you build your query in the Sync Set Criteria dialog window, you might want to make use of the And/Or column to help you group your criteria to indicate the relationship between each set of criteria. For example, if you want to synchronize contacts from three different ID/Status categories you'll want to use the **or** criterion to indicate that you want to include anyone who is **either** a customer, vendor, or employee.

Along the same lines you might want to include parentheses so that specific lines of your queries are grouped together. This is a particularly important step if your query contains both "and" and "or" criteria.

10
Integrating with Google

In this chapter, we will cover:

- ▶ Setting up Google and ACT! integration
- ▶ Synchronizing your ACT! and Google calendars
- ▶ Synchronizing your ACT! and Google contacts
- ▶ Setting the Record History options for Google
- ▶ Setting up Automatic Integration

Introduction

Although you probably use ACT! to help organize all the aspects of your personal and business life, you might also use Google. For example, you may have a Gmail account so that you can easily access your e-mail from any location. Or perhaps you have a Google calendar that you share with the other members of your team. You might even store contacts in Google so that you can synchronize them with your smart phone.

The new ACT! and Google integration that appears in ACT! 2012 consists of three components:

- ▶ ACT! and Google calendar synchronization
- ▶ ACT! and Google contact synchronization
- ▶ ACT! and Google e-mail history synchronization

Depending on your Google usage, you can use any or all of this functionality. For example, you may decide to Sync your contacts to Google so that you can access your ACT! contacts on your smart phone, but opt for Outlook integration when it comes to recording e-mail history in ACT!.

If you are already familiar with ACT! and Outlook integration it is important to understand that Google integration works a bit differently. If you choose to link ACT! to Google, Google will still be responsible for the actual e-mail transmission; you cannot initiate an e-mail from ACT!. That means that although it is possible to have ACT! automatically create a history of all the e-mails you send using Google, you must use Google as the originating point of the message and not ACT!.

Setting up Google and ACT! integration

Before you can start sending Google e-mail in ACT!, you'll need to set up your e-mail preferences. Fortunately, ACT! makes the task fairly easy.

Getting ready

You'll need to have a Google account and have your username and password readily available. Alternatively, you can set up a Google account during the integration process.

How to do it...

1. From any ACT! screen, click the **Tools** menu, point to **Integrate with Google,** and then choose **Google Integration Preferences**. Alternatively, you can click the **Connections** button on the Navbar and choose the **Configure Settings** hyperlink in the **Google Integration** area. The **Google Integration Preferences** dialog box opens like the one you see in the following screenshot:

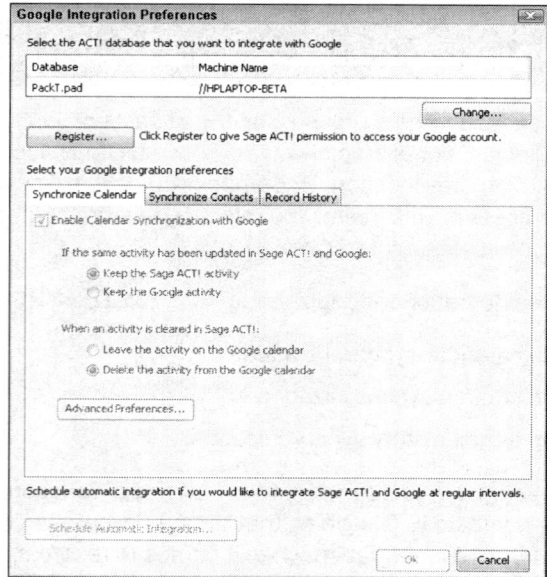

2. Click the **Change..** button. The **Change Sage ACT! Database** dialog window appears. The name of your database should already appear in the **Sage ACT! Database** box. If it doesn't, click the **Browse..** button to navigate to a different ACT! database.

3. Fill in your ACT! username and password and then click **OK**.

4. Click the **Register** button and answer **Yes** at the prompt asking you whether you have a Google account. The **Google Authorization** dialog window opens like the one you see in the following screenshot:

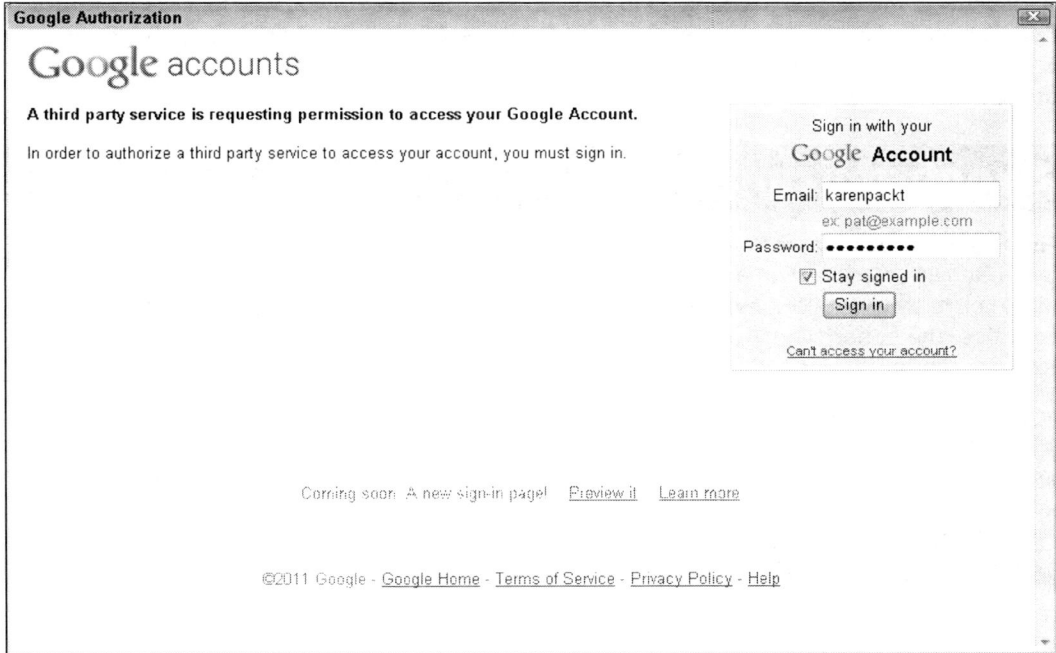

5. (Optional) Click the **Sign in** button to set up a new Google account if you don't already have one.

6. Fill in your e-mail address and password and then click **Sign in**.

7. Click **Grant access** at the prompt.

8. Click **OK** to close the **Google Integration Preferences** dialog window. You'll notice that your Google e-mail address now appears at the top of the window and that the **Register** button is grayed.

9. Click **No** when prompted to integrate ACT! and Google.

There's more...

Once you've set up the connection between Google and your ACT! database, you're ready to determine how closely you'd like the two products to work together. However, one thing you can't do from within ACT! is to change or deactivate the Google account that you are connected to. You'll have to go directly to your Google account to deactivate the current account and then return to the proceeding section to set up the new Google account.

To deactivate the Google account, go to `http:/www.google.com/`, sign in, click on your Google e-mail address, and choose **Account Settings**. Click the **Authorizing applications & sites** hyperlink and then click the **Revoke Access** hyperlink after the **Sage ACT! Google Integration** item.

Synchronizing your ACT! calendar to Google

Although most ACT! users love the ACT! calendar, there are times when you might want to use a Google calendar. For example, you might share the Google calendar with your assistant while you're traveling. Or maybe you use the Google calendar to keep track of your personal activities. The bottom line is that if you use both the ACT! and Google calendar, ACT! will allow you to synchronize your activities between the two.

ACT!'s Google calendar integration functionality allows you to schedule and view appointments, activities, and tasks in either of your ACT! and Google calendars. In addition, you can synchronize appointments, activities, and tasks from one calendar to another.

How to do it...

1. From any ACT! screen, click the **Tools** menu, point to **Integrate with Google**, and then choose **Google Integration Preferences**. Alternatively, you can click the **Connections** button on the Navbar and choose the **Configure Settings** hyperlink in the **Google Integration** area. The **Google Integration Preferences** dialog box opens.

2. Click the **Synchronize Calendar** tab. The **Synchronize Calendar** tab dialog box appears similar to the following figure.

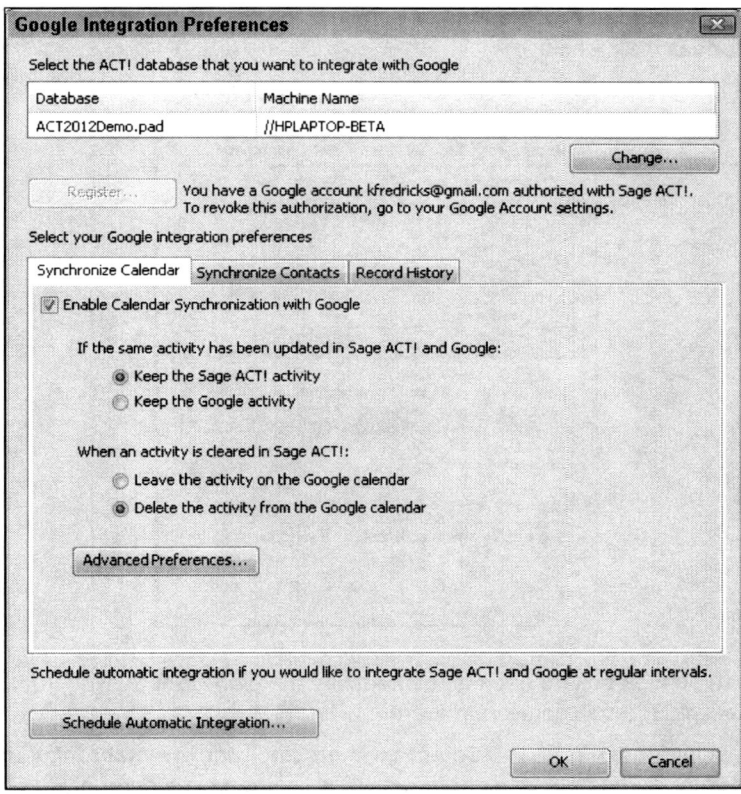

3. (Optional) The name of your database should appear at the top of the dialog window. To select a different ACT! database, click **Change** to navigate to and select a different database.

4. Select the **Enable Calendar Synchronization with Google** check box.

5. Select the following calendar synchronization options from this tab:

   ❑ **If the same activity has been updated in both ACT! and Google**: Select **Keep the ACT! activity** if you want to save the changes made in ACT! when there is a conflict, or **Keep the Google activity** if you want to save the changes made in Google.

   ❑ **When an activity is cleared in ACT!**: Select **Leave the activity on the Google calendar** if you want the activity to remain on your Google calendar, or **Delete the activity from the calendar** if you also want the activity removed from your Google calendar.

6. Click the **Advanced Preferences** button. The following figure shows you the **Advanced Preferences** dialog box:

7. Select the check box for each type of activity that you want to synchronize between your Sage ACT! and Google calendars.

8. Select a date range from the **Select days on calendar to synchronize** drop-downs to determine the date range of the activities that will be synchronized between your Sage ACT! and Google calendars.

9. Use the **Specify where activity alarms will ring** drop down to determine whether alarms will appear in Google, ACT!, or in both programs.

10. Click **OK** to close the **Advanced Preferences** dialog window.

How it works...

Once you've started synchronizing the ACT! and Google calendars, you can view your Google activities in the ACT! **Task List** as well as in any of the ACT! calendars. Conversely, you'll be able to see your ACT! activities in your Google calendar. Best of all, you can make changes to either calendar and know that the changes will be passed to the other calendar the next time you sync.

There's more...

You'll find that it's easy to identify the Google activities in ACT! because they include a gold clock icon, making them Meeting activity types. Because the Google calendar does not allow you to associate a calendar item with a specific contact, all the Google calendar items will be associated with your own Record Manager. You can of course edit any of the Google activities and associate them with specific contact records.

If you don't see your Google activities in the ACT! Task List, it might be necessary to change the filtering options by clicking the **Options** button and selecting **Show Tasks from Other Applications**.

Synchronizing your ACT! contacts to Google

The new Google integration lets you synchronize your ACT! and Google contacts. The integration includes the ability to:

▸ Create new Google Contacts from ACT!

▸ Create new ACT! Contacts from Google

▸ Control which ACT! Contacts are synced to Google

▸ Keep both sets of contacts up to date regardless of where they were created or changed

Getting ready

If there are contacts that exist in both ACT! and Google, there is the potential for duplicated contact records. Ideally, you'll start without any contacts in your Google address book to avoid possible duplication. Fortunately, both ACT! and Google include the ability to find and merge duplicate contact records. However, until you are comfortable that the preference settings you select for synchronizing contacts will work correctly, it's not a bad idea to create a backup of your ACT! data.

How to do it...

1. Click the **Tools** menu, select **Preferences**, and then click the **E-mail & Google sync** tab.

2. Click the **Google Synchronization Preferences...** button.

3. Click the **Synchronize Contacts** tab and select the **Enable Contact Synchronization with Google** check box. The following figure shows you the **Synchronize Contacts** tab:

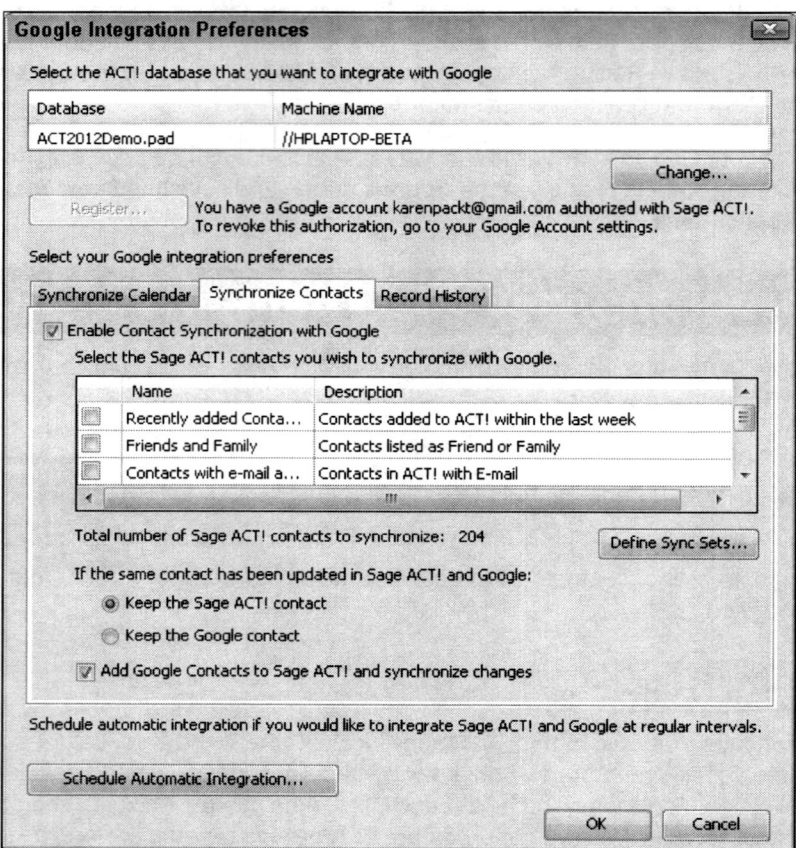

4. (Optional) The name of your database should appear at the top of the dialog window. To select a different ACT! database, click **Change** to navigate to and select a different database.

5. (Optional) Click the **Add Google Contacts to Sage ACT! and synchronize changes** checkbox if you want to be able to add new contacts in Google and have them appear in ACT!.

6. (Optional) Click the **Schedule Automatic Synchronization...** button to set your synchronization scheduling preferences.

7. Click the **Define Sync Sets** button. The **Manage Google Contact Sync Sets** dialog box appears like the one in the following figure:

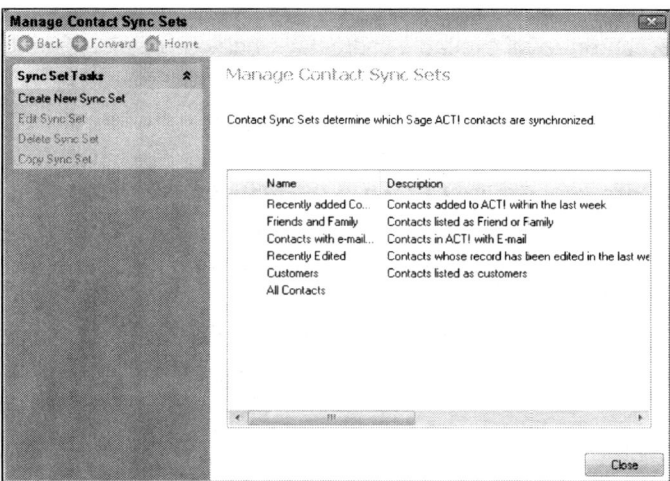

8. Click **Create New Sync Set**. Alternatively, you can select one of the existing sync sets and then click **Edit Sync Set**. The **Manage Google Contact Sync Sets** wizard opens.

9. Enter a name for the sync set or optionally modify the existing one and click **Next** to continue.

10. In the **Google Contact Sync Set Users** dialog window, choose the users who will use this sync set by selecting their names from the **Users to select from:** panel and clicking the single right-pointing arrow to move the name to the panel on the right. The following screenshot shows you what this looks like:

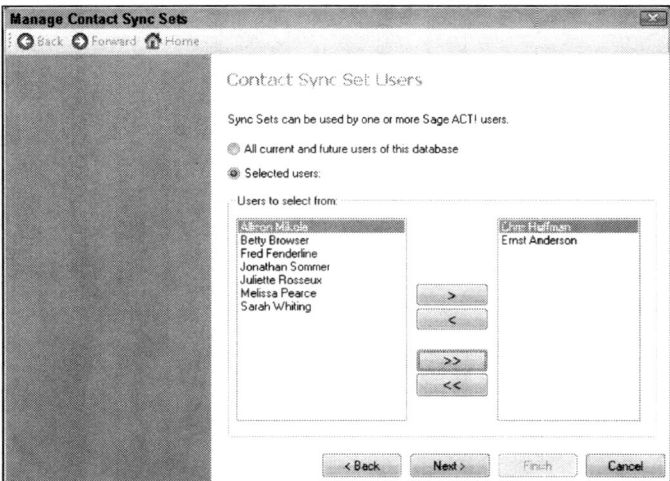

11. Click **Next** to continue.

12. Indicate the number of contacts you will be synchronizing and click **Next** to continue. You have two options here:

   ❑ Synchronize all available contacts: synchronizes all of your Contacts. You can then skip to step 18 below.

   ❑ Define Sync Set criteria: allows you to create a query to determine which contact records will synchronize with Google.

13. Click **Edit Criteria** or **Create Criteria** in the **Manage Contact Sync Sets** dialog window to open the **Sync Set Criteria** window.

14. Define the contact records that will be included in the sync set by selecting the following criteria:

   ❑ **Type**: Your only choice here is to choose **Contact**.

   ❑ Field Name: Select one of the contact fields from the **Field Name** drop-down list.

   ❑ Operator: Indicate whether you're looking for a specific word, a field that contains a part of a word, or even a range of figures or dates. You can search for fields that contain some data, or for fields that are blank and don't contain any data.

   ❑ Value: Select one of the available items that correspond to the selected **Field Name** item.

15. Click **Add to list** to include the criterion.

16. (Optional) Click the **Preview** button to see the number of contacts that match your query criteria.

17. Click **OK** to add the query to the Sync Set and to close the **Sync Set Criteria** dialog window. The following figure gives you an example of a completed **Sync Set Criteria** window:

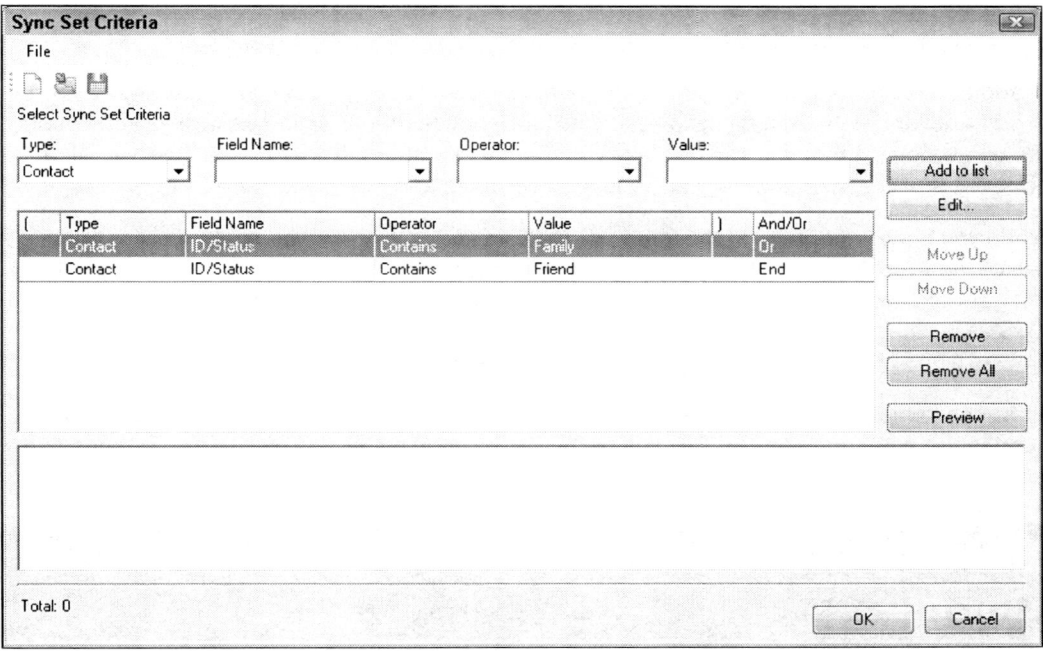

18. Click **Finish** to close the **Manage Contact Sync Sets** wizard and then **Close** to close the **Manage Contact Sync Sets** dialog window.

19. Place a checkmark next to the sync sets that you want to include in your ACT!/Google synchronization.

20. Click **OK** to close the **Google Synchronization Preferences** dialog window.

21. (Optional) Click **Yes** in the **Sage ACT! Google Sync** dialog window to synchronize your ACT! contacts to Google. An indicator will appear measuring your progress and a confirmation screen will appear when your contacts have finished synching.

22. Click **OK** to close the **Preferences** dialog window.

How it works...

Don't be alarmed if you don't see your changes immediately—you might need to **refresh** ACT! by clicking the ACT! View menu and choosing **Refresh.**

Your ACT! and Google contacts will now synchronize according to the criteria you selected. You'll want to take a moment to peruse both your ACT! and Google databases to make sure you got the expected results. If something doesn't look correct, restore your backup and tweak the above instructions until your contacts are synchronizing correctly.

There's more...

In addition to creating new sync sets, the **Manage Contact Sync Set** dialog box allows you to edit and/or delete existing sync sets. You'll also notice that ACT! comes with several 'out of the box' sync sets that you can use 'as is' or modify to better suit your needs. Keep in mind, however, that the sync sets only apply to ACT! contacts and not to your Google contacts.

When you build your query in the **Sync Set Criteria** dialog window, you might want to make use of the **And/Or** column to help you group your criteria to indicate the relationship between each set of criteria. For example, if you want to synchronize contacts from three different ID/Status categories, you'll want to use the **or** criterion to indicate that you want to include anyone who is **either** a customer, vendor, or employee.

Along the same lines, you might want to include parentheses so that specific lines of your queries are grouped together. This is a particularly important step if your query contains both 'and' and 'or' criteria.

Setting the Record History options for Google

Once you've set up the connection between ACT! and Google, you're ready to set your preferences as to how you'd like the history of any Gmail transactions recorded in ACT!.

How to do it...

1. From any ACT! screen, click the **Tools** menu, point to **Integrate with Google**, and then choose **Google Integration Preferences**. Alternatively, you can click the **Connections** button on the Navbar and choose the **Configure Settings** hyperlink in the **Google Integration** area. The **Google Integration Preferences** dialog box opens.

2. Click the **Record History** tab. The following screenshot shows you what the tab looks like:

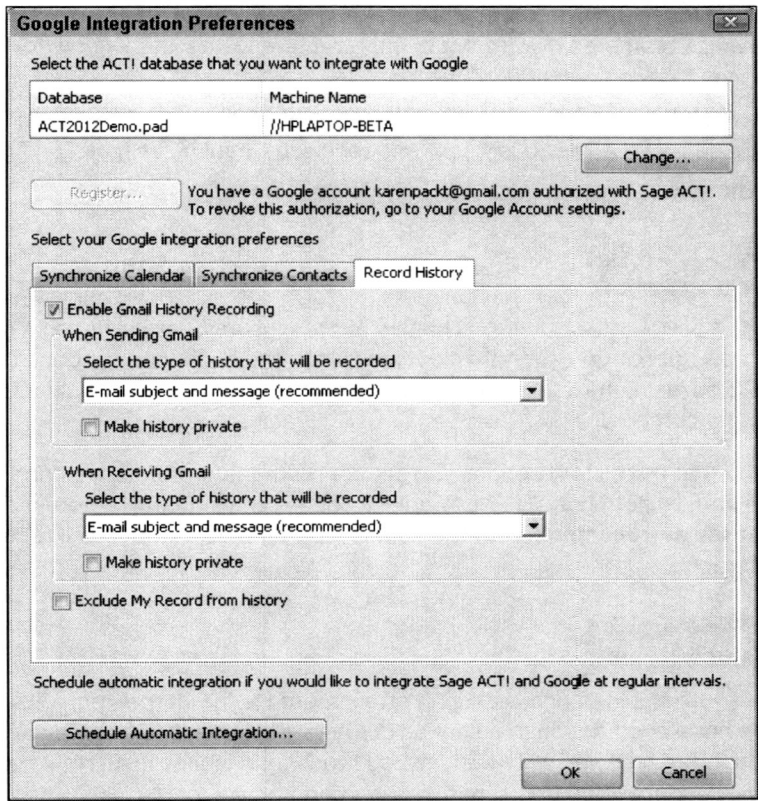

3. Place a checkmark in the **Enable Gmail History Recording** box.

4. Choose an option for sending Gmail. Your options include the following:

   - **None**: no history of the message will be recorded.
   - **E-mail Subject Only**: records only the subject line of the message.
   - **E-mail Subject and Message (Recommended)**: records both the subject line and the contents of the outgoing e-mail message.
   - **E-mail Subject, Message and all Attachments**: creates a file of the outgoing e-mail. This is the only option that will retain the attachments sent with an e-mail.

5. Choose an option for receiving Gmail. You have a choice of the same options as in step 4.

6. (Optional) Place a checkmark in the **Make history private** checkbox in the **When Sending Gmail** area if you want to only create private history items for Gmail messages that you send.

7. (Optional) Place a checkmark in the **Make history private** checkbox in the **When Receiving Gmail** area if you want to only create private history items for Gmail messages that you receive.

8. (Optional) If this is the first time you are integrating e-mail history to ACT!, indicate the starting date of the previously sent and received Gmail messages.

9. Click **OK** to save your changes.

How it works...

Depending on the preferences you set, a history of both incoming and out-going e-mail messages will now appear on the contact's **History** tab. The history will go back to the date you set in step 8 above. Future messages arriving from the same contact will automatically attach to the contact record.

You'll also notice that the history options you set are permanent preferences and can't be changed on an item by item basis. For example, if you set the sending preference to **E-mail subject and message (recommended)** then all new Gmail that you send will record to ACT! using that preference.

There's more...

Many ACT! users love the idea of creating an attachment file for **all** their outgoing messages. However, this is not a good option to select as the default option. If you're typical of most ACT! users, over a period of time you will have created thousands of files in ACT!'s **Attachments** folder and placed unnecessary pressure on your computer's resources.

Using Outlook to manage your Gmail

The three areas of the ACT! and Google integration work independently from each other, which means you might use the contact and calendar integration but not the history integration. Many Gmail users prefer to use Outlook as their e-mail client. If that is the case, you might choose to set up Outlook as your e-mail client in ACT!, knowing that all your Gmail ultimately appears in Outlook. This will give you several benefits over the Google history integration:

 ▶ You will be able to initiate new e-mail directly from within ACT! by clicking on a contact's e-mail address

 ▶ You can make use of e-mail templates you create in ACT!

 ▶ You can change the history option on the fly for each message that you send and/or receive

Setting up automatic integration

Once you've set up the ACT! and Google integration and are happy with the results, you might want to put the integration on auto-pilot so that your ACT! and Google data will synchronize automatically at the time intervals you select. Fortunately, ACT! has a service that runs in the background waiting to accomplish this goal.

Getting ready

You'll want to make sure that you have already configured at least one of the ACT! and Google integration options and that you can manually synchronize your data.

How to do it...

1. From any ACT! screen, click the **Tools** menu, point to **Integrate with Google**, and then choose **Google Integration Preferences**. Alternatively, you can click the **Connections** button on the Navbar and choose the **Configure Settings** hyperlink in the **Google Integration** area. The **Google Integration Preferences** dialog box opens.

2. Click the **Schedule Automatic Integration...** button to set your synchronization scheduling preferences. The following figure illustrates the **Schedule Google Integration** dialog window:

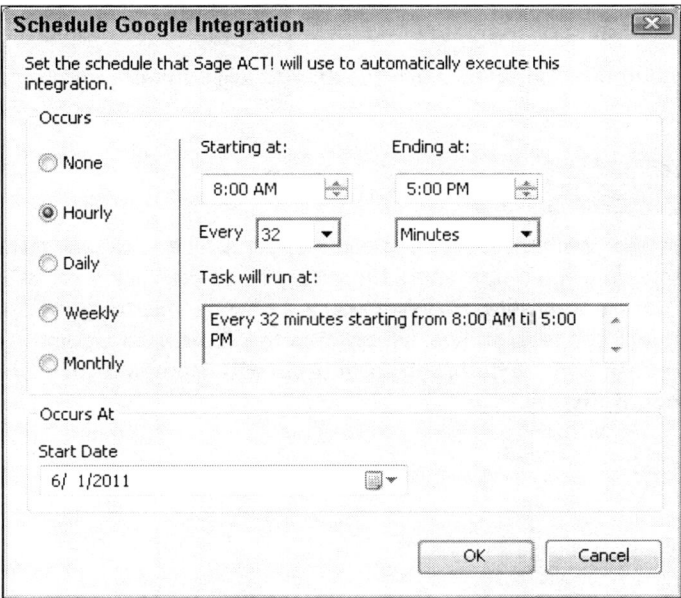

3. Select whether the synchronization should occur **Hourly, Daily, Weekly,** or **Monthly** in the **Occurs** area.

4. Indicate the frequency of the synchronization. Your options change according to your selection in step 2 above. For example, if you chose **Daily** you can set the frequency for once every other day. If you chose **Hourly,** you can indicate both the starting and ending time as well as the intervals between each synchronization.

5. Set the date on which you'd like to start the automatic synchronization.

6. Click **OK** to save your synchronization preferences.

7. Click **OK** to close the **Google Integration Preferences** dialog window. You will be prompted to synchronize; click **Yes** if you'd like to proceed.

How it works...

When the synchronization takes place an indicator window will appear similar to the one in the following screenshot:

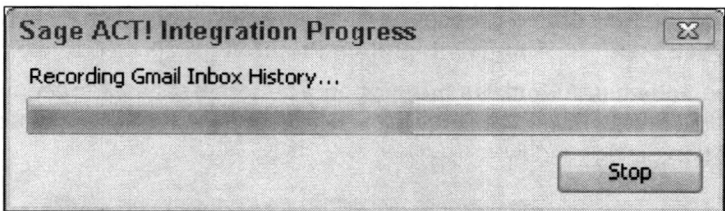

After the initial synchronization takes place the service will minimize and remain in the system tray.

There's more...

Although you're probably content to sit back and let your ACT! and Google data synchronize according to the schedule you determined, there might be times when you'd like to immediately synchronize your data. However, you will only be able to synchronize one component at a time. If the urge strikes, simply click the **Tools** menu, point to **Integrate with Google**, and then chose either **Synchronize Contacts with Google, Synchronize Calendar with Google** or **Record History.**

11
Performing Routine Maintenance

In this chapter, we will cover:

- ▸ Performing routine maintenance
- ▸ Creating a backup
- ▸ Restoring a backup
- ▸ Scheduling automatic maintenance using the ACT! Scheduler
- ▸ Applying ACT! updates
- ▸ Removing old data
- ▸ Merging duplicate records
- ▸ Deleting a database
- ▸ Global edit and replace

Introduction

Some of you might agree that an ounce of prevention is worth a pound of cure. Well, fortunately for you, Sage agrees with this concept and has provided the ACT! user with a whole arsenal of tools to make sure that your ACT! database keeps running smoothly and error-free.

In this chapter, you'll learn how to take care of your database. A database requires periodic maintenance to keep it in good working order. Failure to provide routine maintenance can result in big problems. And, should something go wrong, having a backup makes life a whole lot easier for you.

Your database is also prone to clutter. You sometimes have to bite the bullet, roll up your sleeves, and do a little cleaning to clear out old or duplicate contact records from ACT!. In other cases you might decide that a whole bunch of records need to be changed; for example, you might find that some of your contacts are categorized as prospects and others as suspects and you'd like to inject a bit of uniformity.

Performing routine maintenance

In ACT!, basic maintenance is referred to as checking and repairing. You can run the Check and Repair tool regularly to ensure a healthy database. Check and Repair consists of two procedures: the Integrity Check and the Re-index. These procedures are very similar to the Scan Disk and Disk Defragmenter procedures on a Windows PC. The Integrity Check scours the database for errors. Reindexing squeezes out all the little empty spaces that are left in your database when you delete contact records; reindexing on a regular basis ensures that you'll be able to create lookups as quickly as possible.

Getting ready

You need to have administrative privileges to your database in order to perform routine maintenance. If you don't have them you can skip this section, pass the information on to one of the administrators, or ask that you be given administrative access to the database. And, because every database requires an administrator, if you are the only user of your database you are automatically the administrator.

How to do it...

1. Log in as an administrator and make sure that all other users are logged off and will remain off the database until the reindexing has completed.

2. Click the Tools menu, point to Database Maintenance, and select Check and Repair...

3. The Check and Repair Database window opens, as shown in the following screenshot:

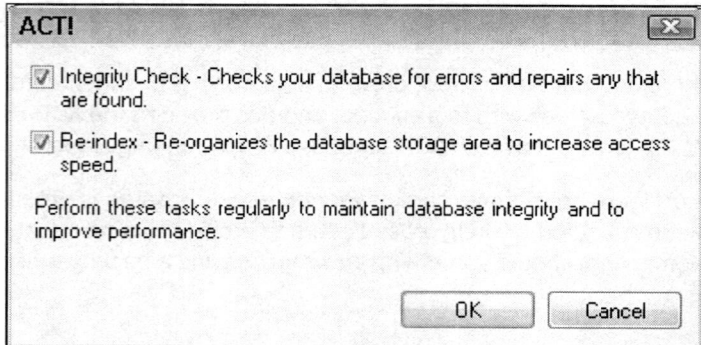

4. Select both the **Integrity Check** and **Re-index** options and then click **OK**.

5. Wait while ACT! runs the maintenance procedure. The following figure gives you an idea of what you can expect:

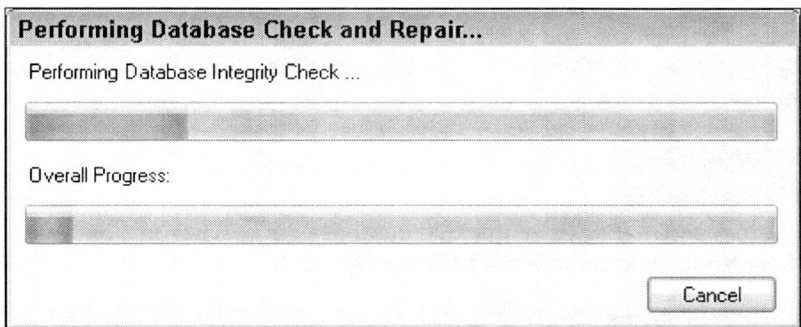

5. Click **OK** to the successful completion message.

How it works...

The required time is directly proportional to the size of your database but normally takes less than a minute to run.

There's more...

Although Check and Repair protects your database from damage, it doesn't actually repair any damage that has already occurred in your database.

See also

Although running the maintenance is extremely simple it is also extremely necessary and something that is frequently overlooked. Fortunately you can put this task on auto-pilot by including it as a part of the ACT! scheduler, which is covered later in this chapter.

Creating a backup

You probably already know the three rules of real estate: location, location, location. Similarly, the three basic rules of computing are backup, backup, backup! With the proliferation of viruses as well as the poor construction of many computers, backing up on a daily basis is imperative. Failure to do so can result in loss of data. Having a recent backup enables you to recover quickly when the unexpected happens. Having multiple backups gives you the luxury of determining the exact point of time you'll use if it becomes necessary to restore a backup.

When you create an ACT! backup, it backs up the entire contents of your database including all records, notes, histories, and opportunities. In addition, an ACT! backup contains all of the supplemental files including reports, layouts, and attachments.

Another important time to create a backup occurs if you are about to make major changes to your database. For example, you might be importing new records, deleting old records, or maybe modifying your layout. It's always a good idea to create a backup before you start, just in case something goes wrong.

Getting ready

Only administrators and managers of the ACT! database get to back up a database. After a database is backed up, only an Administrator can restore it.

How to do it...

1. From any ACT! screen, click the File menu, point to Back Up, and then choose Database. The **Back Up Database** dialog window opens like the one in the image below:

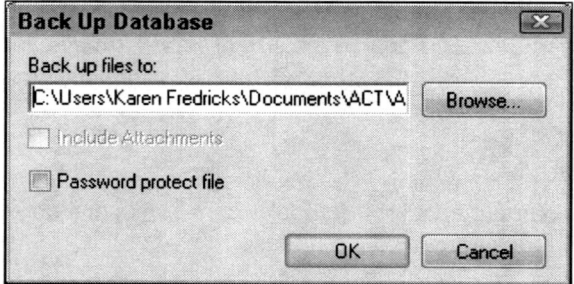

2. Click the **Browse** button, navigate to a new location for your backup file in the Save As dialog box, and then click **Save**.
3. Click **OK**.

How it works...

An indicator bar appears, letting you know that ACT! is creating your backup. The time required to complete your backup varies depending on the size of your database and the supplemental files. When the backup is complete, a message appears telling you that your backup was completed successfully.

ACT! uses a set naming convention for backup files that automatically places the word **ACT!** in front of your database name and uses the .zip extension.

There's more...

ACT! automatically creates a set of supplemental folders when you create an ACT! database. In addition to the folders that contain your templates, reports and attachments, ACT! also creates a backup folder. Although you might think it's a good place to store your backup it's not! Any new backups you create will include any old backup files saved in the backup folder making the backup file way too large.

By default, ACT! tries to save your database to a local folder on your hard drive which is not where you should be creating a backup. One of the main reasons to create a backup is to make sure that you have a copy of your database just in case something goes drastically wrong with your computer. If something bad does happen to your computer and that's where your backup is stored, you'll find yourself without a computer, database, or backup.

Password protecting the backup file

The Back Up Database dialog window includes an option to password-protect your backup file. If you check the option you will be prompted to type and confirm a password. However, you might not feel the urge to password protect your backup file knowing that only database administrators can use the file.

Additional reasons for using an ACT! backup

You'll want to create an ACT! backup even if you are using backup software or store your data on an external site. Remember, an ACT! database consists of more than a single file. The Zip file backup that the ACT! backup creates ensures that you do indeed collect all the bits and pieces of your database.

Sometimes ACT! users feel they don't need to create a backup because they feel that one is already being made. For example, in a corporate setting the ACT! database often resides on a network drive that is backed up on a daily basis. However, you might be feeling a false sense of security knowing that this backup is taking place. ACT! is a Structured Query Language (SQL) database, meaning that unless you have a special tool, a routine network backup will not back up your ACT! database. It's good practice to create ACT! backups and then add the backup file to the regularly scheduled system backup.

Restoring a backup

A backup isn't any good if you don't know how to use it to restore your data should it become necessary. Hopefully you will never have to use your backup but should the need arise the process is a very quick and painless one.

Getting ready

Obviously, if you want to restore a file you'll need a backup file to restore. You'll also need to have physical access to the computer that contains your ACT! database. For example, if you normally access ACT! through a network drive you won't be able to restore the database from your work station; you'll have to take a trip over to the server. Finally, you'll need to be a database administrator in order to restore a backup.

How to do it...

1. Click the File menu, point to Restore, and choose Database. The **Restore Database** dialog box opens like the one you see in the following figure:

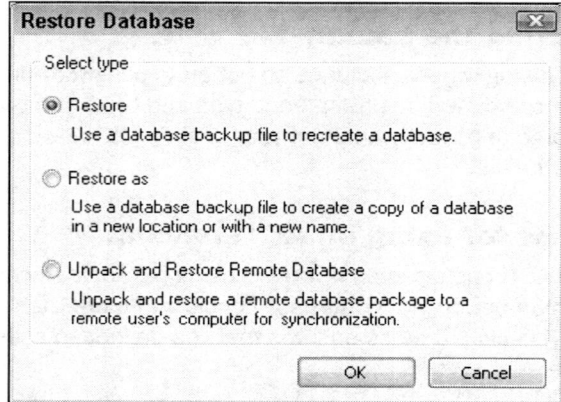

2. Select one of the restoration options and click **OK**:

   - **Restore** restores all files to their original locations; this restoration option is most-commonly used when data is lost or corrupted. The Restore functionality can only be used on the same computer on which the database was originally installed.

   - **Restore As** allows you to restore the database to a new location with a new filename; this option must be used when you want to copy or move a database to another computer.

   - **Unpack and Restore Remote Database** allows you to install a remote database that was created during the synchronization setup procedure.

3. Click the **Browse** button on the second Restore Database dialog window to navigate to the location where the backup file is stored; click **Save** and then click **OK**.

4. Indicate the desired location of the database if you are using the **Restore As** or **Unpack and Restore Remote Database** options (optional).

5. Type the backup file password if prompted and click **OK**.

6. Enter your username and password and click **OK**.

7. Click **Yes** to the warning that you see in the figure below:

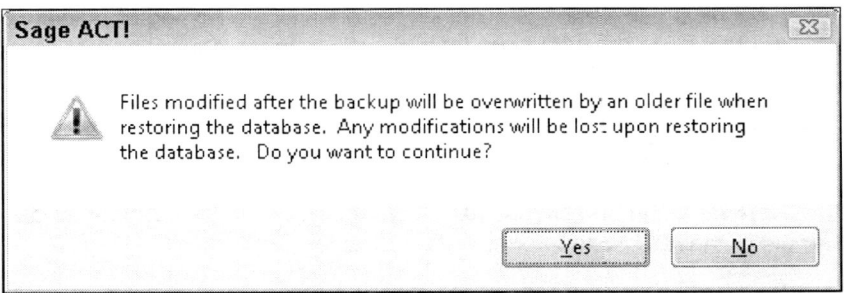

How it works...

When you restore a backup file, your current database will be overwritten with older files. Your entire database will be replaced with the contents of the backup file right down to all the supplementary folders that contain items such as your layouts, templates, and reports. If your current database is a corrupted mess, that's a good thing; if your database is perfectly fine, that could be a bad thing!

There's more...

Backup files end with the .zip extension. This is a somewhat unfortunate coincidence because there are several other software programs that use the .zip extension to archive and/or compress files. If you've worked with other software that uses that same extension, don't be tempted to unzip an ACT! backup file with a program other than ACT!. The files contained in the backup won't be placed in the correct locations, and the backup file will probably be rendered useless!

Using the ACT! Scheduler

As you can see throughout this chapter, the database administrator and manager have a lot of responsibility. The **ACT! Scheduler** automates database maintenance and backups. And, if you're working on a remote, synchronized database and the administrator has given you his permission, you can use the ACT! Scheduler to automate the synchronization process.

The ACT! Scheduler is actually a **service** or "mini program" that runs alongside ACT!; if the Scheduler is running, you see an icon in your system tray that looks like a gold clock. The great thing about the Scheduler is it will run your previously scheduled tasks even if no one is logged into the database. You might think of it as a "set it and forget it" ACT! feature.

Getting ready

Because you need to be a database administrator or manager to create and perform backups and maintenance you'll need to be one in order to schedule those tasks. By default the ACT! Scheduler does not have permission to access directories located on other machines, which means you'll want to access the ACT! Scheduler directly from the computer that contains your database.

How to do it...

1. Click the **Tools** menu and choose **ACT! Scheduler**. The following figure shows an example of the ACT! Scheduler dialog window:

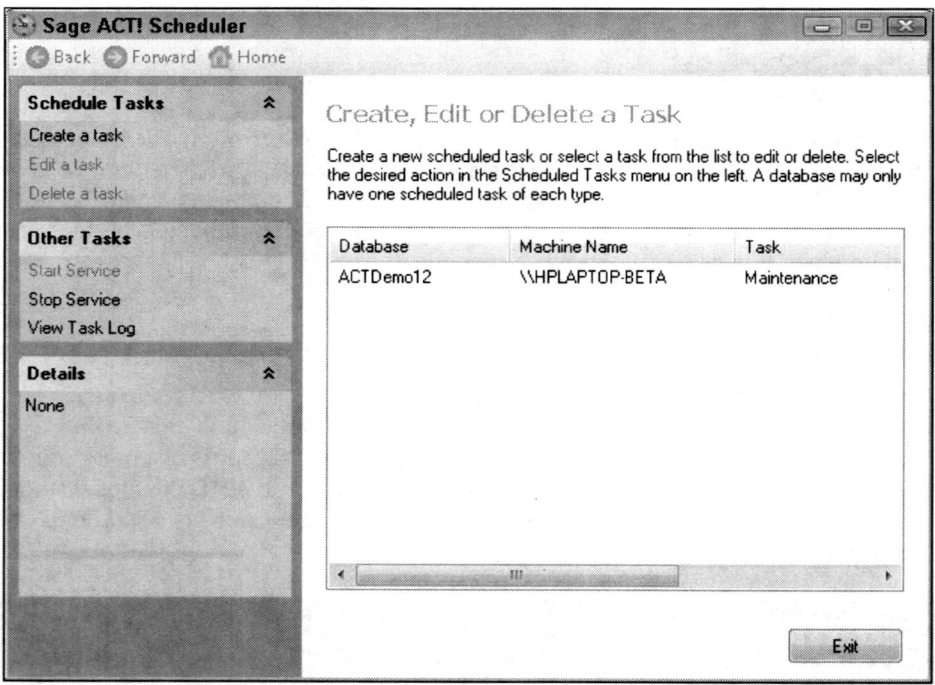

2. Click **Create a Task** to open the first screen of the ACT! Scheduler wizard.

3. Fill in the name and location of your database, username, and password and then click **Next** to continue. The following figure gives you an idea of what this step of the Scheduler wizard should look like:

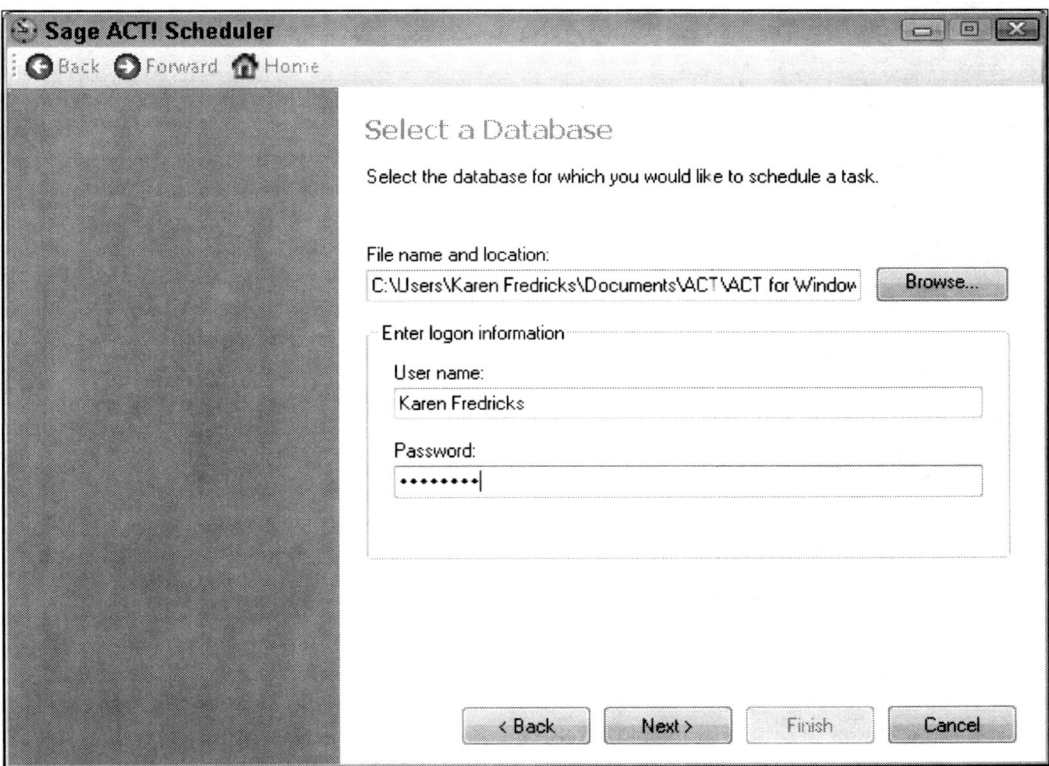

4. Select the task you want to schedule from the **Task:** drop-down list and then click **Next**.

5. Fill in the specifics of the selected task and click **Next**:

   ❑ **Database backup**: indicate the location for your backup files, whether or not you'd like to include attachments, and the number of backup files that you'd like to keep

   ❑ **Database maintenance**: indicate whether you want to do an integrity check, re-index, or both

6. Indicate when you'd like the task to run. As you can see in the following figure you can run the tasks on an hourly, daily, weekly, or monthly basis at the exact time you want:

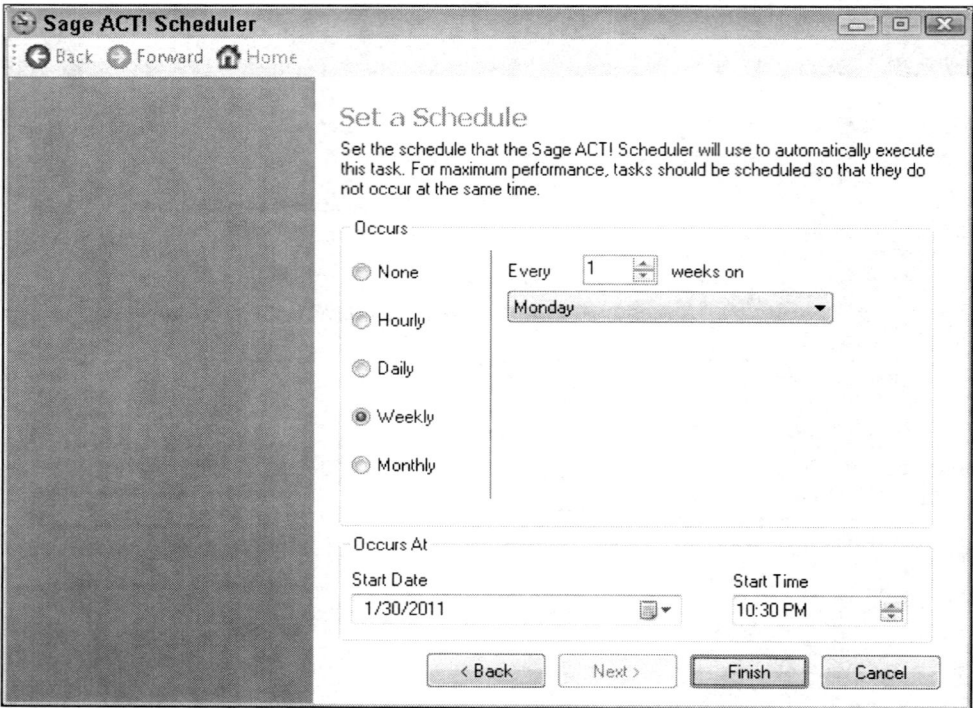

7. Click **Finish** to return to the ACT! Scheduler dialog window.
8. Repeat steps 2 through 7 to add additional tasks (optional).
9. Click **Start Service** to start the ACT! Scheduler.
10. Click **Exit** to close the ACT! Scheduler.

How it works...

The tasks will now run automatically according to the schedule you created. This means that you will no longer have to worry about running routine backups and maintenance.

There's more...

Although you might heave a big sigh of relief knowing that you are no longer responsible for the routine upkeep of your database, there are still times when you might need to run these tasks manually. For example, it's a good practice to run a backup prior to importing new information into your existing database.

Checking on the Scheduler

From time to time you may want to take a look at your scheduled tasks to make sure they are running as planned. Of course, you can always take another trip to ACT!'s Tools menu to launch the Scheduler. Alternatively, once the ACT! Scheduler icon appears in your system tray you can give it a right-click and choose **Open ACT! Scheduler** from the contextual menu to reopen the Scheduler. In either case, the ACT! Scheduler opens just like you asked it to do.

The ACT! Scheduler includes a few other options:

- **Edit a task** allows you to select an existing task to review or edit it
- **Delete a task** removes a task from the Scheduler
- **View Task Log** opens a dialog box that will show you the data, time, results and any errors that occurred in the course of running the tasks

Although theoretically the ACT! Scheduler service will automatically restart even if you reboot your computer, it's never a bad idea to double check that it's running. Needless to say, if the Scheduler isn't running your scheduled tasks won't run. If the service shuts down, a red diagonal line will appear across the clock; right click the icon in the task tray to open the Scheduler and click **Start Service** to get it up and running again.

Determining a good time for the Scheduler to run

Theoretically, you can run tasks as often as you'd like. One rule of thumb is to run backups on a daily basis, and to run the maintenance at least once a week. As to the specific time you choose there are two things to keep in mind:

- Tasks must be scheduled at least 15 minutes apart to allow sufficient time for one task to finish running before the next one begins
- If your server is also running its own maintenance and backup procedures you'll want to schedule your ACT! activities at a different time to avoid any conflict and to make sure that the ACT! backup is captured as part of the server's own backup

Applying ACT! updates

Nobody's perfect. From time to time a few of those dreaded **bugs** slip by the programmers and annoy the heck out of you. Enter the update.

When you purchased ACT! you paid for a specific **version**. For example, you might have purchased ACT! 2012, which is also known as version 13. From time to time Sage will issue a **service pack** that is an update specific to that version and fixes an existing problem; sometimes the service packs also include enhancements to the product. Over a period of time a **hotfix** or **patch** might be released that actually contains files to fix known problems or provide enhancements.

It's important to realize three things about ACT! updates:

▶ It is essential to apply them

▶ Although you must pay for a new version, **updates** to your existing version are free

▶ If you are sharing an ACT! database all users should have the same updates installed

In ACT!, applying an update is actually a two-step process. First, you apply the update, and then you need to update your database.

There are two ways to update your version of ACT! to the latest release patch: manually or automatically. With an automatic update, ACT! informs you when a new update is available when you open ACT!. You also see a blinking message in the bottom-right corner of ACT!. I highly recommend that you resist the urge to use the automatic update. By using the manual method, you can update your version of ACT! at your leisure. This is especially important if you are using a shared database because everybody needs to be updated at the same time.

Getting ready

When it comes to your database, surprises are generally not a good thing. You might want to read up on any updates before doing the deed. An easy way to do that is to click the **Help** menu, point to **Service and Support**, and choose **Knowledge Base Articles**; information about new updates is generally listed there.

You'll also want to make sure that you know the version, release, and Hot fix number of your current ACT! version. You can find that information by clicking the **Help** menu, and choose **About ACT!**. A window similar to the one in the following figure appears, giving you the complete details:

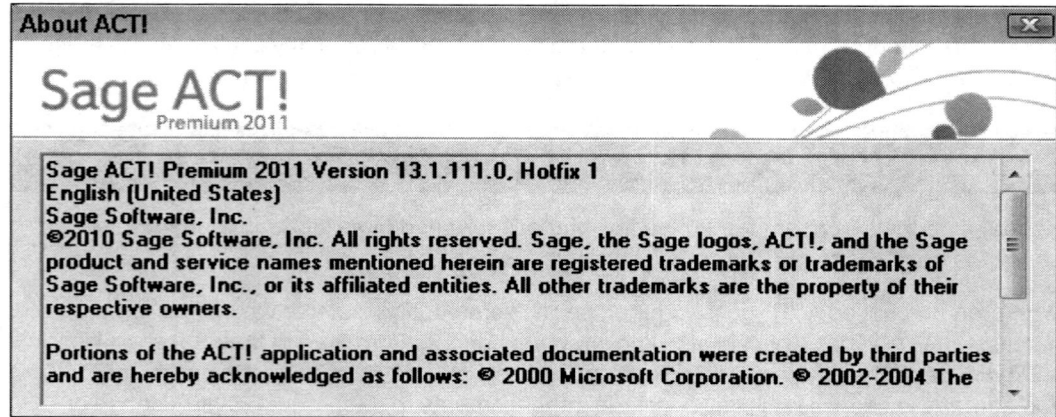

How to do it...

1. Click the **Help** menu and choose **ACT! Update...**
2. Click **Next** to continue updating ACT! to the latest release patch.
3. Close ACT! and any Microsoft products if prompted.
4. Create an ACT! backup when prompted.
5. Continue through the prompts by clicking **Next** to update your database.

How it works...

You can double-check that your version of ACT! is now updated to the latest release patch by heading back to the **Help** menu and choosing **About ACT!**.

There's more...

If you're responsible for a multi-user database, you want to make sure that a renegade user doesn't attempt to update the database prematurely. In a multi-user environment, you should update the server copy of ACT! first and then update the database itself directly from the server. Only then should the local workstation copies of ACT! be updated. The same procedure holds true for remote databases; remote ACT! users should update their copies of ACT! and their databases only after receiving the go-ahead from the database administrator.

Changing the automatic update preference

If you are the only one using your ACT! database you might like having the automatic preference turned on to notify you that a new update release or hot fix is available. You can change your automatic updating with a simple change in the preference settings. If you're the database administrator you might prefer to turn off that preference so that users don't give the update the green light without your prior consent.

Follow these steps to change the preference setting:

1. Click the **Tools** menu and choose **Preferences...**.
2. Click the Startup tab.
3. Uncheck the **Automatically check for updates** item to turn off the automatic updating.

Removing old data

ACT! users tend to be extremely loyal; it's not unusual to run into ACT! users who have been using ACT! for over 20 years. It's only natural that the longer you use ACT! the larger your data file becomes. In addition, some of that older data can become less and less important. Fortunately, ACT! provides you with a simple tool for clearing the clutter from your database. The removal tool allows you to remove notes, histories, cleared activities, and/or documents based on a given time period.

Getting ready

You'll want to analyze your database before running this utility to get an idea of how far back your history and notes records go, and decide on the cut-off date that you will be using to removing those old items. And, because you'll be asked for the number of days back that you want to go, you might consider grabbing your calculator to translate years into days. For example, if you wanted to remove data that more than 10 years old you'd need to know that ten years is equal to approximately 3650 days.

If you're not feeling really comfortable with blowing away some of your older information, you can always make an archival database so that you can refer to that information if necessary. And of course, creating a backup copy of your database prior to removing data goes without saying.

How to do it...

1. Click the **Tools** menu, point to **Database Maintenance**, and choose **Remove Old Data...** The following figure shows you the **Remove Old Data** dialog window:

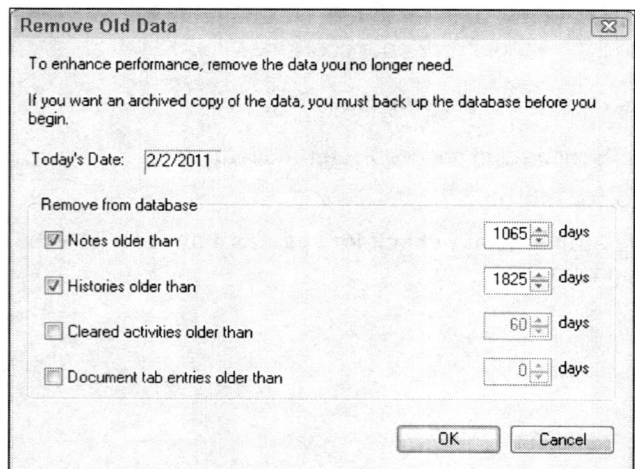

2. Select the type of data you want to remove and indicate the number of days that you want to use to remove that data in the **Remove from Database** area.

3. Click **OK**.

4. Answer **Yes** at the warning prompt like the one you see in the following figure:

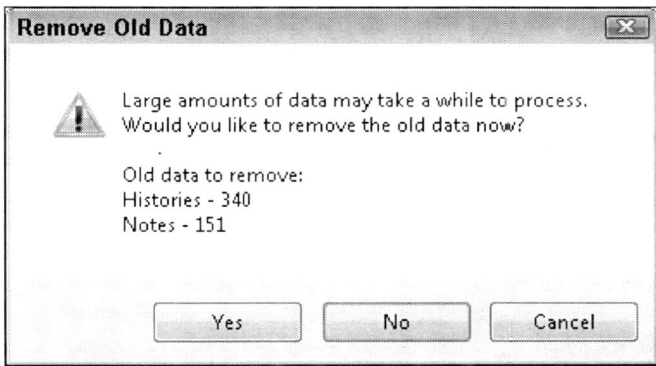

5. Click **Yes** when prompted to reindex your database.

6. Click **OK** to close the dialog box when ACT! has finished reindexing your database.

How it works...

ACT! will scour through your database looking for any notes, histories, cleared activities, or documents that match your criteria and remove them from your database. The time it takes to scrub your database is directly proportional to the size of your database and the number of items that will be removed.

There's more...

If you're concerned about deleting old cleared activities, remember that a history record is automatically created when you clear an activity. So, even if you delete an old, cleared activity, the history of that activity remains safe and secure on the contact's History tab.

Merging duplicate records

If you've been using your database for a while, chances are that you have some duplicate records. And, if there are multiple users accessing your database the chances are good that you have lots of duplicate records. Unfortunately, simply deleting duplicates is not a good way to solve the problem; you'll often find that one record contains one key piece of information and the duplicate record contains several different pieces of information.

Removing duplicates in your database is tricky but not impossible. Because having duplicate records is a common problem, ACT! lets you easily check for duplicate records based on predefined criteria. Once ACT! creates a lookup based on your criteria you can then merge the duplicate records together.

Merging duplicates is a slow process; you have to merge your duplicates on a pair-by-pair basis. This involves going through a seven-step wizard. One of the records will become the **source** record and will be subject to deletion. The other contact record will become the **target** record and will ultimately contain the combined contents of the two original records.

Getting ready

After contacts are merged together, there's no undo function. Proceed with caution! And, just to make sure that all your bases are covered, it's a good idea to make a backup prior to merging duplicate records.

How to do it...

1. Click the Tools menu and choose **Scan for Duplicates....** The **Scan for Duplicate Contacts** dialog box opens like the one in the following figure:

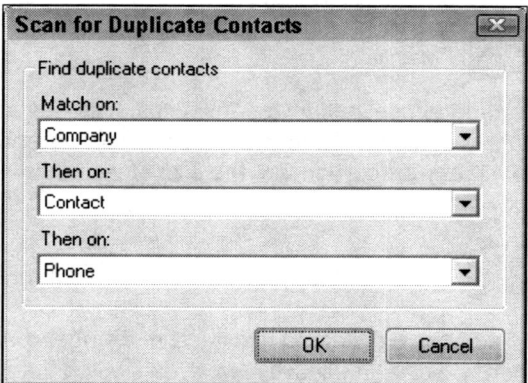

2. In the **Find duplicate contacts** area, choose the three fields you want ACT! to use to search for duplicate contact data and then click **OK**.

3. Click **Yes** at the prompt if you want to combine duplicates and open the Copy/Move Contact Data wizard.

4. Click **Next** to continue.

5. Select a set of duplicates by selecting one record and then holding down the *CTRL* key to select the duplicate record. You can see this step of the wizard in the following figure:

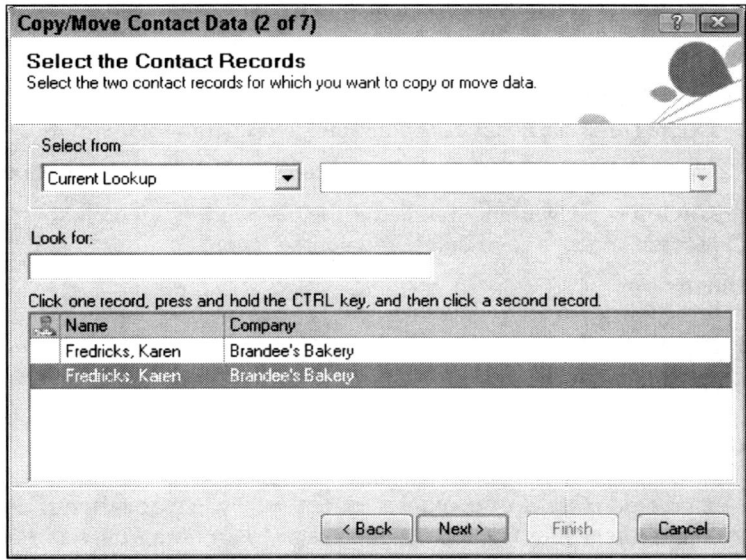

6. Click **Next** to continue.

7. Decide which contact will be the source contact and which one will be the target by selecting the appropriate radio button and then clicking **Next** to continue.

8. Click on a field and then click the **Copy** button if you want to retain information from the Source column. The following figure illustrates the fourth step of the wizard:

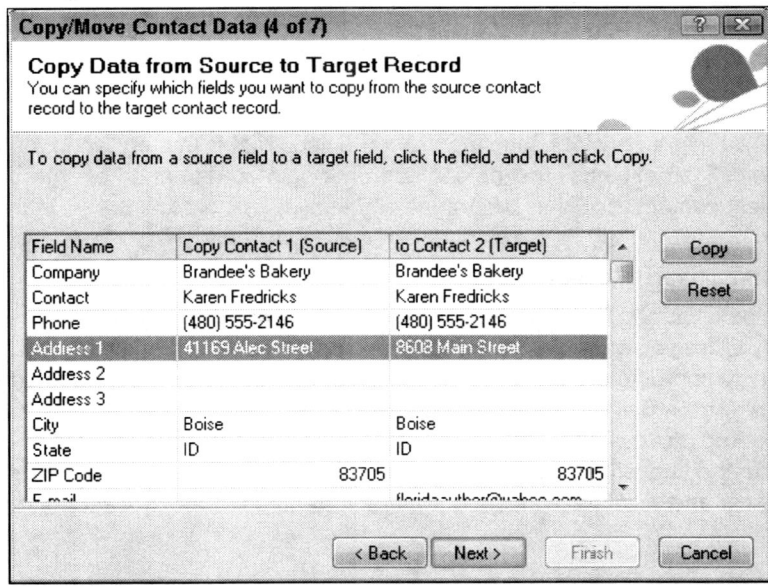

9. Scroll down the list of fields and copy as many fields as needed.

10. Click **Next** to continue.

11. Select the additional items that you want to merge together: notes, histories, activities, opportunities, secondary contacts, and documents, and then click **Next**.

12. Indicate whether to keep or delete the source record and then click **Next**.

13. Click **Yes** on the scary warning that confirms that you will not be able to recover the contact recordif you decide to delete the source record.

14. Click **Finish**.

How it works...

After a momentary pause you will be returned to the Contact List where you'll notice that the contact you selected as the source record is now gone from the list.

You can't undelete deleted records or contact information. If you inadvertently delete important information, run to your backup file and restore your data from a previous backup.

There's more...

By default, ACT! looks for duplicate contact records based on the company name, contact name, and phone number. Contact records must meet all three criteria to be considered duplicates. If records only match on two of the three fields they will not be considered duplicates. Therefore, you'll want to switch around your duplicate criteria in order to find additional duplicate records. For example, you might search by contact name and phone number but not company name to weed out duplicates with misspelled company names. Or you might search just on the email address to find duplicates with misspelled contact names.

ACT! users are often confused as to which contact should be the source and which one should be the target. You might consider scrolling down the list of fields in step 7 and focusing on the Create Date field. System fields can't be copied from one record to another so you might want to pick the oldest contact record as the target to preserve that date.

Copying or moving duplicates

The above recipe assumed that you were actively seeking out duplicate contact records. However, many times you stumble on duplicate records by accident and you may as well take the opportunity to combine the records. For example, your search for "Jones" might turn up both a "William" and a "Bill" with exactly the same contact information. If this is the case you can skip the lookup process and immediately start combining the two records by clicking on the **Tools** menu and choosing **Copy/Move Contact Data...**. The Copy/Move Contact Data wizard will appear and you'll have skipped the first four steps of the proceeding recipe.

Deleting a database

You might wonder why you would ever want to delete your database. That's good thinking because you're right: you probably don't want to delete your database. However, you might have inherited several databases that you no longer use or perhaps you created a database or two for specific, temporary purposes. Some ACT! users create a multitude of databases not realizing that there are more efficient ways to segment their data.

In general, allowing users to have access to more than one database isn't a good idea; chances are pretty good that one of your users will end up in the wrong database. And, because each database contains its own separate calendar, the users would have to access several databases to keep track of all of their appointments. Having a multitude of extraneous databases can also put extra strain on your resources and create a great deal of confusion.

Getting ready

Before you set about deleting a database you'll want to make pretty darn sure that you are deleting a database that you no longer use. The first thing you should do is access your current database, make note of its name (displayed in the ACT! title bar), and create a backup. At that point you should open the database which you wish to delete and verify that the name is different from the current database.

If your database is shared on a server you will need to have direct access to the server; you cannot delete a database over a network drive.

How to do it...

1. Open the database that you wish to delete.
2. Click Tools, point to Database Maintenance and choose Delete Database.
3. Click Yes on the Delete Database dialog window to delete your database, or No or Cancel if you change your mind.
4. Click Yes to confirm the deletion of your database.

How it works...

In an incredibly short period of time your database will be removed from your computer. In addition, all the database sub-folders that contain the database supplemental files such as layouts and templates will be removed as well.

There's more...

Deleting a database is ridiculously simple but impossible to undelete once deleted. Proceed with caution. You might also consider moving the database to another location for safekeeping rather than deleting it.

Performing a global edit and replace

One of the challenges of maintaining a database is ensuring that your database remains consistent. For example, some of your contacts might have the city listed in all capitals, but others don't. Or perhaps some contacts are listed in the **USA** whereas other contacts reside in the **United States**. This lack of consistency makes it extremely difficult to query your database and can make the results of your merges look rather sloppy. Correcting these errors on a record by record basis could be extremely time-consuming. Fortunately, ACT! provides you with the ability to correct these errors **globally**.

Getting ready

At this point in the chapter you might be feeling like you're listening to a broken record. However, I cannot stress enough the importance of creating a safety backup copy of your database before proceeding! Unfortunately, there is no Undo button to reverse your changes once you replace the information in the fields of your database.

How to do it...

1. Perform your lookup of inconsistent data.

2. Click the Edit menu and choose Replace Field. The **Replace Data** dialog box that you see below appears:

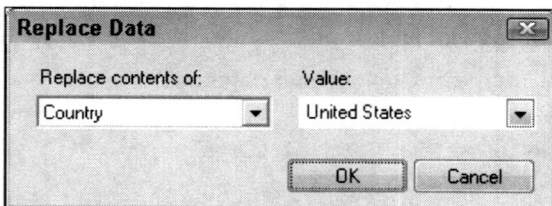

3. Select the desired field from the **Replace contents of:** drop-down list.

4. Enter the desired information in the **Value** field.

5. Click **OK**.

6. Read the warning that appears and then click **Yes** if you are ready and willing to proceed.

How it works...

ACT! will zip through your database and replace the information in the field you indicated in step 3 with the information you entered in step 4. The changes will only affect the records that are in the current lookup.

There's more...

Unless you're planning on changing field data for every contact in your database, make sure you perform a lookup prior to replacing data. These changes are irreversible! For example, if you notice 100 instances of USA that you want to change to United States you'll want to verify that your current lookup contains exactly 100 contacts. If you fail to do a lookup first, you end up changing the country field for every contact in your database to United States rather than just for the original 100 that you intended to change.

Generally speaking, when life—or ACT!—gives you a warning, it's a good idea to heed it. ACT! wants confirmation that you intend to change all the contact records in the current lookup to the value that you indicated in step 4 above. If you're not sure as to the exact number of contacts in your current lookup it's a good idea to hit the Cancel button and head over to the Contact List to verify that you are working with the correct portion of your database. You might also customize the columns of the Contact List to include the field in question just to make sure the changes you are about to make are good ones.

You can change the data in virtually any of your contact fields with the exception of the system fields. And, to make life even easier, if the field you want to change is a drop-down field, ACT! supplies you with the appropriate drop-down list.

Swapping or copying fields

aCT! provides you with two variations of the replace fields functionality, which you'll also find located in the Edit menu:

- ▶ Swap Field: This option swaps the information between two fields
- ▶ Copy Field: This option copies information from one field and pastes it into a second field

These two functions work in a similar fashion to the Replace Field function so needless to say the same instructions—and warnings—apply!

12
Creating an E-marketing Campaign

In this chapter, we will cover:

- ▶ Creating an E-marketing account
- ▶ Moving a Template to the Local Library
- ▶ Editing a Local template
- ▶ Importing a HTML template
- ▶ Sending E-marketing messages
- ▶ Updating ACT! with E-marketing History
- ▶ Analyzing an E-marketing Campaign
- ▶ Creating Lookups of your Campaign Results
- ▶ Creating Surveys
- ▶ Creating Web-Forms

Introduction

You are probably already familiar with the concept of a mail merge, and you know what an email is. The ACT! E-marketing module, also known as **Swiftpage E-mail**, gives you a safe and easy way to merge your ACT! contact information into a graphic-rich template.

ACT! E-marketing is actually an **e-mail service provider**, or ESP, which is an outside service that helps manage some of the more problematic parts of an e-blast. They make sure that your emails are spam compliant and that your email won't get blocked by the larger service providers such as AOL, Yahoo, or Gmail. They automatically suppress sending to duplicate email addresses, and to individuals who have previously opted out of your list.

An ESP also offers many additional benefits. They send your email from their own email servers, which means that you don't have to worry about sending limitations imposed on you by your Internet Service Provider. You can upload your graphics to the ESP so that creating an HTML email becomes a relatively simple task. You can send your e-blast to a Lookup or Group of your ACT! contacts. And, when combined with the Smart Task functionality, you can time when or how often you'd like your emails to be sent based on the value in a specific field.

Sending out your e-blast is only the beginning of the E-marketing process. Once sent, you can track the response to your email campaign directly from within ACT!. You'll be able to run searches for who opened—and who ignored—your email. You'll also be able to see what parts of your email they found the most interesting. And you'll be able to focus in on the individuals who showed the most interest in buying your product.

As if all of this wasn't enough, ACT!'s ESP will allow you to create web forms that your contacts can fill in from your website; that information will automatically appear in ACT!. You can even create a web-based survey and have the ESP track and compile the results.

ACT! E-marketing is bundled into ACT! and provides you with a free, limited ESP account which you can try out for 60 days or upgrade at any time.

In this chapter, you'll learn about three of the most popular functions of ACT! E-marketing:

- ▶ **E-mail** – Create email templates and send them out to select portions of your database.
- ▶ **Results** – Track the results of your email campaign, create histories of the email on the individual contact records, and use the information to take care of opt-outs, duplicated and bad email addresses.

- ► **Surveys and Web Forms** – Easily compile a survey, send it out to your contacts, and track the results. Or, create a web form so that new contacts are automatically added to your ACT! database and existing contacts can be updated easily.

When you create ACT! E-marketing templates you actually do it from a series of Swiftpage email websites. That means that your templates will be stored online in the Swiftpage Template Manager and not on your computer. Although you originate the process in ACT!, all the heavy lifting is actually done on the Swiftpage website. And, because Swiftpage is "cloud based," the format of the various windows may change periodically. Your templates, however, will remain unscathed.

Adding your E-marketing account credentials

The ACT! E-marketing account requires a paid subscription. If you have already set up an account you'll need to add your credentials to ACT!. If you do not already have an account you can create a 60 day free trial account by going to: `http://swiftpage.com/partners/partneractinternational.asp?Partner=TechBenders`. At the end of the 60 day period you can opt to continue the service or discontinue its usage.

Getting ready

You'll need three important pieces of information in order to start using your ACT! E-marketing account:

- ► Your ACT! E-marketing account name
- ► Your ACT! E-marketing user name
- ► Your ACT! E-marketing password

How to do it...

1. Click the Write menu and choose **Manage ACT! Services**.

2. Select the **Services Account** tab. You can see an example of the **Services Account** tab of the **Sage Connected Services Account Management** dialog window in the following screenshot:

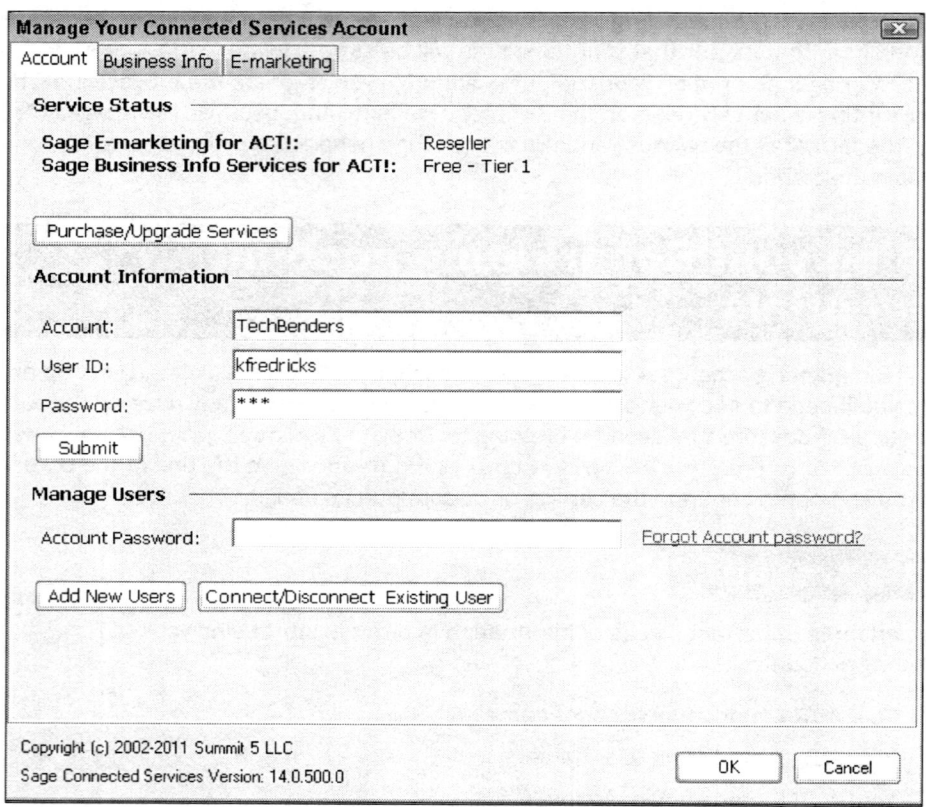

3. Enter your **Account**, **UserID**, and **Password** information.
4. Click **Submit**.

How it works...

You'll now be able to work with the ACT! E-marketing functionality for 60 days. This is a great opportunity to master ACT! E-marketing and set up some of your templates before actually paying for the service. At the end of the 60 day period you'll be prompted to both upgrade and start paying for your account or you will no longer be able to take advantage of the E-marketing capabilities. You can upgrade your account at any time by returning to the **Services Account** tab and clicking the **Purchase/Upgrade Services** button.

There's more...

You'll receive a Welcome email message that you'll need to respond to prior to sending out your first email blast.

Turning off the Marketing Results tab

By default, ACT! adds a Marketing Results tab to the Contact Detail view. This tab is designed to allow you to view the results of your various campaigns directly from within ACT!. If you decide that you don't want to use ACT! E-marketing, or don't want to take advantage of the Marketing Results tab, you can remove it from your layout. However, the tab must be removed from ACT!'s E-marketing Account area:

1. Click the **Write** menu and point to **Sage E-marketing for ACT!** and select **E-mail Marketing**.

2. Click the **Account** button. The E-marketing tab of the **Sage Connected Services Account Management** dialog window appears like the one you see in the following figure:

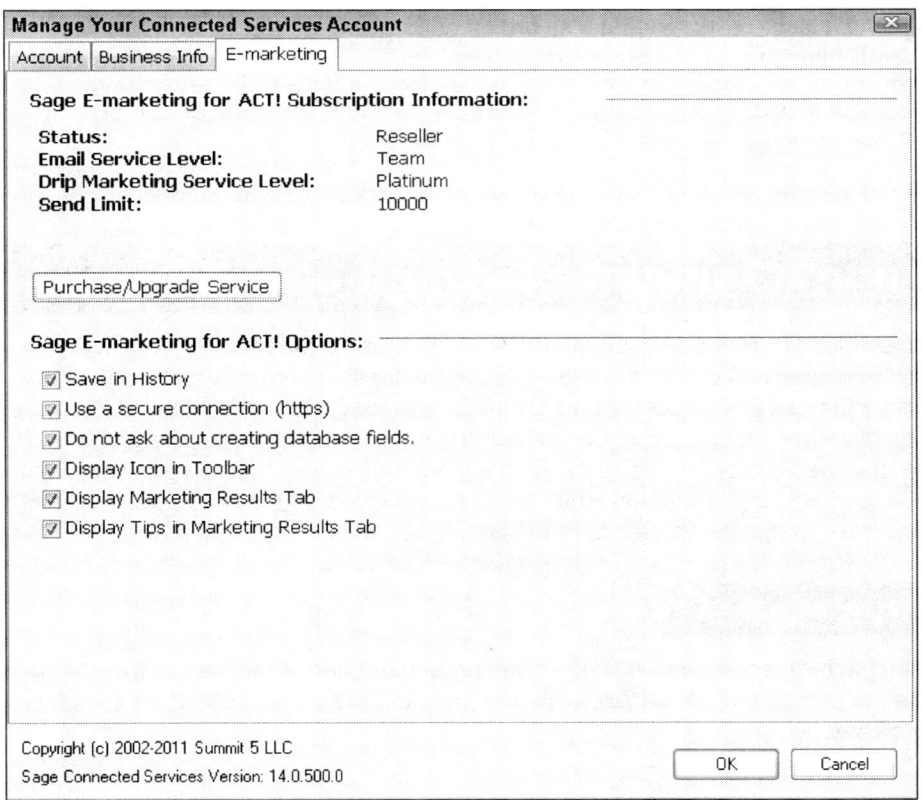

3. Remove the checkmark from the **Display Marketing Results Tab** field.

4. Click **Submit** to save your changes.

Why can't I just use ACT! email?

As you learned earlier, ACT! E-marketing includes many additional benefits in addition to the ability to just send email. You might be wondering why, if the ACT!'s email functionality works so well, you would need to use an additional service.

If your email blast follows either of these parameters then you'll want to use ACT! E-marketing rather than just ACT! email if:

- The email needs to be sent to over 50 people
- You wish to include graphics in the body of your email
- You'd like to be able to track the open rates and clicks that your message garnered
- You want to make sure that you are completely anti-spam compliant

There are several processes that come into play when you send ACT! email using a template. Each email address is merged with the template so that each recipient receives their own message. ACT! also creates a history record for each of the recipients. All this takes time and can severely hamper your computer's resources.

In addition, most ACT! users integrate with Outlook, which means that any graphics in the body of your message must also appear as an email attachment.

ACT! E-marketing supplies you with a great solution for both of these problems.

Moving a template to the local library

Your subscription to ACT! E-Marketing includes a number of **global** templates that you can use. These templates are stored in the Template Manager. In order to make changes to these templates you must first select a global template and copy it to the **local** templates area of the Template Manager. Once copied, you can edit the template by changing the graphics, verbal content, and even the design using the ACT! E-Marketing design tools. In addition, if you or someone you know is proficient in HTML they can custom design a template using their own software; you can then import those HTML templates into the Template Manager.

Getting ready

You'll need to have set up your ACT! E-marketing account and responded to the welcome email before proceeding. Of course, it will also help to have an idea about the template you wish to create.

How to do it...

1. Click the Write menu, point to **Sage E-marketing for ACT!**, and choose **E-mail Marketing**. The following image shows you an example of the ACT! E-marketing dialog window:

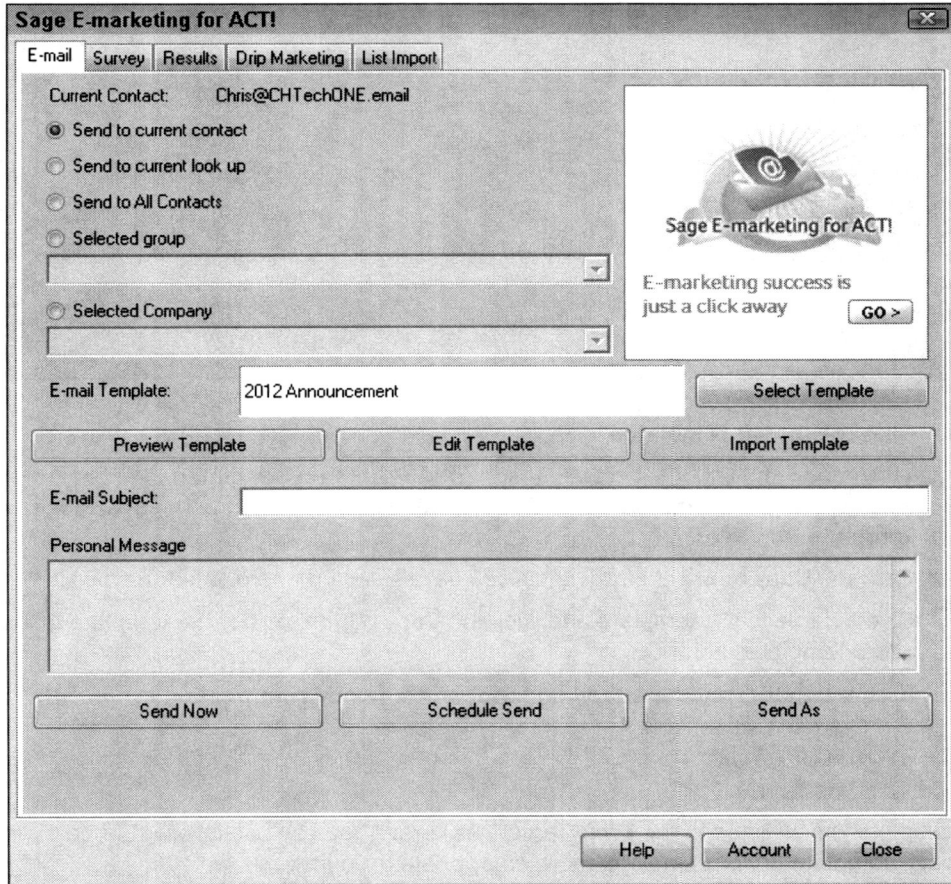

2. Click the **Edit Template** button which opens your browser to the Swiftpage Template Editor.

3. Click the **Manage Templates** button which opens the Swiftpage Template Manager. The following image shows you what this looks like:

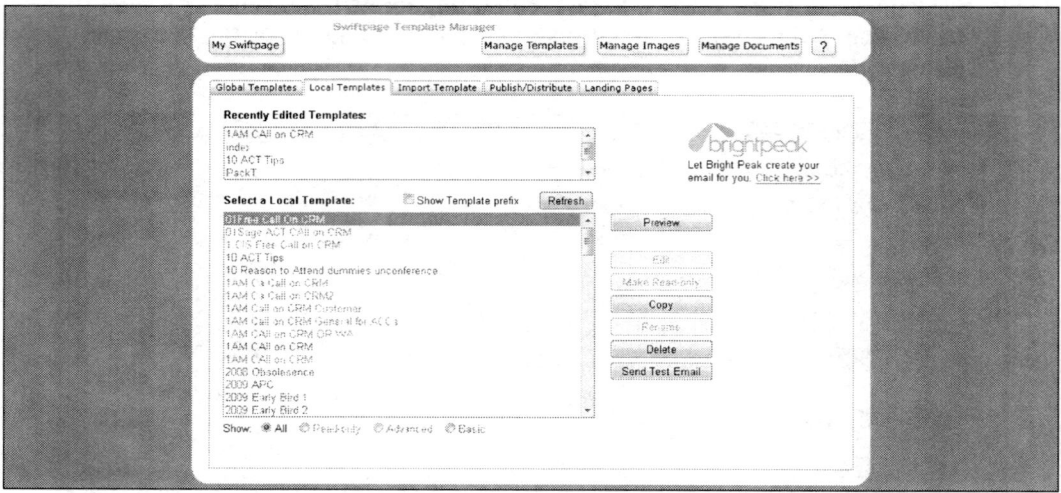

4. Click the **Global Templates** tab.

5. Scroll down the list of templates and then click the **Preview** button to preview the selected template and then click the **<<Back** button to return to the **Swiftpage Template Manager**.

6. Click the **Copy to Local** button once you have selected a template that you like.

7. Give a name to the template and click the **Copy** button to copy the template to the Local Templates library.

8. Click the **Edit Template** button on the **Template Copy confirmation** screen.

How it works...

Your template is now listed in the Local Templates library. You can use it "as is" or edit it in the Swiftpage Template Editor to make it more appropriate to your needs.

Each template is divided into a series of **windows** arranged in columns and rows. You can edit or remove any of the windows, add new windows, or change the order of the windows.

Editing a local template

Sending an email that contains graphics is not as easy as it looks. You've all seen examples of bad **HTML** (hypertext markup language) email templates. They might arrive to you missing graphics, or maybe you're seeing big red X's where the graphics should be. Or the email might arrive with lots of attachments and no graphics in the body of the email.

If you've ever grappled with HTML, you know that it can be a very tedious process. Fortunately for you, ACT! E-marketing makes designing a new template a fairly painless procedure.

Getting ready

You can only edit templates that are in the Local Templates library. If you have not done so already, take a moment to peruse the Global Templates library, select one, and copy it to the local library.

How to do it...

1. In ACT!, click **Write**, point to **Sage E-marketing for ACT!**, and then select **E-mail Marketing** to open the ACT! E-marketing dialog window.

2. Click the **Select Template** button to select the name of the template you wish to edit if the correct template doesn't already appear in the **E-Mail Template:** field (optional).

3. Click the **Edit Template** button to open the Swiftpage Basic Template Editor. The following screenshot shows you what it looks like:

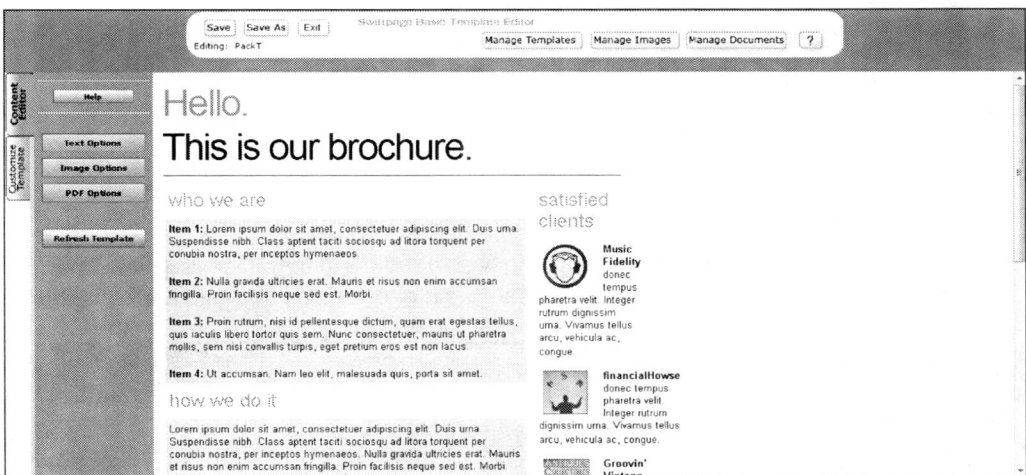

4. Notice the menu buttons in the top navigation pane that will allow you to perform the following functions either now or in the future:

   - **Save**: Saves any changes you've made to the currently opened template. You must save a template before you can edit another template.

   - **Save As**: Saves the template with a new name.

   - **Exit**: Cancels any changes you have made and returns you to the Template Manager screen.

- ❑ **Manage Templates**: Returns you to the Template Manager screen.
- ❑ **Manage Images**: Opens the Swiftpage Image Library where you store the graphics that are used in your templates.
- ❑ **Manage Documents**: Opens the Swiftpage Document Library where you store any attached documents that are used in your templates.

5. Click the **Content Editor** tab on the left-hand side of the Template Editor and then click **Text Options** to open the text options window that you see in the image below:

6. Select a window by clicking it and then click the **Erase Window Text** button to erase all of the text in the selected window (optional).

7. Click a window to select the window you wish to edit and then click the **Edit Text** button to access the Text Options similar to the one you see in the following image:

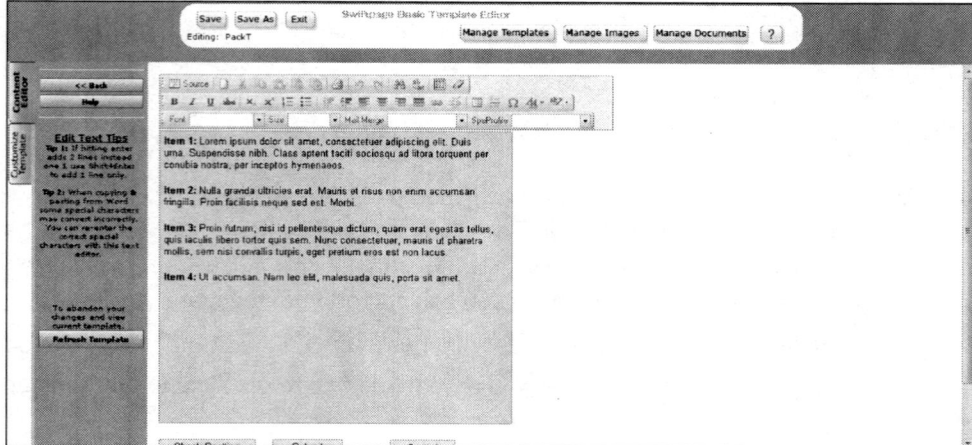

8. Change the text wording and make any necessary formatting changes including changes to the font and font size.

9. Click the **Mail Merge** drop down and select an ACT! field to insert into the body of your text so that personalized content from each ACT! record will flow into your email message when transmitted (optional).

10. Click the **SPE Profile** drop down and select a field to insert into the body of your text if you want information about yourself to appear in your email message (optional).

11. Click the **Submit** button when you've finished editing the current window to return to the main screen of the Template Editor and review your changes.

12. Click the **Undo Text Update** button to undo the last changes you made in the text editor if you're not happy with them (optional).

13. Click the **<<Back** button to return to the main screen of the Template Editor and then click the **Image Options** button. The **Image Options** area of the Content editor opens like the one you see in the following screenshot:

14. Select a window and then choose from the following options:

   ❏ **Add/Replace an Image**: Adds an image to your template or replaces an existing image. You will be prompted to select an image from your Image Library or upload a new image. Each window can contain only one graphic.

   ❏ **Replace Header Image**: Gives you the ability to replace the header image in your template with a new uploaded image or an image from Swiftpage's Header Library.

   ❏ **Remove Logo**: Removes the logo that appears across the top of your template.

   ❏ **Change Position**: Allows you to change the position of your image within its window.

- ❑ **Change Width**: Allows you to change the width of your image; the height of the graphic changes proportionately.

- ❑ **Link to Survey/Web**: Allows you to create a hyperlink from your image to a URL or one of your Swiftpage surveys.

- ❑ **Remove Image**: Removes the image from the selected window.

15. Click the **<<Back** button.

16. Click on the **PDF Options** button to access the PDF Options area like the one you see in the following image:

17. Click **Upload a PDF** to upload your document to the window you select. You then must choose one of the following options:

- ❑ **Link Text to PDF**: links the PDF to specific text in your document.

- ❑ **Link Image to PDF**: links the PDF to a specific graphic in your document.

18. Click the **Customize Template** tab. The Customize Template options open similar to the ones you see in the following screenshot:

19. Choose from the following options:

    ❑ **Set Column Width**: Changes the width of the left-hand column even if you select a window on the right-side column.

    ❑ **Background Colors**: Changes the background color for a specific window column, or for the entire template.

    ❑ **Horizontal Lines**: Inserts a horizontal line above the currently selected window.

    ❑ **Add/Delete Window**: Adds, deletes or duplicates a window. However, you cannot delete the top window in a column.

    ❑ **Move Window**: Moves a window up or down within a column.

    ❑ **Lock/Unlock Window**: Allows you to lock a window so that no changes can be made to it, or unlock a previously locked window.

    ❑ **Refresh Template**: Displays all the recent changes you've made to the template.

20. Click **Save** to save all the changes to your template.

21. Click **Exit** to exit out of the Swiftpage Basic Template Editor.

How it works...

Your template is now ready to send out to the your chosen contacts. Or, should it require some additional tweaking, you can follow the steps above to make more changes.

If your goal is to create a series of related templates and you're happy with the final product, you can click the Save As button to **clone** the template by giving it a new name. Once copied, you can edit the newest template variation.

There's more...

As nice as the existing Global Templates are, you might prefer to start a template entirely from scratch. In that case you'll want to begin with the **Blank Template – 1Col No Header No Border Template** which you can find in the **Global Template** library.

Editing a template directly from the Internet

You might have noticed that when you navigate to ACT! E-marketing from within ACT!, it actually takes you to a series of external Swiftpage email websites. You can also access these sites directly by going to www.swiftpagee-mail.com and supplying your ACT! E-marketing credentials to open up the web page you see in the following image:

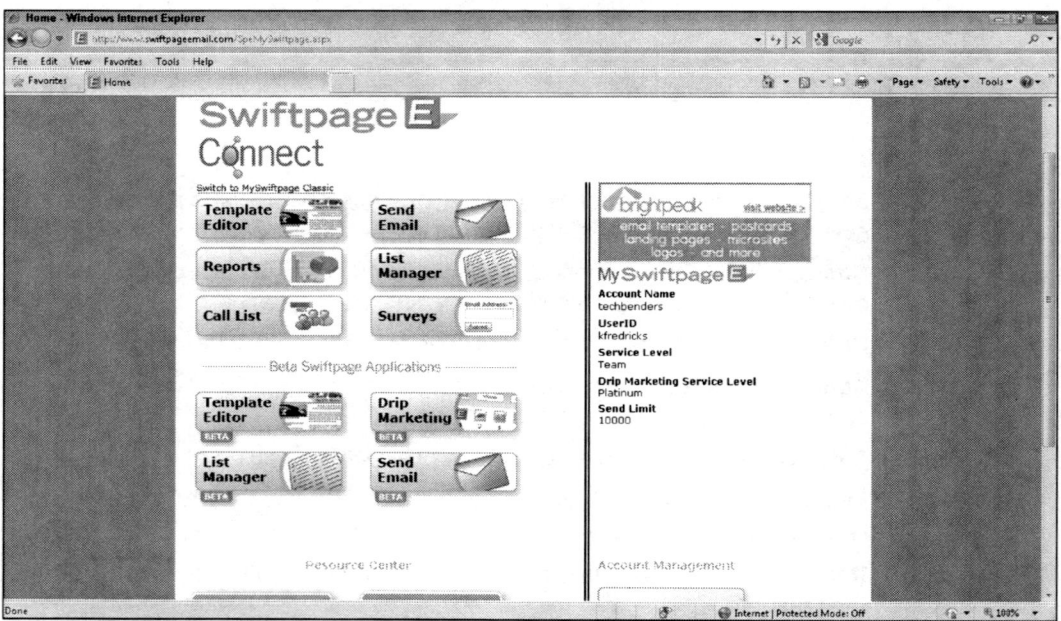

From there click the **Template Editor** button to return to the last template that you were working on.

Creating a plain text template

Several years ago the rage was to send HTML E-marketing messages. Today, however, more and more companies are finding greater success with plain text messages. For one thing, recipients often use a preview pane and routinely delete messages with graphics thinking that they're spam. Many other recipients access their email on mobile devices that will only accept plain text email.

To create a plain text email you will simply need to save your email template with the word **PlainText_** in front of the template name. You can name the email whatever you want as long as the name starts with **PlainText_**.

If you want to convert an existing global template to plain text, select the template from the Global Templates, click **Copy to Local**, and save the template with **PlainText_** in front of the existing name. If you want to convert a local template select the template, click Copy, and save the template with **PlainText_** in front of the existing name.

Remember that there are a few limitations with plain text email templates:

> ▸ You cannot add line breaks in plain text emails.

> ▸ You cannot add images in plain text emails although you can spell out a URL address that links to a graphic on your website.

> ▸ You cannot add hyperlinks in plain text emails. However, you can include links by spelling out the entire URL.

> ▸ ACT! E-marketing cannot send a single email in HTML format to some recipients and in plain text format to others; you'll have to actually create two separate templates.

Determining template column widths

The Swiftpage templates are 600 pixels wide and can have a maximum of two columns. If you want two equal columns each one will be set to 300 pixels; if you don't want any columns in your template you can set the left column to 600 and remove the windows on the right-hand side of the template. If you want one column to be twice as wide as the other you'll set one to 400 pixels and the other to 200. If you are creating your templates using HTML you can have as many columns as you'd like and set the width of your template accordingly.

Adding a personal message

You might have noticed the **Personal Message** option that appears at the top of the Mail Merge drop-down box. Unlike the other Mail Merge fields that correspond to fields in your database, this field inserts a place holder that you can populate as you send the template to one or more of your contacts on an ad-hoc basis.

For example, you might want the date that you send your marketing message to appear in the top-right corner of your template; by using the Personal Message field you'll have the opportunity to input that data when you send your email. Alternatively, you might send out a newsletter template to thousands of contacts and leave the personal message blank. However, you might then decide to send the newsletter to a single, brand-new prospect and want to add a personal message.

Importing an existing HTML template

You might be fortunate enough to be able to create templates using an HTML editor. Or perhaps you work with a media company that creates HTML templates for you. Either way, it's a snap to add those templates to your existing Swiftpage templates.

Getting ready

Once you or another person has created the HTML template you'll need to have access to the .html file as well as all of the graphics included in the document unless the graphics are already hosted on your website.

How to do it...

1. In ACT!, click **Write**, point to **Sage E-marketing for ACT!**, and then select **E-mail Marketing** to open the ACT! E-marketing dialog window.

2. Click the **Import Template** button to open the Import Template folder of the Template Manager. The following screenshot shows you what it looks like:

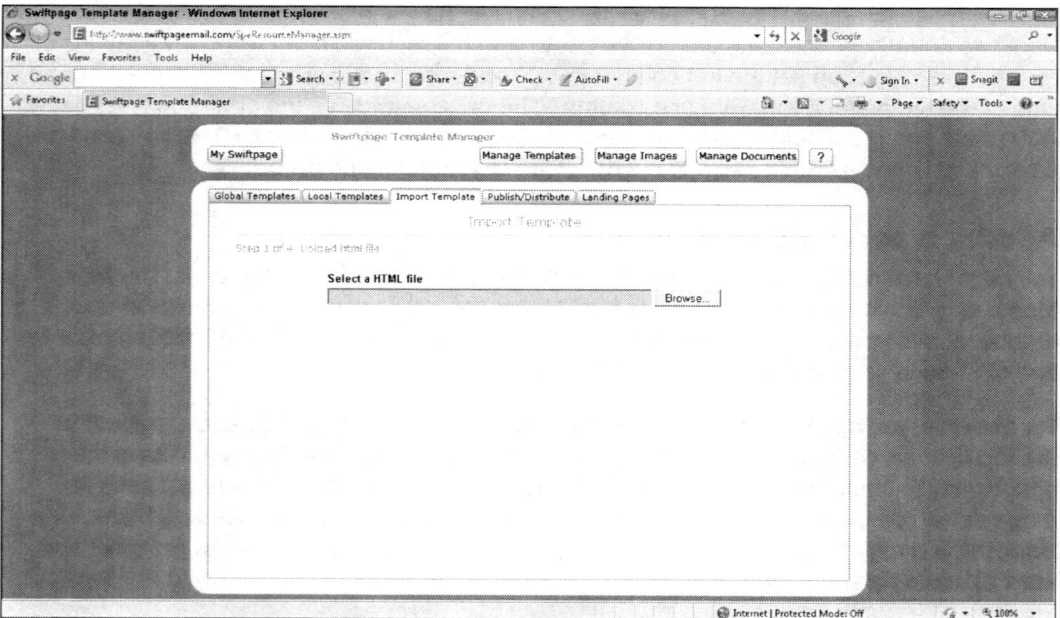

3. Click the **Browse** button to navigate to the .html file and then click **Next**.

4. Click the **Browse** button to navigate to the referenced graphic and click **Next** to continue. The following figure shows you what this step of the template import wizard looks like:

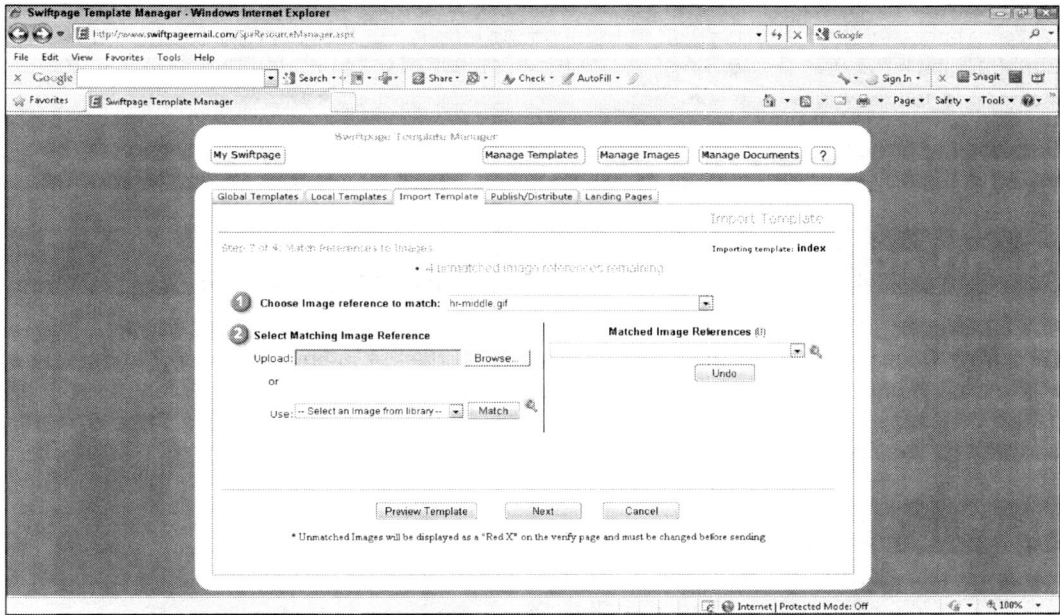

5. Click **Match** to accept the uploaded file.

6. Repeat steps 3 through 5 to upload all the graphics to your imported template.

7. Click **Preview Template** when you are prompted that all required graphics have been uploaded.

8. Click **Next** to continue.

9. Swiftpage will now add the required spam compliant footer; you'll need to scroll to the very bottom of the template and click the **Click here to Verify** link.

How it works...

Your imported email will be automatically saved with an **e_** and followed by the name of the original HTML document. Best of all you can edit the template using the Advanced Template Editor.

There's more...

If the images contained in your original HTML are hosted by you on your own website you won't need to go through the process of uploading all of the template graphics; you just need to make sure that the HTML content references the location of the graphics. Simply import the template, click the Preview button to insure the accuracy of the imported template, and then click the template verification link.

Because imported templates were originally created using an HTML editor, they can only be edited in the Advanced Template Editor which makes use of tables, frames, and text sockets.

Sending an E-marketing pieces

ACT E-Marketing is designed to both send email blasts and to track the results of your campaign. Once you've created a template you can send it out to any portion of your database at the click of button. You can even integrate templates in to ACT!'s Smart Task feature so that future templates will be sent out at regular intervals. At that point you can then sit back, relax, and wait for the results of your campaign.

Getting ready

There are two requirements for an email blast: a template and a contact with a valid email address. Although you can send an E-marketing template to an individual, most ACT! users want to send blasts out to multiple contacts. The easiest way to segment your database for your marketing efforts is to create dynamic groups prior to sending your marketing pieces.

How to do it...

1. (Optional) Create a lookup of the contacts you'd like to send the blast to.
2. In ACT!, click **Write**, point to **Sage E-marketing for ACT!**, and then select **E-mail Marketing** to open the ACT! E-marketing dialog window.
3. Select whether you'd like to send your email blast to the current contact, the current lookup, all contacts, a selected group, or a selected company.
4. Click **Select Template** and choose the name of the template you'd like to send.
5. Enter a subject line.
6. Fill in a message in the **Personal Message** area (optional). If the area is greyed out it means that you did not add the Personal Message field to your template.
7. Choose from one of the following options (optional):
   - ❑ **Schedule Send**: allows you to schedule the blast for a date in the future if you have a Pro or Team level account

- ❑ **Send As**: allows you to send the blast out on behalf of another team member if you have a Team level account
- ❑ **Account**: allows you to change your account credentials if you manage multiple accounts

8. Click **Send Now** to send your template on its way to the specified contacts. The dialog box you see below will appear confirming your selectiors:

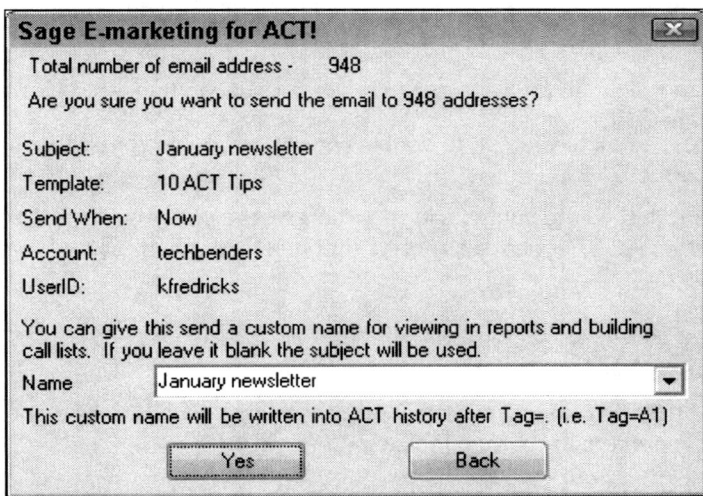

9. Fill in a name for the mailing so that you can recognize it in reports; if you don't provide one the subject of the email will be used (optional).

10. Click **Yes** to send your e-blast on its way.

How it works...

Once sent, your email will be sent via the Swiftpage mail servers. Your email template will be transmitted to the designated contacts and personalized based on the merge fields you added to the template and the data that is contained in your database.

You'll receive a confirmation email from Swiftpage telling you that your message has been successfully sent. You may also begin to receive a flurry of "bounced" emails messages indicating that the email addresses contained in your ACT! database are either incorrect or no longer valid.

There's more...

One other area you might consider customizing is the subject line. For example, you might want the subject line of the email to read *Tom, I think you'll want to see this*. You can accomplish this by adding a mail merge field surrounded by a double set of square brackets to the subject line of your Swiftpage emails. The field should be an exact match to the corresponding database field name to which you want to merge. In the example above you'd use the **First Name** field and the subject line would read *[[First Name]], I think you'll want to see this*.

Before sending out the email you will want to make sure of two things:

- ► Send a test email to yourself to double check that you've set up the mail merge field(s) correctly.
- ► Make sure that all the contacts in your merge have data in the merge field. If one of your contacts does not have any data in that field, the name of the mail merge field will display.

See also

- ► For more help on creating dynamic Groups you might want to look at the *Adding dynamic members to a Group* recipe in Chapter 4.

Updating ACT! with E-marketing history

Now that the hard part is done and you've successfully created a template and sent it off to a segment of your database, it's time to see the fruits of your labor. ACT! E-marketing will update each contact record with the results of your e-blast. And, once your database is updated with the results of your marketing campaign, you'll be able to query that information to find those contacts who are really interested in your message as well as those contacts that aren't.

Getting ready

Once you've sent out an email campaign there's not much left to do except to wait for the recipients to open (and hopefully read) your message. Your results will begin to appear within 24 hours of your initial send.

How to do it...

1. In ACT!, click **Write**, point to **Sage E-marketing for ACT!**, and then select **E-mail Marketing** to open the ACT! E-marketing dialog window.

2. Click the **Results** tab, check the boxes next to email blasts for which you want to write results, and then click the **Submit** button.

3. Click **OK** at the prompt asking if you'd like to update the Swiftpage results into ACT!.

How it works...

The ACT! History tab of all the contacts included in your e-blast will only be updated with open, click, and send information when you perform this process. It's important to remember that the results are not updated **automatically**; you will need to continue to update the results following the method above until new results stop appearing.

Once you've transmitted an ACT! E-marketing message the results of your campaign will be updated on a daily basis. Typically you'll receive the greatest number of results within 24 hours of your transmittal as your recipients begin to open your message. The results will continue to trickle in, sometimes for as long as a month after the initial send, as recipients continue to view your message.

If there are not any campaigns listed in the Results area then there are no new results to report.

Analyzing an E-marketing campaign

One of the biggest differences between a mail merge and a true E-marketing campaign is the ability to track results. You'll be able to see who opened—or didn't open—your email transmissions. In addition you can also track other results such as opt-outs and bounces.

Getting ready

Once you've sent out an email campaign there's not much left to do except wait for the recipients to open (and hopefully read) your message. Your results will begin to appear within 24 hours of your initial send.

How to do it...

1. In ACT!, click **Write**, point to **Sage E-marketing for ACT!,** and then select **E-mail Marketing** to open the ACT! E-marketing dialog window.

2. Click the **Results** tab.

3. Click on **Reports**.

4. Select the email that you wish to see results from.

5. Click **View Report**. A summary of your campaign will open similar to the one you see in the following figure:

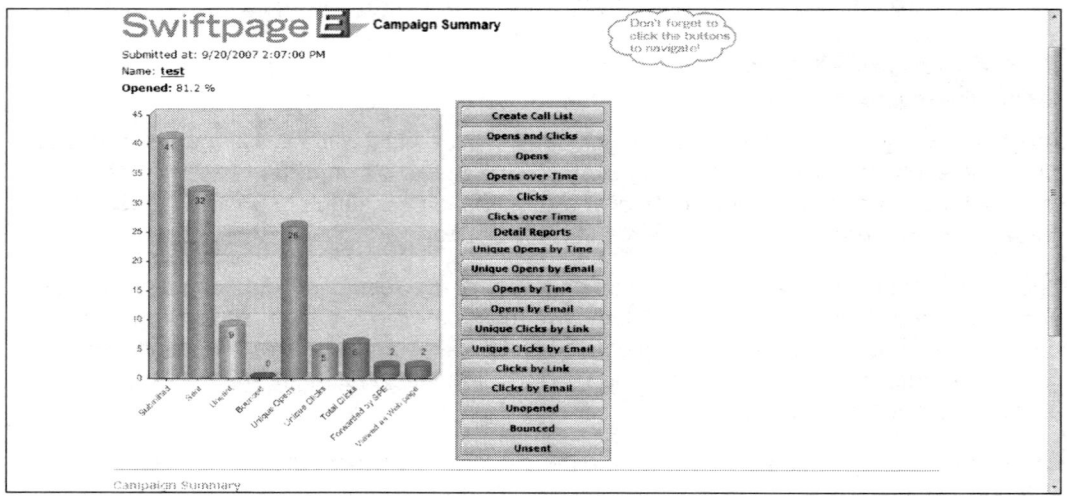

6. Observe the name of the campaign and the Opened rate percentage at the top of the screen.

7. View the following statistics:

    ❑   **Submitted**: Lists the total number of emails that you included in your e-blast.

    ❑   **Sent**: Lists the total number of emails that were actually sent.

    ❑   **Unsent**: Lists the total number of email addresses that were not sent because the email address was a duplicate, invalid, belonged to someone who had previously opted-out, or had bounced on three previous occasions.

    ❑   **Bounced**: Lists the number of emails that bounced.

    ❑   **Unique Opens**: Lists the number of individuals that actually opened the message.

    ❑   **Unique Clicks**: List the number of links that recipients clicked on.

    ❑   **Total Clicks**: Lists the total number of times any of the links were clicked.

    ❑   **Forwarded by SPE**: Shows the number of times recipients clicked on the "Forward to a Friend" link at the bottom your template.

    ❑   **Viewed as Web Page**: Shows the number of times recipients clicked on the "View as a Web page" link at the bottom of your template.

8. Select from one of the following reports (optional):

   ❑ **Create Call List**: provides you with a ranked list of your most interested recipients based on the number of times they opened the message and the number of times they clicked on links

   ❑ **Opens and Clicks**: lists all the recipients and how many times they opened the message, clicked on links, and forwarded the message

   ❑ **Opens**: shows you pie charts depicting the percentage of people that read your email

   ❑ **Opens over Time**: displays a graph showing the time of day recipients opened your email

   ❑ **Clicks**: displays a graph showing you which links were the most popular

   ❑ **Clicks over time**: displays a graph showing you the time of day the various links were clicked on

9. Select one of the Detail Reports to see the list of recipients that corresponds to the details of the statistics listed in step 7 (optional).

How it works...

Statistics can only be measured when a recipient actually clicks one of the links in your message. For example, messages that are forwarded using the email client's forwarding mechanism rather than the forward button that appears in your templates will not be counted.

There's more...

With ACT's E-marketing module you'll be able to find out who's really interested in your products and services, who never opened your email, and who never even received your email. You might even experiment by sending different templates to different portions of your database so that you can measure the effectiveness of each one.

Requesting a CSV file of your results

In the next recipe you'll learn how to create lookups in ACT! of the various results of your campaigns. However, you might also like to see the results of your campaigns in the form of a spreadsheet. For example, you might want to share this information with non-ACT! users. If you scroll down to the bottom of any of the Detail Reports you'll notice the **Send .csv file** to field. Simply fill in the email address you'd like the report sent to and click **Send** and within minutes a copy of the report will arrive in your Inbox.

Creating a Lookup of your Campaign Results

When you send a campaign using ACT! E-marketing a history of the transmittal is automatically created for each intended recipient. When you update ACT! with the results of an E-marketing campaign the history item is modified to reflect pertinent information, such as how many times the message was opened or whether the recipient chose to opt out of future mailing. The following image shows you a sample of the history message created by ACT! E-marketing:

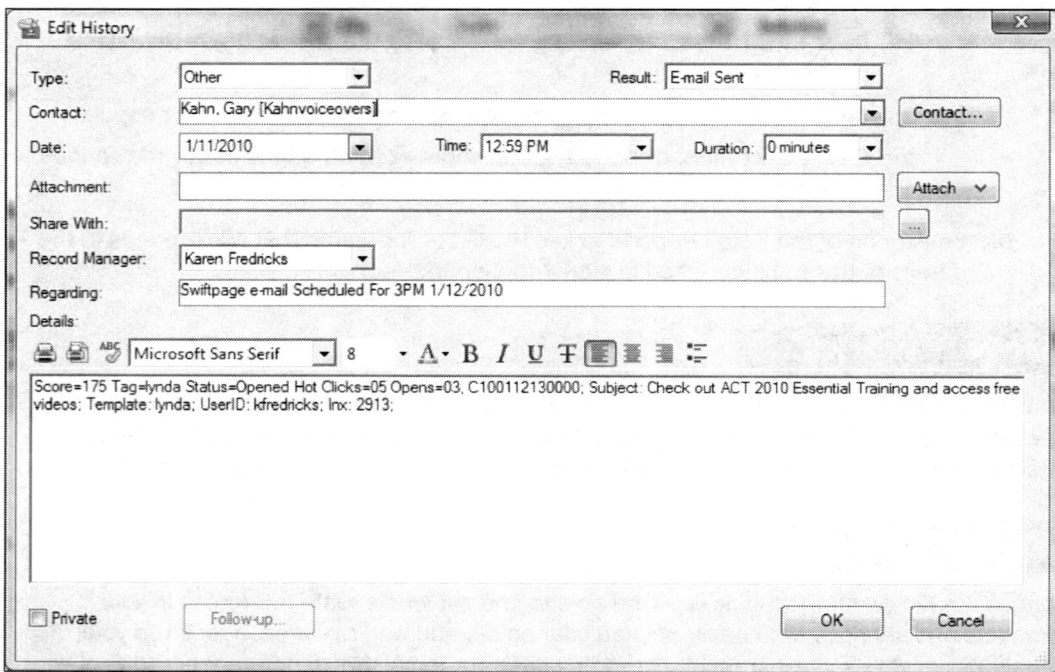

Although that information appears a bit cryptic, it holds the key to being able to track important results about an email blast from within ACT!.

Getting ready

You'll need to have sent an email blast and updated ACT! with the corresponding results before you can start tracking the results of your campaign from within ACT!.

How to do it...

1. In ACT!, click the **Marketing Results** tab on the **Contact Detail** view. The following screenshot shows you what it looks like:

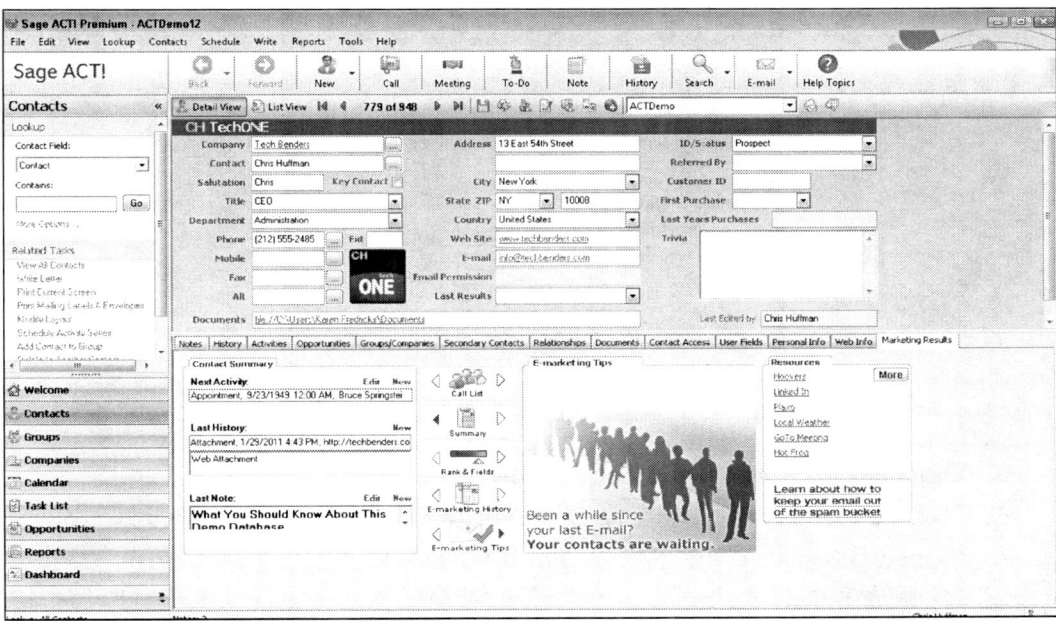

2. Click the **E-marketing History** icon.

3. Scroll through the E-marketing History using the right-pointing arrow until the subject line appears that corresponds to the campaign you are tracking (optional). You can see an example of this in the following image:

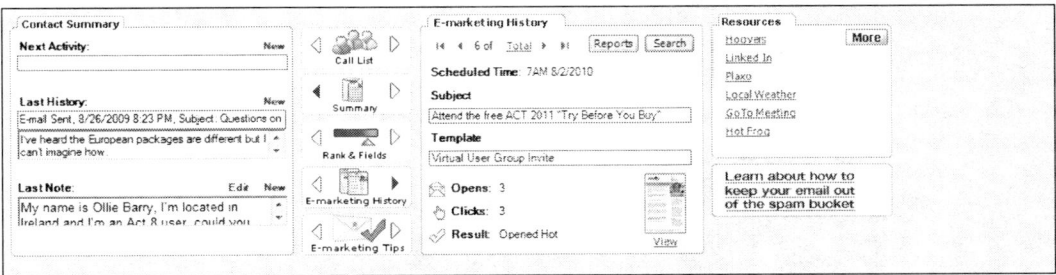

4. Click the **Search** button. As you can see in the following figure you can search for **Unopened**, **Opt-outs**, **Invalid**, **Bounced**, and **Duplicates** responses:

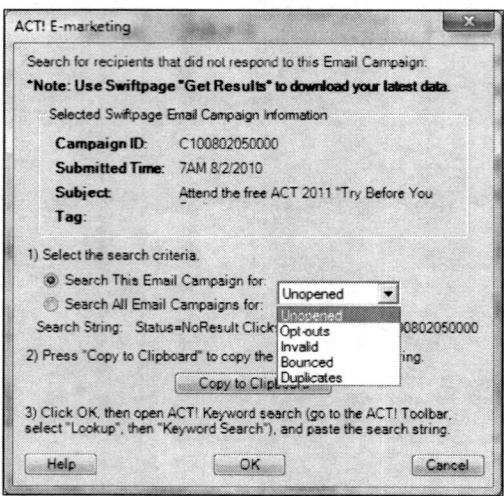

5. Click **Copy to Clipboard** and then Click **OK**.

6. Click the **Lookup** menu and select **Keyword Search**.

7. Paste the contents of the clipboard into the Search for field of the Search on Keywords dialog box. You can see what this looks like in the following screenshot:

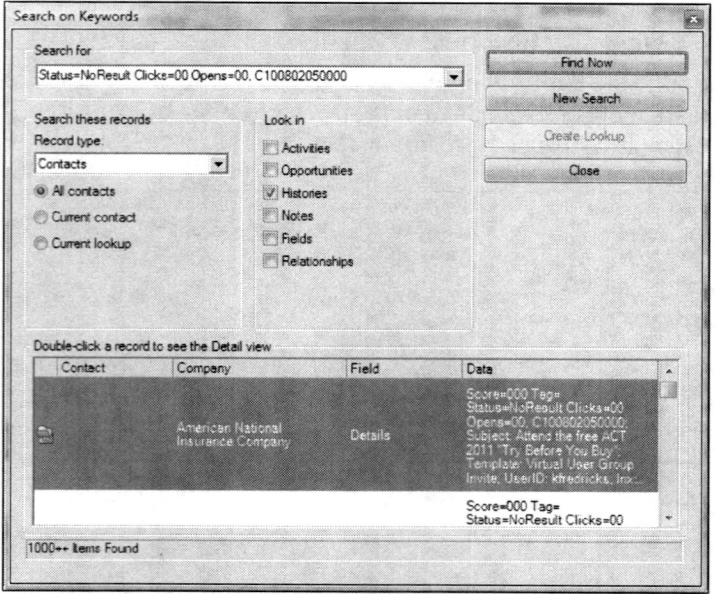

8. Check the Histories item; remove all other checkmarks if you want to speed up the time it takes to perform the search.

9. Click **Find Now** and wait for ACT! to find the records that match your criteria.

10. Click **Create Lookup** to create a Lookup of the matching records.

There's more...

Once ACT! presents you with those records that match your search criteria you can easily make whatever changes you need. For example, if you searched for Invalid or Duplicate records you might scroll through the Lookup and make necessary corrections to the email addresses. If you were searching for the Opt-outs you might globally update all of those records with this new piece of information. And, if your search provided you with the names of the people who didn't open your message you might move all of those names into a group and start contacting those contacts use a different method than email.

Creating a survey

The ACT! E-marketing module contains the ability to create **surveys**. You're probably already familiar with traditional surveys that poll your contacts for their preferences. For example, you might want to find out your customer's preferred method of contact or their product color preference. Once you've transmitted a survey you can view the survey statics or request that they be sent to you in an Excel spreadsheet.

How to do it...

1. In ACT! click the **Write** menu, point to **Sage E-marketing for ACT!**, and then choose **Survey/Web** Forms. The Sage E-Marketing for ACT! dialog window opens on the Survey tab.

2. Click **Survey Editor**. The **Swiftpage Survey** screen opens like the one you see in the following screenshot:

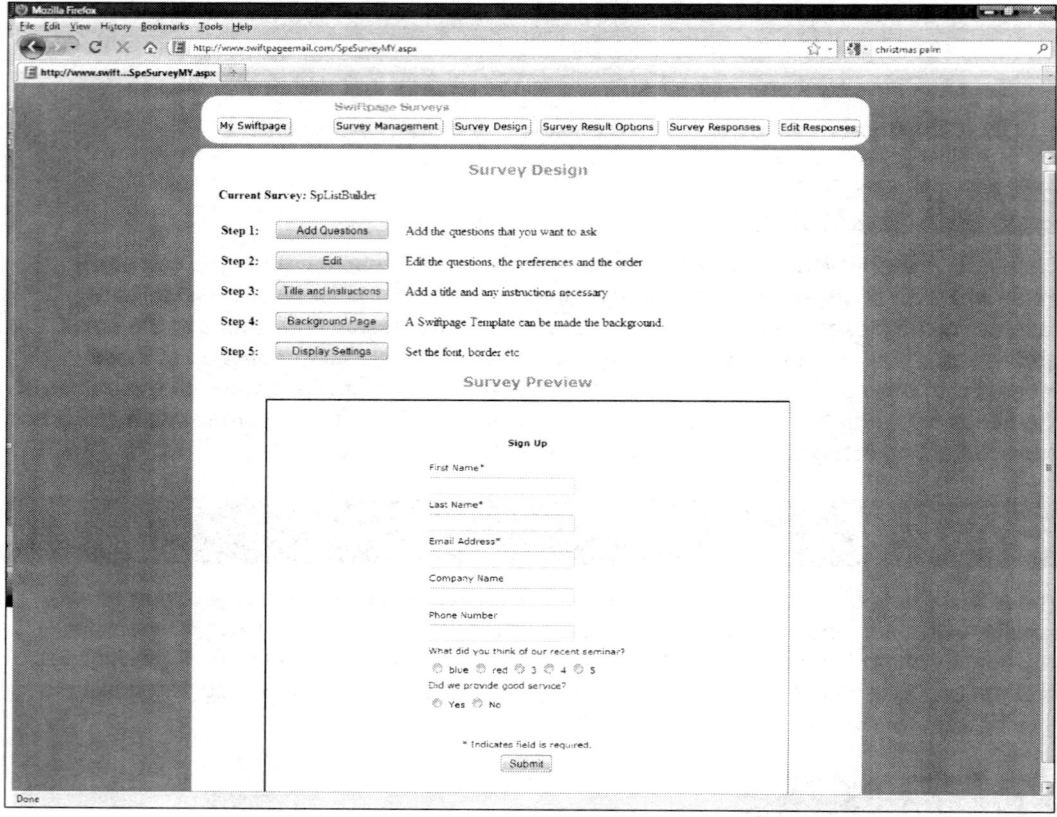

3. Click **Survey Management** and then click **New**.

4. Give your new survey a name.

5. Select an existing survey from the **Copy Questions From** dropdown (optional).

6. Click the **Submit** button to return to the main survey window.

7. Click **Survey Design** and then choose **Add Questions**.

8. Fill in a survey question in the **Enter the question that you want to ask** field and indicate the type of answer you want. The following image shows you how to add a new question:

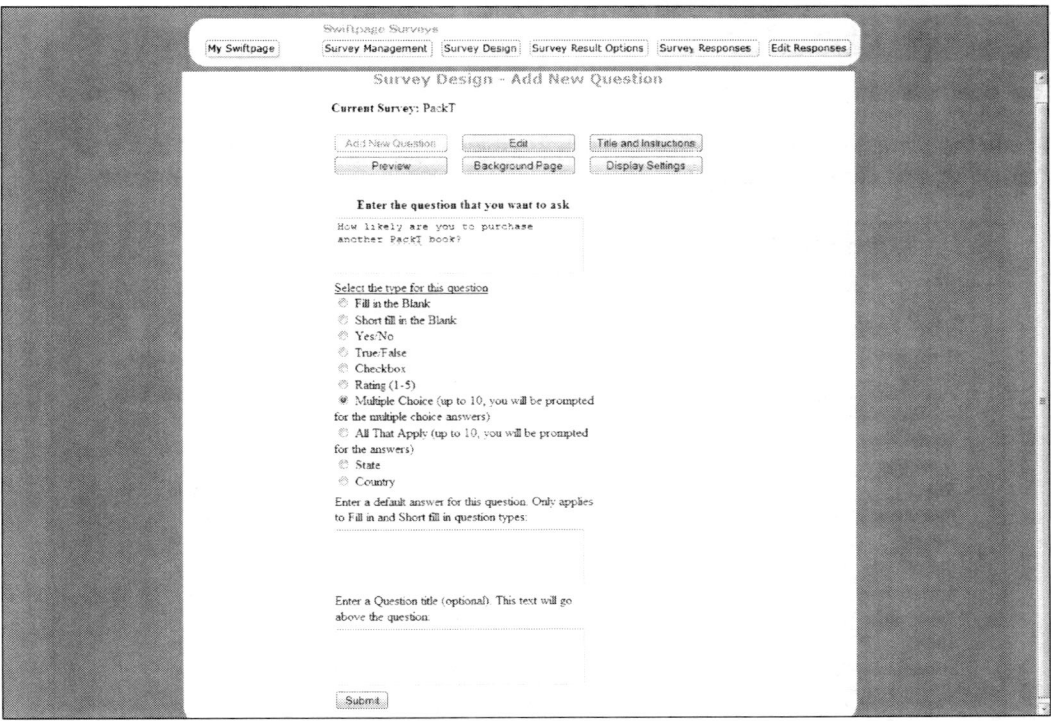

9. Click **Submit**.

10. Depending on the type of question you selected in Step 8 above you will be asked to provide question responses (optional). Fill in your answer(s) and click **Submit**.

11. Repeat steps 8-10 to add additional questions to your survey (optional).

12. Click **Edit** to change the order of questions or to edit or delete a question.

13. Click **Title and Instructions** to add these items to your survey.

14. Click **Background Page** if you have a Pro and Team level accounts to change the background and text color or to change the font and then click **Submit** to save your changes (optional).

15. Click **Preview** to preview your survey (optional).

16. Click **Survey Management** to return to the Survey Management page.

17. Copy the Survey Link if you'd like to place a hyperlink to your survey on your website or in a template (optional).

18. Click **Short Link** if you'd like to create a shortened form of the survey link (optional).

How it works...

Your contacts can now access your survey by clicking on the web link you provide them.

To see the compiled survey information click **Sage E-marketing for ACT!**, point to E-mail marketing, and click the **Survey** tab which will look similar to the following screenshot:

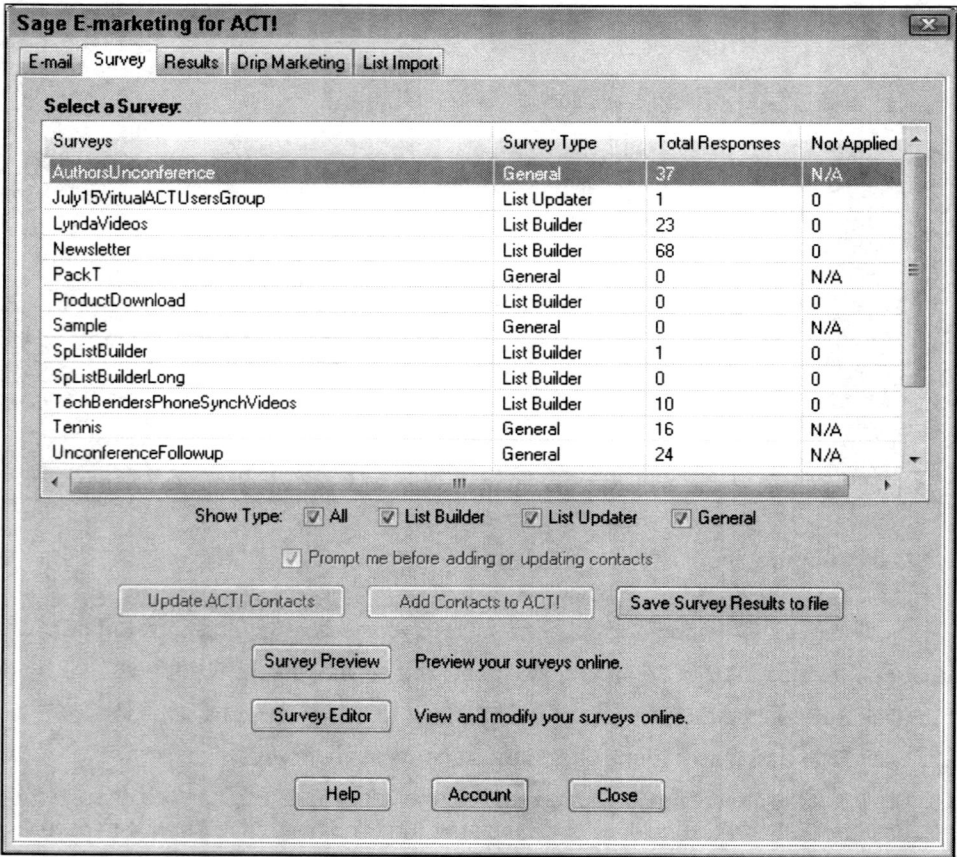

From there you'll select a survey and click **Save Survey Results to file** to receive an Excel spreadsheet showing individual responses for each participant as well as a compilation for each question.

Once you get familiar with surveys you'll find that you can use them in a variety of ways. You might use them to guage the success of your webinars; alternatively you might use them to see how well your customers like your new product line or to poll them for their opinion about an upcoming conference.

There's more...

Once your survey is set up, you can put the survey into an E-marketing template or include it on your website.

There are two ways to put a survey in your template: you can link it to text or link it to an image.

To link your survey to text, create a template and include a phrase that you want to link to a survey. For example, you might include the words **Click here to take the survey**. Then choose Text Options from the Content Editor and click Link to Survey. In the white box on the left-hand side of the screen, type the words exactly as they appear in the template so in the example above you'd type **Click here to take the survey**. Select your survey from the dropdown list, and click Submit. Your survey will now be linked to the specified text.

To link a survey to an image, add the image you want linked to your survey into a template. Then select the window your image is in, click on **Content Editor** and choose **Image Options** and then pick **Link to Survey / Web**. Select Link to Survey and then choose the name of the survey from the drop-down list and click **Submit**.

Creating a web form

A lot of companies have forms on their websites that they're hoping prospects will complete and thus provide them with new and or updated contact information. Well guess what? You can create these forms in ACT!, integrate them to a website, and have the information automatically appear in ACT! at the click of a button. The versatility of creating a web form—and getting that information directly into ACT!—is a feature you'll certainly want to take advantage of. It will not only save you lots of time but it will help you keep your data up to date!

In the preceding recipe you learned how to create a **general** survey designed to poll your contacts on the topics of your choice. However, ACT! E-marketing includes other types of surveys that allow your contacts to add new contact information or update existing information in ACT!. This survey information will automatically be added to your ACT! database saving you countless hours of data processing time.

There are two forms of these special surveys:

- **List Builder**: Adds new contacts to your database
- **List Updater**: Updates existing contacts in your ACT! database with additional or corrected information

Getting ready

You can include links to your List Builder and List Updater surveys to your E-marketing templates.

How to do it...

1. In ACT! click the **Write** menu, point to **Sage E-marketing for ACT!** and then choose **Survey/Web Forms**. The Sage E-Marketing for ACT! dialog window opens to the Survey tab.

2. Click **Survey Editor**. The **Swiftpage Survey** screen opens.

3. Click **Survey Management** and then click **New**.

4. Give your new survey a name.

5. Select an existing survey from the **Copy Questions From** dropdown. Choose **UpdateContactInformation** for a List Updater survey and **SPListBuilder** or **SPListBuilderLong** for a List Builder survey.

6. Click the **Submit** button to return to the main survey window.

7. Scroll to the bottom of the Survey Management window to review the questions in the current template. You might want to make note of the questions you'd like to modify, delete, or add.

8. Click **Survey Design** and then choose **Add Questions**. Fill in a survey question in the **Enter the question that you want to ask** field and indicate the type of answer you want.

9. Click **Submit**.

10. Depending on the type of question you selected in step 8 above you will be asked to provide question responses. Fill in your answer(s) and click **Submit** (optional).

11. Repeat steps 8-10 to add additional questions to your survey (optional).

12. Click **Edit** to change the order of questions or to edit or delete a question.

13. Click **Title and Instructions** to add these items to your survey.

14. Click **Background Page** if you have a Pro and Team level accounts to change the background and text color or to change the font and then click **Submit** to save your changes (optional).

15. Click **Preview** to preview your survey (optional).

16. Click **Survey Management** to return to the Survey Management page.

17. Copy the Survey Link if you'd like to place a hyperlink to your survey on your website or in a template (optional).

18. Click **Short Link** if you'd like to create a shortened form of the survey link (optional).

How it works...

You can include links to your List Builder and List Updater surveys in your E-marketing templates. In fact, sending a List Updater survey to your existing contacts is a great way to ensure that your database stays "up to date." When a recipient fills in their content data you'll be able to update the contents of your database with the new, improved information.

Connecting a List Builder survey to the Contact Us link on your website is a great way to collect new contact information because the information will automatically add to ACT! saving you the bother of having to input new contact data!

There's more...

When a contact fills in one of your list surveys, you'll receive a notification email. You'll then want to return to the Survey tab of the Sage E-marketing for ACT! dialog window and click the Add Contacts to ACT! button. If a duplicate record is found you'll be given the opportunity to either ignore the contact or decide which fields you'd like to update. All new contacts will be put into the Swiftpage Imported Contacts group in your ACT! database so that you'll be able to find them easily.

13
Working Smarter with Smart Tasks

In this chapter, we will cover:

- ▶ What are Smart Tasks?
- ▶ Editing existing Smart Tasks
- ▶ Creating a Smart Task template
- ▶ Adding a Smart Task step
- ▶ Changing Smart Task steps
- ▶ Putting Smart Tasks on Auto Run
- ▶ Running Smart Tasks manually
- ▶ Checking the progress of a Smart Task

Introduction

When ACT! arrived on the scene over 20 years ago it was labeled as **contact management software**. Simply put, this means that ACT! allowed you to create a group of contacts and associate a variety of activities with them, including **notes** and **activities**.

As software evolved, **CRM** (Customer Relationship Management) software became popular. CRM software takes contact management software to the next level by relying more heavily on automated processes. **Workflow** is the term generally used to describe the automated process found in CRM software. Sage Software knew they had to step up to the plate and they did just that by adding the new **Smart Steps** feature to ACT! 2012.

You might find it easier to understand the difference between contact management and CRM software if you contrast ACT!'s traditional Activity Series with the new Smart Tasks feature. Both processes are similar in that they allow you to automatically schedule a series of related activities or steps. Here are some of the subtle yet important differences:

- An Activity Series is based on a target date. Alternatively, Smart Tasks are based on a defined query of field or opportunity information.
- An Activity Series will schedule an ACT! Activity; a Smart Task can automatically send an email.
- An Activity Series can be set to run multiple times for same contacts whereas an option within Smart Tasks allows you to define that it will only run once per contact.
- An Activity Series must be run manually; Smart Tasks can be run manually or be scheduled to run automatically. Smart Tasks can be run automatically based upon completion of the previous step.

Smart Tasks are a series of steps that automatically perform tasks or actions based on contact opportunity or field information. For example you might set up a Smart Task to let you know if you haven't had any contact with a key customer in over 90 days; you might want to receive a notification via email or have an activity schedule to remind you to follow up with the contact.

Smart Tasks can contain more than one step and are organized by creating a template. For example, you might want to send out several emails to a new customer once they've signed on the dotted line.

Working with Smart Tasks is actually a three part process. The entire process is covered in this chapter but for now, here's an overview of the process in its entirety:

1. Create a Smart Task template.
2. Run the Smart Task—or have the Smart Task set to run automatically.
3. Monitor the Smart Task progress.

A Smart Task can run automatically or manually. Automatic Smart Tasks run based on a trigger that specifies when the Smart Task will run and criteria that specifies which records (contacts or opportunities) the Smart Task should include. If a Smart Task is run manually the criteria is ignored and the user has the option to run the Smart Task for all contacts or just the current lookup.

It is important to note that Smart Tasks can only run when your ACT! database is open. Unfortunately, Smart Tasks cannot be added to the ACT! Scheduler and run automatically in the same way that routine maintenance and backups can run regardless of whether or not your database is open. If you're not logged into ACT! when the Smart Task is scheduled to run, the Smart Task won't run.

Learning about the existing Smart Tasks

It might seem a little backwards to have a section on managing Smart Tasks appear before the section on creating them. You can use the included Smart Tasks templates or create your own custom Smart Tasks to help manage your day-to-day operations. Nine Smart Tasks come right out of the box and you may as well try your hand at editing them before you plunge into creating a new Smart Task from scratch. Besides, you might find that at least one of the Smart Task is perfectly suited to your needs.

How to do it...

1. Open the **Manage Smart Tasks** dialog window. There are a number of ways to get to this window:

   ▸ Click the **Schedule** menu and choose **Manage Smart Tasks**.

   ▸ In the **Contact Detail** or **Contact List** view, click **Manage Smart Tasks** in the **Related Tasks** area of the **Navbar**.

   ▸ In the **Opportunity Detail** or **Opportunity List** view, click **Manage Smart Tasks** in the **Related Tasks** area of the **Navbar**.

2. All of these methods will take you into the **Templates** tab of the **Manage Smart Tasks** dialog window that you see in the following screenshot:

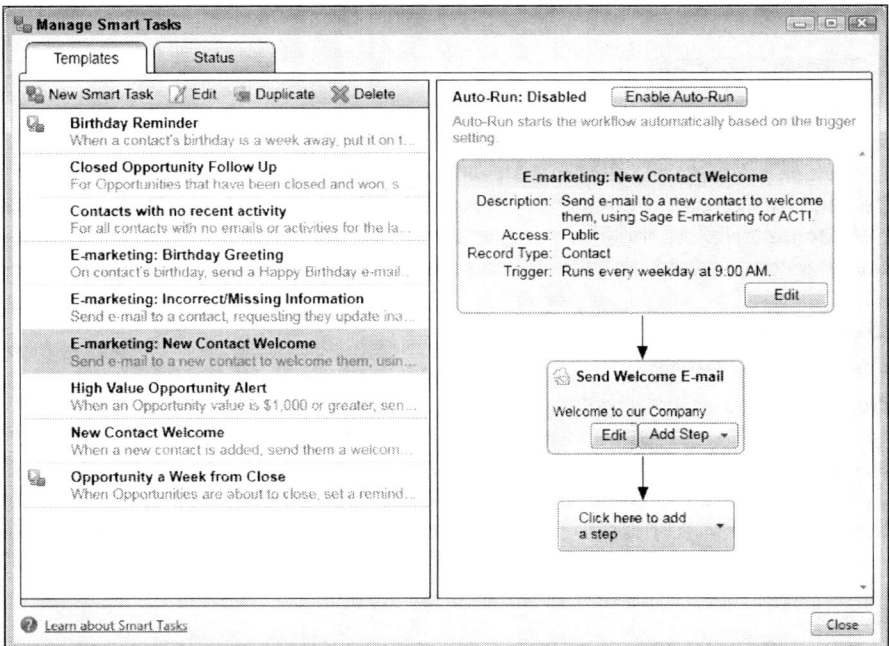

3. Click the template name that you'd like to investigate further. The list of Smart Task templates runs along the left side of the **Manage Smart Tasks** dialog window. The steps of the selected Smart Task template appear in the right pane. You might notice a small icon to the left of a few of the template names; this indicates that the template is set to Auto-run.

4. Click the **Delete** button to remove a template if you don't think you'll ever use it.

5. A warning like the one you see below will pop up. It's important to realize that the template will disappear for all users of your database and not just you. Deleting a template does not delete the scheduled tasks already associated with the template.

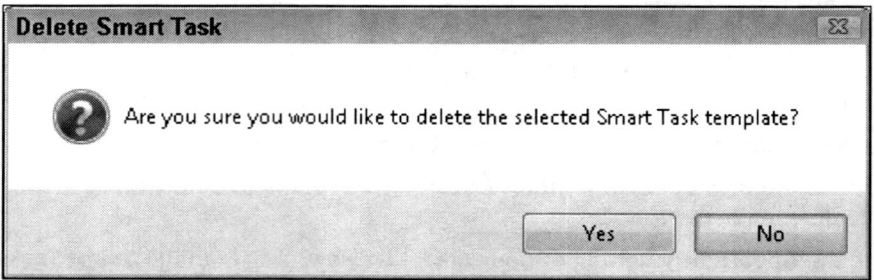

6. Click the **Duplicate** button if you'd like to clone one of the Smart Task templates and make it your own. This is a much safer option than permanently deleting a template.

7. Click **Close** to close the **Manage Smart Tasks** dialog window.

How it works...

You'll notice that all of the Smart Task templates have at least two steps. The first step determines which contacts the Smart Task will touch and how often you'd like to run the query. The second step determines the action that will take place. For example, in the **New Contact Welcome** template the first step indicates that the task will run everyday based on information in a contact field, and the second step indicates what exactly is going to happen.

There's more...

You'll notice that some of the templates have more than two steps. That's because you might want to have several things happen when you run a Smart Task. For example, you might want to send a thank you email to all new customers, follow that up seven days later with a personal phone call, and then send out a satisfaction survey three months later. It's important to note that each step won't happen until the previous one has been completed.

I've included a brief description of each template to make things a bit easier for you:

- **Birthday Reminder**: This will add a To – Do to your calendar to remind you a week in advance that one of your contacts is having a birthday.

- **Closed Opportunity Follow Up**: This will schedule a follow-up call on your calendar seven days after you close an opportunity.

- **Contacts with No Recent Activity**: If one of your users has not sent an email or had any other contact with a contact in the last 90 days, ACT! will automatically schedule an activity for the user to follow up.

- **E-marketing: Birthday Greeting**: An e-mail will automatically be sent to a contact on his birthday. This is different from the Birthday Reminder template that schedules a task but doesn't actually send anything out.

- **E-Marketing: Incorrect/Missing Information**: This sends an e-mail web form to a contact requesting to update inaccurate or missing information. The recipient's responses will be updated in ACT! automatically.

- **E-Marketing: New Contact Welcome**: This sends a welcome email to new contacts.

- **High Value Opportunity Alert**: An email will be sent to a user if an opportunity over a specific value is created.

- **New Contact Welcome**: This will send an email to all new contacts in your database.

- **Opportunity a Week from Close**: This will create a reminder for a user a week before an opportunity is expected to close.

Using Smart Tasks with ACT! E-marketing

Several of the template names begin with E-marketing. Those templates use email templates and require an ACT! E-marketing subscription. Unfortunately Sage didn't consistently incorporate this naming convention because a few of the other templates also require an ACT! E-marketing subscription. However, unless you need to send out a web form and/or track other parameters such as open rates, you can incorporate an email message into a Smart Task step.

Editing an existing Smart Task

If you like any of the existing Smart Tasks you can "make them your own" very easily by changing one or all of the three major elements of a Smart Task:

- The contacts or opportunities that will be affected by the Smart Task

- How often and when the Smart Task runs

- The activity that the Smart Task accomplishes

How to do it...

1. Click **Manage Smart Tasks** from the **Schedule** menu. This will open the **Manage Smart Tasks** dialog window.

2. Select the template that you want to change from the list, and then click the **Edit** button. You might be wondering which Edit button to click—the one in the **Manage Smart Tasks** menu bar or the one that you see in the first step of the Smart Task. It doesn't matter; both buttons will open up the **Edit Smart Task** dialog window that you see in the following screenshot:

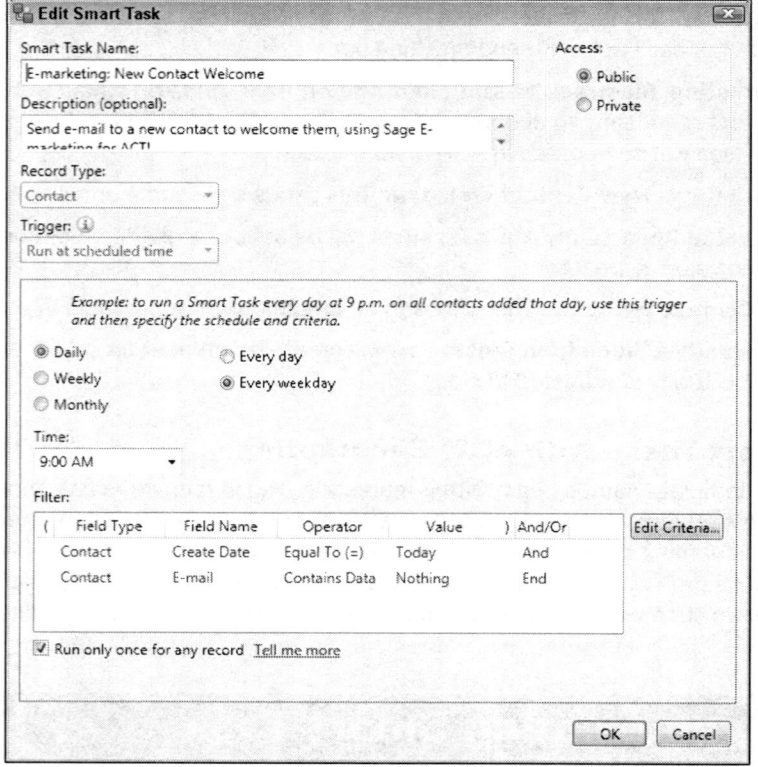

3. Type a name for the Smart Task template In the **Smart Task Name** field. All templates must have a unique name.

4. Optionally, add a description in the **Description** box to further describe the template.

5. Select **Public** if the template should be available to other users, or **Private** if the template should be available only to you in the **Access** area.

6.   Set the scheduled time that the Smart Task will run:

- ❏ **Daily** – This option is a bit confusing a first glance. If you choose **Daily** then you must also select either **Every day** to run the task, every day including Saturday and Sunday, or **Every weekday** to run it every day except Saturday and Sunday.

- ❏ **Weekly** – Select the day(s) of the week that the task should run.

- ❏ **Monthly** – Select the day of the month to run the task. As you can see in following screenshot, you can either select a specific day of the month that the Smart Task will run such as on the 15th of each month, or the week and day of the month such as the **First Monday** or the **Second Thursday**:

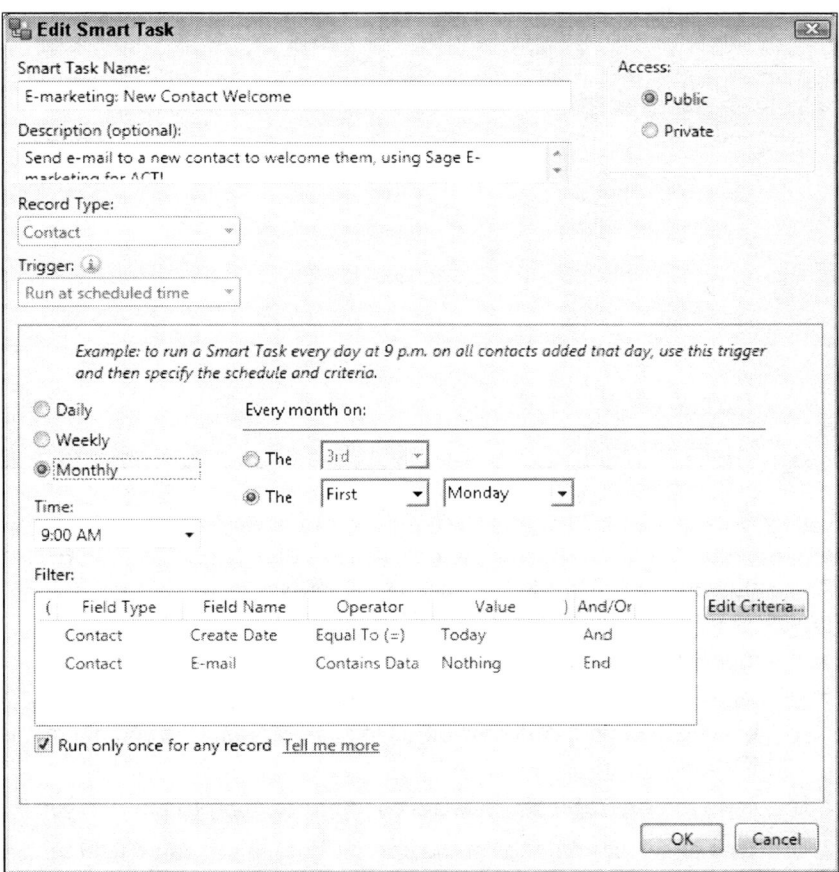

7. Although you can select the time of the day to run the Smart Task from the **Time** list drop-down, you might find it easier to just type it in. The list displays time settings in 30-minute increments, but you might want to run the task at a different interval such as 12:15 AM or 1:45 PM.

8. Click **Edit Criteria** in the **Filter:** area of the **Smart Task** dialog window. The **Smart Task Criteria** dialog window opens like the following one:

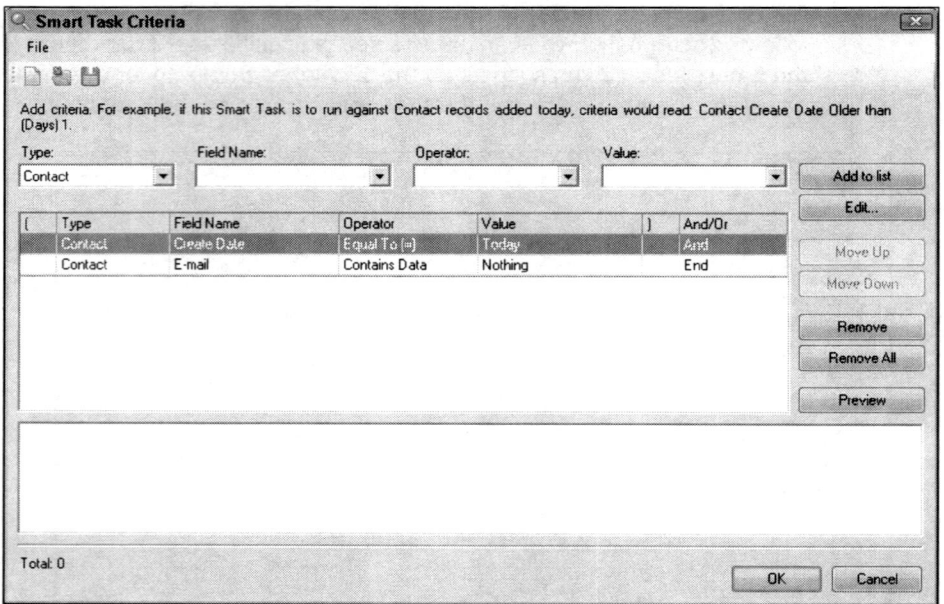

9. If you've worked with ACT! queries in the past, this is very familiar territory, with one major exception. With traditional queries, you are able to use data from Contact, Group, Company, and Opportunity records. However, the Smart Task Criteria window only allows you to create a query for a **Contact** or **Opportunity** record.

10. Create a query following these steps:

    ❑   From the **Field Name** list, select a field to search on. For example, if you are looking to send a Welcome email to all new prospects you might choose the ID/Status field.

    ❑   From the **Operator** list, select a condition to apply to the field you selected.

    ❑   Type or select from the list the specific data in the **Value** field that you are looking for. Following the same example above, you might add the value **Prospect** to the field if your purpose is to send a welcome letter to all new prospects.

❏ Click **Add to list**.

❏ To add another criterion to the query, repeat the process.

❏ To save the query, click **OK**.

11. Select **Run only once for any record** if you want a Smart Task to run only once per user. For example, you probably want to send out a welcome letter once to each record, but you want to run the Smart Task on a regular basis to send those letter out to any new prospects.

12. Click **OK** to close the **Edit Smart Task** dialog window.

13. Click the **Edit** button on the second step of the Smart Task. The **Smart Task Step** window opens. The window that opens will vary depending on the task that the Smart Task is going to run. The figure below shows you an example of a task that sends out an ACT! E-marketing template:

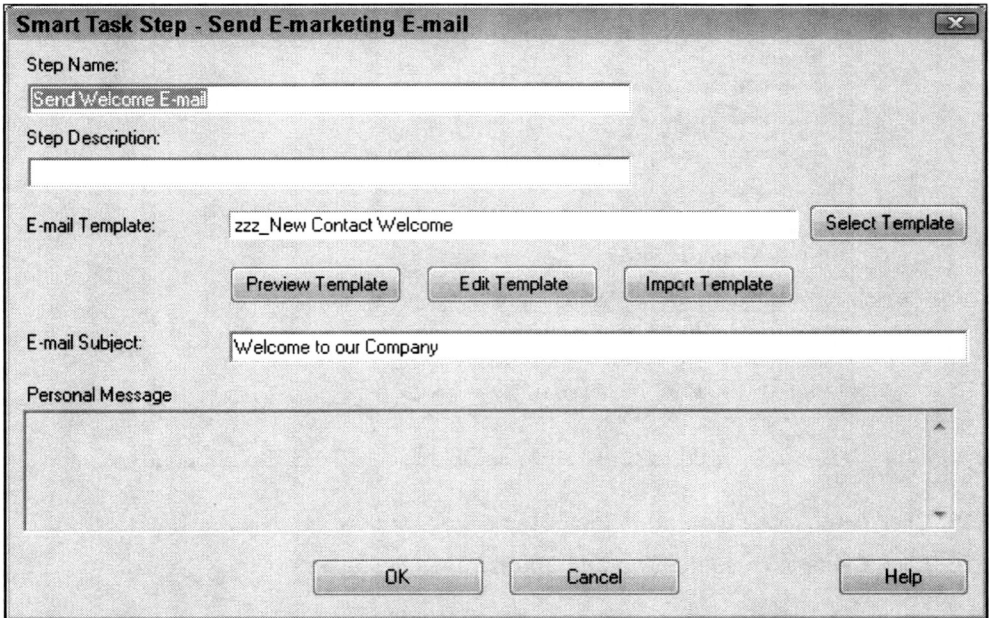

14. Change the task options. For example, if you are sending an ACT! E-marketing template you can select a different template, or change the contents of the email subject. The following screenshot shows you an example of a step that schedules an activity rather than physically doing the activity:

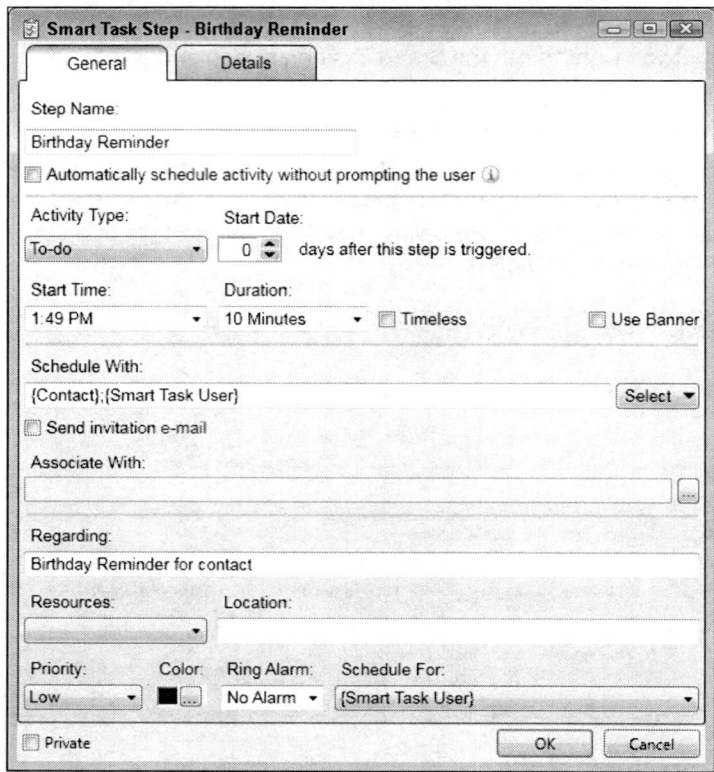

15. Click **OK** to close the **Smart Task Step** dialog window.
16. Click **Close** to close the **Manage Smart Tasks** dialog window.

How it works...

Once you've become familiar with the various Smart Task templates, the fun begins and you're ready to begin customizing those templates. For example, you might want two weeks' notice that someone is going to have a birthday, or you might only want to send a welcome email just to those contacts that you have identified as prospects.

There's more...

Unfortunately, at the time of writing you cannot change the Record Type or Trigger when you edit or duplicate a Smart Tasks template. You'll need to delete the Smart Task and create an entirely new Smart Task if you need to change either of these options. However you can run a Smart Task against manually selected records or disable Auto-Run to prevent the Smart Task from running automatically.

If you edit a Smart Task template, the changes will not take effect until the next time the Smart Task runs, and changing a Smart Task will not change any activities that are already scheduled to run.

Creating a Smart Task template

Editing or duplicating an existing Smart Task template is probably a bit easier than creating a new one from scratch. However, there might be times when you want to start with a clean slate. Or, if you're working with an existing template and need to change either the record or trigger type you will most definitely need to build the template from the ground up.

Getting ready

If your Smart Task is going to include the sending of email, you need to make sure that you have an ACT! E-marketing account set up as well as the template you plan on including.

I have often heard that 25% of the typical database is made up of "**dead wood**." That dead wood can consist of contacts with inaccurate contact information, or prospects that we just let fall through the cracks of our database.

A good way to plug up the holes in your database is to determine what you could do differently to ensure that "no one gets left behind." This is where the Smart Tasks can help. You might also find it a good idea to put a bit of planning into your Smart Task template by thinking about four of the "**4 W's**":

- ▶ Who: What portion of my database is going to be included by the Smart Task?
- ▶ What: What will happen when the Smart Task runs? Will a reminder be set up, or will an email be sent?
- ▶ When: How often do I want the Smart Task to run?
- ▶ Why: Why am I using a Smart Task? What am I trying to accomplish?

For example, you might sell a great product but never remember to send out a thank you note. Here's how that would translate into a Smart Task:

- ▶ Who: Customers who have purchased my products within the last seven days
- ▶ What: Send them a thank you email
- ▶ When: Run the Smart Task every day
- ▶ Why: I need to let my customers know I appreciate their business

How to do it...

1. Click **Manage Smart Tasks** from the **Schedule** menu. You'll want to make sure you're on the **Templates** tab.

2. Click the **New Smart Task** button. The **New Smart Task** dialog window will open just like the one in the following screenshot:

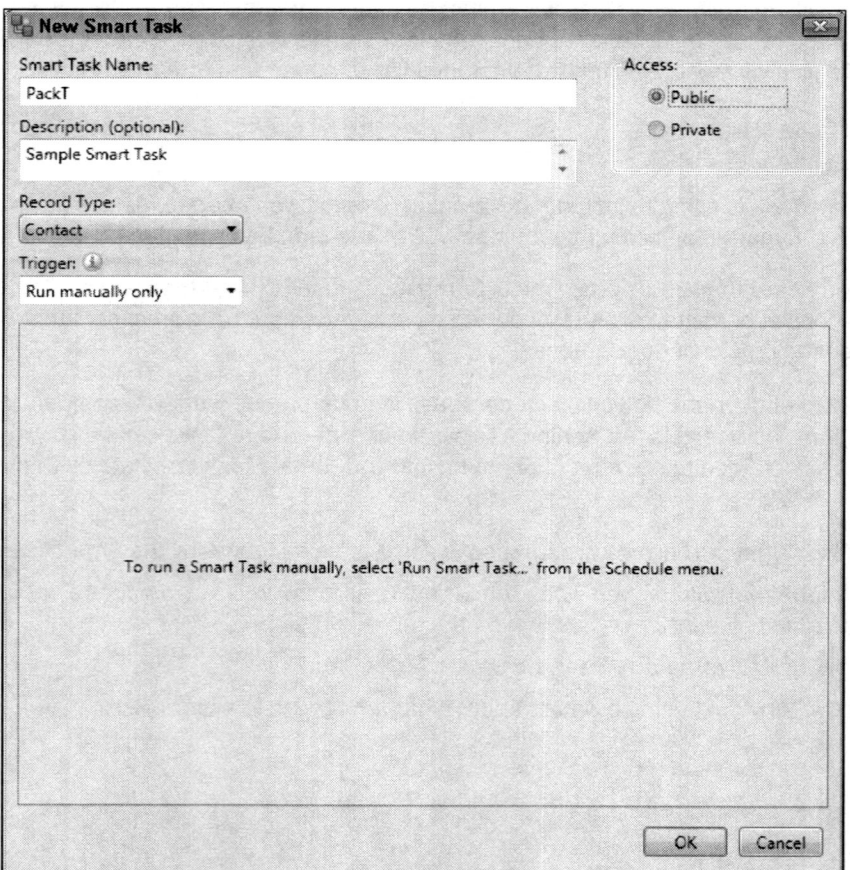

3. Type a name for the **Smart Task** template In the **Smart Task Name** field.

4. Select the access for **the Smart Task** template. Select **Public** if the template will be available to all users, and **Private** if the template will only be available to you.

5. Add additional information to describe the template in the **Description** box (optional).

6. Select the type of record (Contact or Opportunity) from the **Record Type** drop-down that the **Smart Task** will be run on. Remember, you cannot change **the Record Type** later if you edit or duplicate an existing template.

7. Select **Run manually only** or **Run at scheduled time** from the **Trigger** drop-down. Remember, you cannot change **Trigger** type if you edit or duplicate an existing template. However, you can run the **Smart Task** manually or disable Auto-Run to prevent the Smart Task from running automatically.

8. If you select **Run at scheduled time**, the **New Smart Task** window will expand to allow you to add frequency options. You can review those options in the previous section.

9. Click **Edit Criteria** in the **Filter** area to set criteria for the Smart Task. If you don't add any criteria then the Smart Task will run for the entire database. Alternatively, you can set the Trigger to Run manually only and create a Lookup or use a saved query every time you want to run the Smart Task. Remember, even if you add criteria, the criteria will not apply if you run a Smart Task manually. You can review the query process in the proceeding section.

10. Select **Run only once for any record** if you want a Smart Task to be run against a record only once per user.

11. Click **OK** to close the **New Smart Task** dialog window.

How it works...

Once you've created a new Smart Task it will appear alphabetically in the list of templates on the **Templates** tab of the **Manage Smart Tasks** dialog window.

There's more...

I know I sound a bit like a broken record here, but there are a few things you'll want to keep in the back of your mind as you create new Smart Tasks. After all, the only thing worse than spending hours on something is having to do it all over again.

Once you create a Smart Task it is not possible to change either the Record Type or the Trigger options. If you run a Smart Task manually you have the option to run the Smart Task on either your current Lookup or on the entire database; any filtering options you created as part of the Smart Task will be ignored.

Adding a Smart Task step

I mentioned earlier that using Smart Tasks is a great way to plug up database cracks. In the previous section you set up a Smart Task to perform a single task. However, you might want to accomplish several things using a Smart Task. For example, you might want to send a customer a thank you letter, follow it up a week later with a phone call, send out a satisfaction survey three months later, and then contact them six month down the road to see if they are ready for reorder. Many traditional ACT! users rely much too heavily on alarms to remember those touch points; unfortunately, if you forget to set an alarm the contact falls through the cracks—and you might lose a sale. In addition, adding so many alarms and activities to your calendar will make using it very cumbersome.

So, what's the solution? Glad you asked! By adding additional steps to a Smart Task you can ensure that your contacts will be contacted as often—or as little—as you want.

Getting ready

It's probably easiest to begin with an existing Smart Task. You can either create a new one, or clone an existing one. For example, you might duplicate the **Opportunity A Week from Close** Smart Task and change the filtering to find all opportunities that have closed in the last seven days.

Once you have the core Smart Task it's a snap to start adding additional steps. The thing to keep in mind here is that the **first** step is the one that contains the query; additional steps simply add additional tasks.

How to do it...

1. Click **Manage Smart Tasks** from the **Schedule** menu. The **Manage Smart Tasks** dialog window opens. Make sure you are on the **Templates** tab.

2. Select the name of the Smart Task that you wish to modify.

3. Click the **Add Step** button on the second step of the Smart Task. Remember, you see the steps of a Smart Task in the right-hand pane of the **Manage Smart Tasks** dialog window. You'll see the contextual menu shown in the following screenshot:

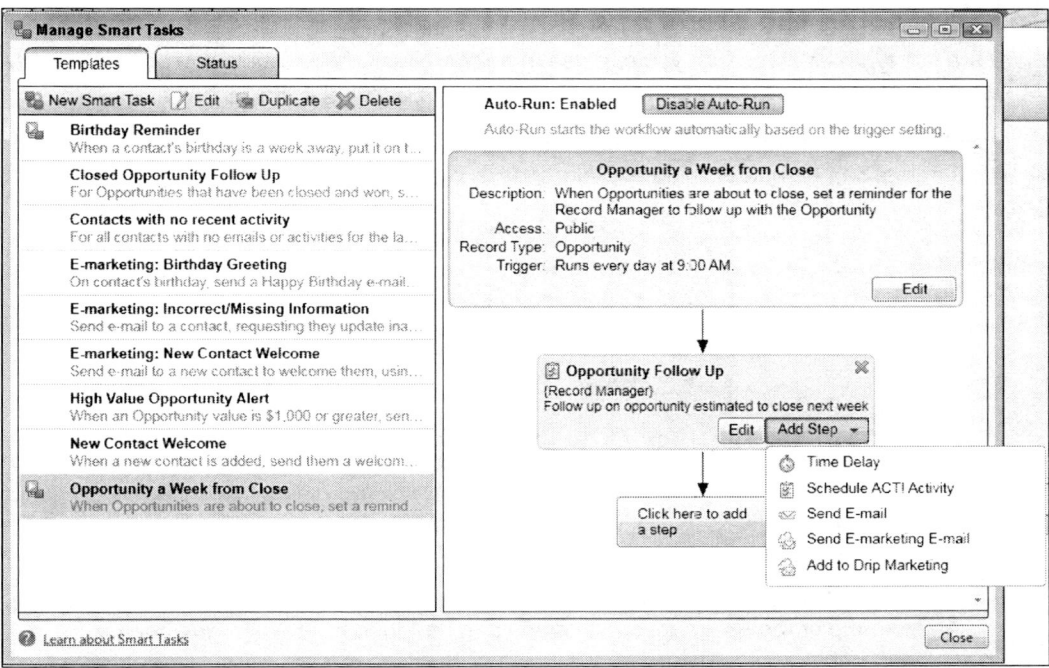

4. Choose a step option from the contextual menu.

5. Click **OK** to save your changes. You'll return to the Manage Smart Tasks dialog window where you'll see the new step displayed below the original two Smart Task steps.

How it works...

I like to think of ACT! like a set of building blocks; you can start out with a relatively small structure and expand as the need arises. Once you design a Smart Task, you will undoubtedly think of another step. Or, as your business grows you might introduce new products and/ or processes into your business and want to include those in with your existing Smart Tasks. There is no limit to the number of steps that you can include in a Smart Task, although it's probably better to create a Smart Task around a specific part of your day to day operations.

Understanding the steps of a Smart Task

There are five types of steps that you can use in a Smart Task. And, should you be so inclined, you use each step type as many times as you'd like when building a Smart Task:

1. Time Delay: This allows you to add spacing between the steps of the Smart Task. The interval can be one of minutes, hours, days, or months.

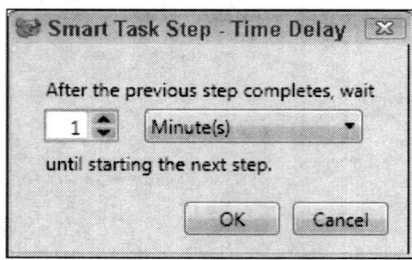

2. Schedule ACT! Activity: Allows you to set up an ACT! activity. You can see what that screen looks like in the figure above.

3. Send E-mail: This option lets you compose an email and even include an attachment. An example of the `Send E-mail` option can be found in the following image:

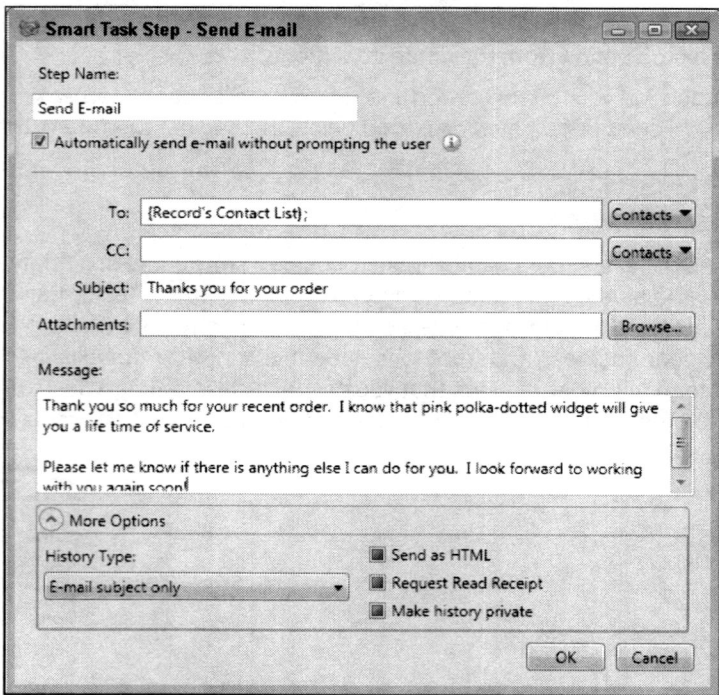

4. Send E-marketing E-Mail: This option will send an ACT! E-marketing template. Remember, the e-marketing template must be created prior to including it in a Smart Task step. The following screenshot shows you an example of sending an E-Marketing E-mail:

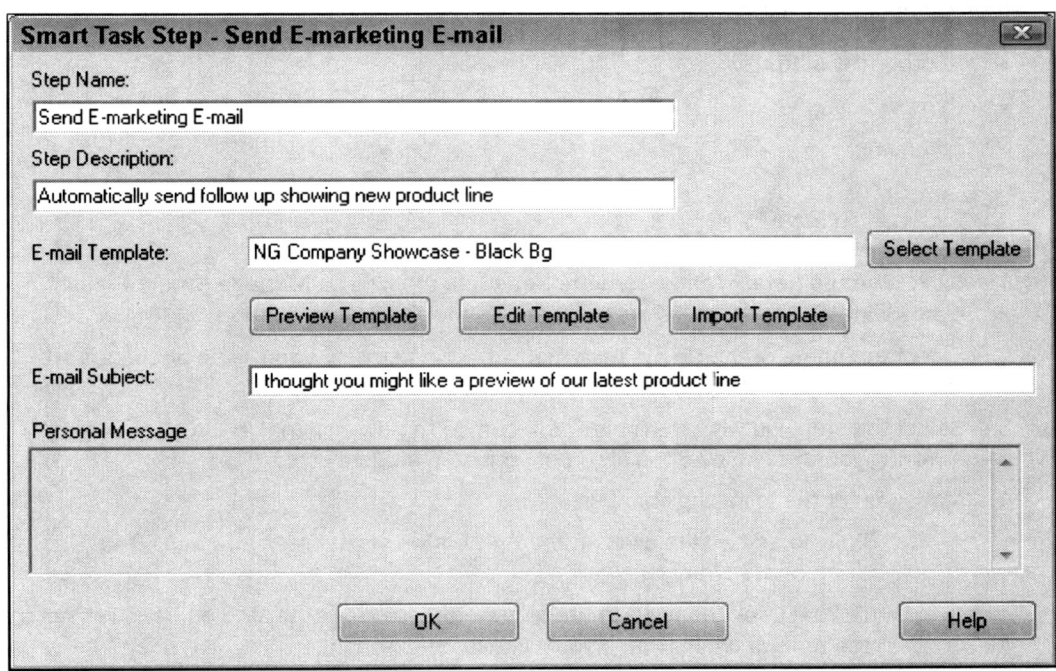

5. Add to Drip Marketing: This is how you can really set your database on auto-pilot. A drip marketing campaign is designed to continuously send out a string of emails. For example, you might have a drip marketing campaign that's designed to send out a newsletter to your customer base every month. By adding this step to the Smart Task you are in essence adding any new customers into the existing newsletter drip marketing campaign.

Changing Smart Task steps

As you begin to add more steps to your Smart Tasks and start to feel more comfortable with the overall process, it's only natural that you'll want to tweak things a bit. If you're like me you'll probably have a flash of genius shortly after you finish creating a Smart Task.

In the previous section, you saw how to add additional steps to an existing Smart Task. But what if you want to remove or change a step? Or what if you'd like to rearrange the order of things? You might think that you'd have to completely redo the Smart Task; don't worry, that won't be necessary.

Getting ready

It's only logical that in order to change the steps of a Smart Task that you already have a Smart Task with a number of steps. That's going to be your starting point. From there you have a number of options including:

- Reorder the steps
- Remove a step
- Edit a step

How to do it...

1. Click **Manage Smart Tasks** from the **Schedule** menu. The **Manage Smart Tasks** dialog window opens. Make sure you are on the **Templates** tab.
2. Select the name of the Smart Task that you wish to modify. You'll see all the **Smart Task** steps in the right-hand pane.
3. Select the step you wish to change. You can do that by clicking on the step, or simply hovering your mouse over the step until the step changes color.
4. Make one of the following changes:
    - Edit: To edit a step click on the **Edit** button of that step and make the appropriate changes.
    - Delete: Click the red x in the upper right corner of the step and answer **Yes** to the prompt asking you if you'd like to delete the step.
    - Change the step order: Select the step you want to move and then drag and drop it before or after another step in the Smart Task template. A dark line will appear which is the indicator showing you where the step will appear once you let go of your mouse.
5. Click **Close** to close the **Manage Smart Tasks** dialog window.

Setting a Smart Task to Auto-Run

Now that you've created a Smart Task and edited it to your liking, you're ready to actually **run** the Smart Task. And what could be smarter than a Smart Task that can be set to run automatically run without intervention?

Getting ready

There are two requirements for putting a Smart Task on Auto-Run:

- The Trigger type of the Smart Task must be set to **Run at scheduled time**

> ▶ The Smart Task must contain a query that specifies which records the Smart Task will apply to

Unfortunately, as I've mentioned earlier, you can't change the Trigger type of an existing Smart Task. If you decide you want to run a Smart Task automatically and you've already set the Trigger to **Run manually only** then you will have to re-create the Smart Task using the **Run at scheduled time** option.

How to do it...

1. Click **Manage Smart Tasks** from the **Schedule** menu. The **Manage Smart Tasks** dialog window opens. Make sure you are on the **Templates** tab.

2. Select the name of the Smart Task that you wish to modify. You'll see all the **Smart Task** steps in the right-hand pane.

3. Click the **Enable Auto-Run** button at the top of the Smart Task's steps like the one you see in the screenshot below. The button will change to **Disable Auto-Run**:

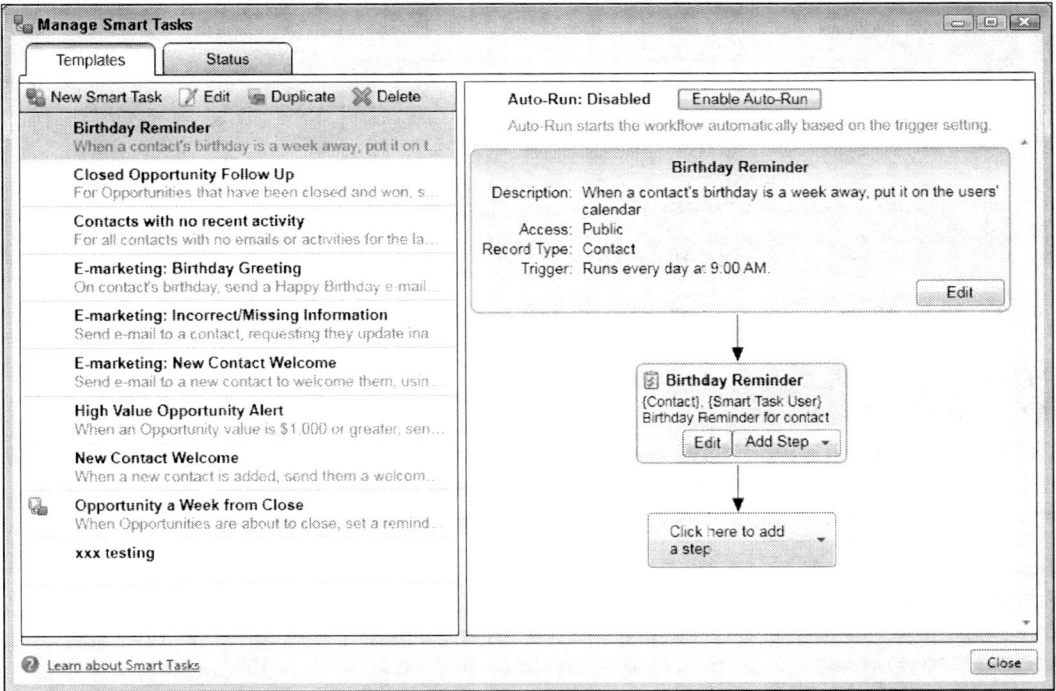

4. If a Smart Task has been set to **Manual run only** you'll notice that the **Enable Auto-Run** button is missing from the top of the Smart Tasks on the right-hand side of the window. See screenshot below:

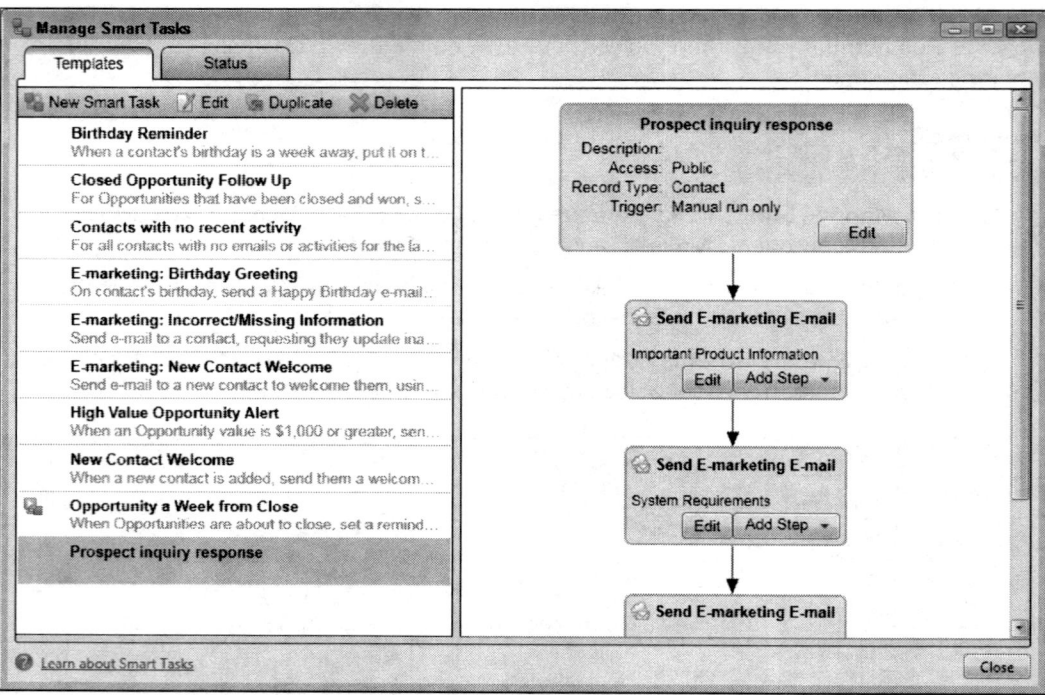

5. Click **Close** to close the **Manage Smart Tasks** dialog window.

How it works...

The Enable Auto-Run button works like a toggle: click it once to start the Auto-Run process and click it a second time to turn it off. You can easily access the Manage Smart Tasks area and scroll through the list of Smart Tasks to see which ones are set on Auto Pilot.

The Auto-Run will begin to run the Smart Task at the time designated in the first step of the Smart Task. At that point it will perform the query that you indicated in the query portion of the Smart Task. It will then begin to process the second step of the Smart Task. After the second step is processed the next step will process, and so on until all the steps have been completed.

If your Smart Task contains a Time Delay step, then the Auto-Run will pause until the allotted time has passed.

There's more...

Although most of us love the idea of being able to "set it and forget it" when it comes to work, there are a few words of caution:

Unless you've designated a Smart Task as **private**—meaning that only you have access to it—any of the standard users, managers and administrators of your database can enable—or disable—the Smart Task at the click of a button.

If the database is closed and none of the users are currently accessing it, the Smart Task will not run—even if Auto-Run is enabled. The ACT! database must be open in order for the Smart Task to run automatically.

Running Smart Tasks manually

There are times when you might want to run a Smart Task manually. Maybe you've targeted a select number of contacts to receive a special offering and based your decision on instinct rather than on a specific query of your field information. Or perhaps you'd like to immediately send out a welcome packet each time you land a new client but don't want to wait for the next time the Auto-Run runs.

Getting ready

When you run a Smart Task manually, any criteria defined in the first step of the Smart Task is ignored. That's because you should be selecting the records manually instead of having the Smart Task run using the query defined in the first step. If you select to run a Smart Task for all records, you might be putting a great deal of strain on your database. The average ACT! database contains somewhere between 2,000 and 7,500 contacts; if you were to schedule an activity for each one of them you'd have a lot of clutter on your Task List!

How to do it...

1. Create a Lookup of the Contact or Opportunity records for which you want to run the Smart Task for.

2. Click the **Schedule** menu and choose **Run Smart Task**. Because Smart Tasks only run against Contact or Opportunity records, you'll need to be in one of those views. The Run Smart Task dialog window will open like the one in the following screenshot:

3. Select the Smart Task that you wish to run by clicking on it once.

4. Make a selection in the **Apply To** area to indicate the contacts you'd like to apply the Smart Task to. You'll notice that ACT!, being the smart software program it is, will actually give you a count of the number of records that match each selection:

   ❑ **Selected records**: That's the Contact or Opportunity record that you are currently on

   ❑ **Current Lookup**: That includes all the records that match the Lookup in step 1 above

   ❑ **All Contacts**: This would run the Smart Task for all of your contacts

5. (Optional) Place a checkmark in the When manually running the selected Smart Task, apply the defined criteria checkbox if you want to limit the records you selected in Step 4 above to just those records that match the criteria you specified when defining the Smart Task.

6. Click **Run**. You'll be confronted by a confirmation prompt like the one you see in the following screenshot. If you do not want to see this message again the next time you run a Smart Task select **Do not show this message again**:

7. Click **OK** to close the Run Smart Task dialog window.

8. The **Pending Smart Task Steps** dialog window you see in the next screenshot may open depending on the Smart Task that you selected in step 3. That's ACT!'s friendly way of letting you know that there might be a few steps that are still waiting to process:

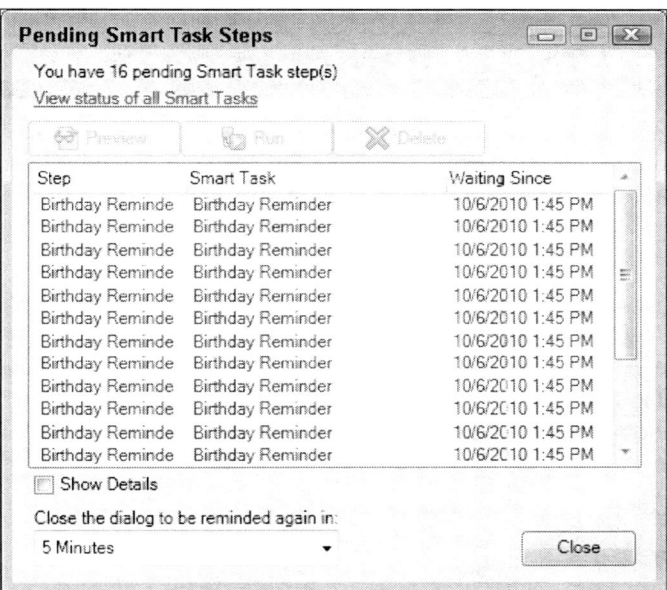

9. Click **Close** to close **the Pending Smart Task Steps** dialog window.

How it works...

When you run a Smart Task manually it basically by-passes the first step of the Smart Task that contains the query information and moves on to the second step that contains a task. And if there are additional steps, they will run as well according to the original design of the Smart Task.

It's important to keep in mind that the steps defined in the second and subsequent stages of the Smart Task will run for every one of the contacts in either your Lookup or your entire database, depending on the criterion you selected in step 4 above.

There's more...

Although running a Smart Task manually might seem like a good idea, you'll want to be careful before you run it because you may not get the results you were hoping for. If you are going to run a Smart Task manually you'll want to do it on a regular basis and be very familiar with its contents and how it works.

Remember, the **Run only once for any record** option is found on the first step of a Smart Task and thus is ignored when you run a Smart Task manually. Let's say, for example, that you have a Smart Task designed to send out a whole group of welcome information to new customers. If you run the Smart Task manually every morning for your customers, chances are that the same customers will receive that welcome packet over and over again!

Checking the status of a Smart Task

If you're new to Smart Tasks, you might make an assumption about a Smart Task and find out too late that your assumption was inaccurate. For example, you might make the decision that you'd really like to be proactive about sending a newsletter to your customers. You create the Smart Task and soon are bombarded with complaints from your customers that they are receiving the same newsletters over and over again. Yikes!

You make a trip to the Manage Smart Tasks dialog window, see the error of your ways, and make a change to the Smart Task to make sure that each customer will receive the newsletter only once. But hold on! The Smart Task has already run many times, and most of your customers are still in line to receive a whole new batch of newsletters. Changing a Smart Task does not change the status of actions that were triggered by a Smart Task that has already run. You can, however, manually remove any pending actions.

Getting ready

Obviously, if you've never created or run a Smart Task there are no actions for you to edit. However, if you have run a Smart Task and want to make sure all systems are working as planned, it's nice to know that you can check the status of your existing Smart Tasks.

How to do it...

1. Click **Show Pending Smart Task Steps...** from the **Schedule** menu. The **Pending Smart Task Steps** dialog window will open showing you any of the Smart Task steps that are still waiting to run.

2. Click on a task to select it (optional). To select several tasks hold the *Ctrl* key on your keyboard while selecting tasks and choose one of these actions:

   ❑ Click **Preview** to see the scheduled action that will be performed

   ❑ Click **Run** to start the action immediately

   ❑ Click **Delete** to cancel the action

3. Click **View status of all Smart Tasks**. The **Manage Smart Tasks** dialog window opens to the **Status** tab. Alternatively, if the **Manage Smart Tasks** dialog window was already open you could have simply clicked the **Status** tab. In any event, the **Status** tab displays a list of all the Smart Task actions that are scheduled to run. The following screenshot shows you what the **Status** tab looks like:

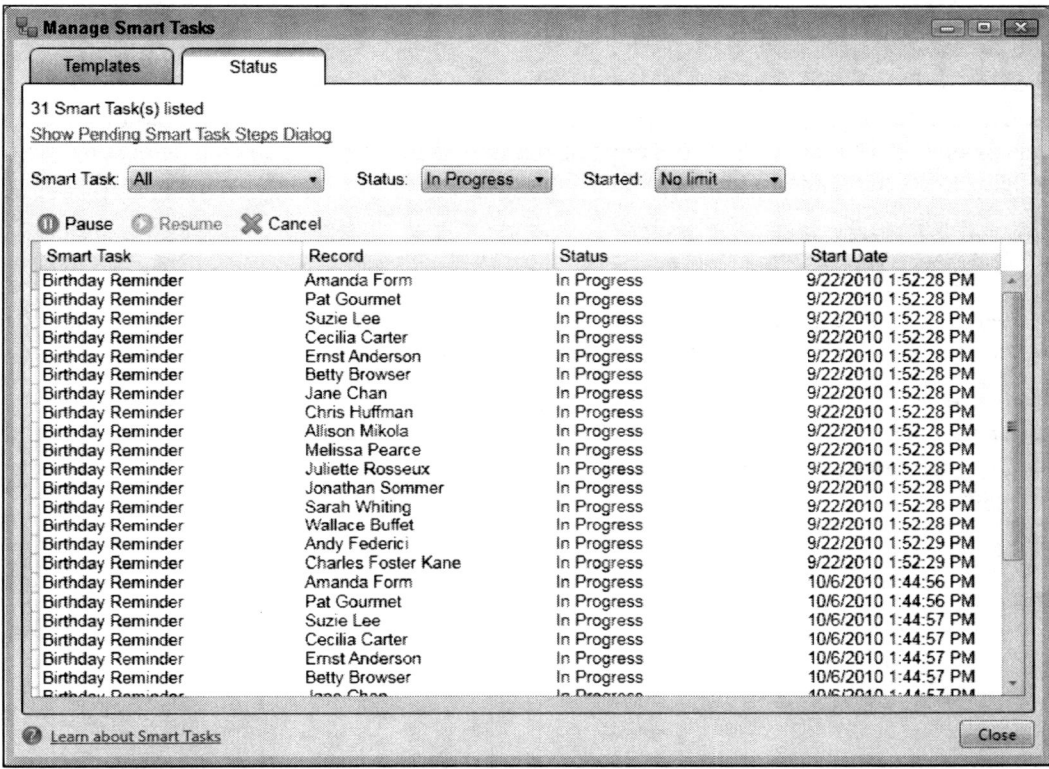

4. To sort the list of pending actions click a column heading to sort the scheduled tasks by Smart Task name, record, status, or Smart Task start date (optional).

5. To filter the list choose of one of these options (optional):

    ❏ Click the **Smart Task** drop-down to select a specific Smart Task

    ❏ Click the **Status** drop-down to select all tasks or only those tasks that have been cancelled, are in progress, or waiting for a further action on the part of a user

    ❏ Click the **Started** drop-down to select a time range from within the last six months to within the last day

6. Select the action(s) that you'd like to change and choose one of the following options:

    ❏ Click **Pause** to pause a Smart Task

    ❏ Click **Resume** to resume a paused Smart Task

    ❏ Click **Cancel** to cancel a Smart Task

7. Click **Close** to close the **Manage Smart Tasks** dialog window.

How it works...

Making changes on the Status tab only changes pending actions that were triggered by the running of a Smart Task. It will not prevent future actions from appearing if the Smart Task runs again in the future. Conversely, deleting a Smart Task template does not delete any pending tasks associated with the template.

There's more...

Remember, pausing or removing pending actions will not to prevent the Smart Task from running automatically again in the future unless you have also disabled Auto-Run.

You'll also want to be very careful about editing a Smart Task template that is in the process of running. Changes you make to a Smart Task will not change any pending actions. And if you do edit a Smart Task, canceling and re-running the in-progress steps may cause duplicated actions.

Index

Symbols

4 W's 243
.zip extension 180

A

account centric 93
ACT!
  about 5, 112, 161
  Accounting Software, linking to 18
  Annual Event Date field 35
  backup, creating 179
  backup, restoring 181
  calendar, synchronizing to Outlook 150
  Connected Services products 16
  connecting, to other services 16
  database, deleting 195
  date field 35
  differences 234
  duplicate records, merging 191
  existing web link, editing 65
  Global Edit, performing 196
  Group 77
  incoming Outlook email, linking to 146
  integrating, with Microsoft Outlook 135
  Internet link, creating 70
  Lookup 29
  new Outlook contact, creating 148
  new Web Link, creating 67
  old data, removing 190
  opportunity 111, 112
  opportunity view, working with 112-114

  Outlook, setting up as email client 136
  probabilities, working with 127
  relational database 49
  Relationships feature 49
  routine maintenance, performing 178
  Sage ACT! 20
  Sage Connected Services, accessing 17
  Sage Connected Services, setting up 17
  Sage Connected Services, working 17
  Secondary Contacts 50
  SideACT! 19
  special pricing, extending 127
  Startup options 8
  Task List 19
  updating, E-marketing history used 218
  using 135
  view specific menus 33
  Web Info tab 62
  web link, deleting 69
  Website Link, adding to History Tab 72
ACT! 2012
  ACT!-Google integration 161
ACT! Calendar
  synchronizing, with Google 164-166
  working 166
ACT! contact, in Outlook
  email, sending 144-146
ACT! contacts
  refreshing 171
  synchronizing, to Google 167-171
  working 171

ACT! Contacts to Outlook
synchronizing 154-158
working 159
ACT! email message
email template, sending 143
sending, Outlook used 141, 142
sending, to multiple contacts 143
sending, to single contact 141
**ACT! email message, sending to multiple
    contacts**
about 143
steps 143
ACT! email message, sending to single contact
email template, sending 143
process 141
requirements 142
steps 142
working 142
ACT! E-marketing
about 216
functions, e-mail 200
functions, results 200
functions, Surveys and Web Forms 201
mail sending, pre-points 218
requirements 216
sending 216
Smart Tasks, using with 237
working 217
ACT! E-marketing account
about 201
ACT! email, using 204
credentials, adding 201, 202
Marketing Results tab, turning off 203, 204
requirements 201
working 202
ACT!-Google integration
components 161
setting up 162
ACT!-Google integration set up
about 162
steps 162-164
activities 233

ACT! Outlook calendar
synchronizing 150-153
working 153
ACT! Scheduler
about 183
Delete a task option 187
Edit a task option 187
requirements 184
specific time, selecting 187
using 184-186
View Task Log option 187
working 186
ACT! Updates
about 187, 188
applying 189
Automatic Update preference, changing 189
working 189
Add/Modify Fields link 7
Add Remove dialog window 90
**Add Selected Contacts to Group dialog
    window 85**
Add to List button 41
Advanced Edit dialog window 69
Advanced Preferences button 152
Advanced Query
about 39
creating 40, 41
working 41
Annual Event Lookup
about 35
creating 35, 36
working 37
Annual Events Search dialog window 37
Attach to ACT! Contacts icon 146
Automatic Integration
about 175
setting up 175, 176
working 176

B

Back button 46
backup
creating 180

file password protection 181
restoring 182, 183
using, benefits 181
working 180
Back Up Database dialog window 180
basic Lookup
group, creating from current Lookup 33
performing 30-32
returning, to a previous Lookup 33
view specific menus 33
working 32, 33
bugs 187
Business Address tab 57

C

campaign results
lookup, creating for 222-225
collapse icon (<<) 12
companies detail view
companies, creating from 95
company
and contact fields, linking 106-108
company activity tab, working with 106
company opportunities tab, working with 106
contact, adding 103
contact and company records, linking 101, 102
contact and company records, moving
between 102
contacts, lookup creating 109
contacts name, adding to notes tab 105
creating, from companies detail view 95, 96
creating, from contact record 97
deleting 100
division, adding 98, 99
divisions, viewing 100
history and document tabs, working with 106
hyperlink, removing 102
list view, divisions viewing from 99
lookup, creating from company list view 109
new companies, entering from company list
view 96
record, working with 103, 105
company activity tab 106

company and contact fields
linking 106-108
company contacts
lookup, creating 109
company list view
divisions, viewing from 99
lookup, creating from 109
new companies, entering from 96
company opportunities tab 106
company views 94, 95
Configure Settings links 18
Contact Activity dialog window 38
Contact Activity lookup
about 37
creating 37, 38
creating, System Date fields used 39
working 39
contact and company records
linking 101, 102
contact centric program 93
Contact Detail view
Group Tab, using 85-87
contact management software 233
contact record
company, creating from 97
contacts
adding, to company 103
relating 50
Contacts button 94
contacts name
adding, to notes tab 105
Copy/Move Contact Data 194
CRM 233
current Lookup
using, for Group creation 84, 85
working 85
Current View
about 13
modifying 13
starting with 13
tree 14
working 14
Customer Relationship Management. *See* **CRM**

D

database
  deleting 195
default history option 141
Delete button 23
Delete Secondary Contact... option 59
Detail View 13
division
  adding, to company 98, 99
  viewing, from company list view 99
duplicate records
  copying 194
  merging 192, 194
  moving 194
  removing 191, 192
  working 194
dynamic members
  adding, to Group 82, 83
  working 84

E

Edit Smart Task dialog window 241
E-mail - Outlook Address Books dialog box 137
e-mail service provider 200
E-marketing campaign
  about 219
  analyzing 219, 220
  CSV file of results, requesting 221
  working 221
E-marketing history
  using, for ACT! update 218
  working 219
Enable Auto-Run button 251
existing HTML template
  importing 214, 215
  working 215, 216
existing Smart Task
  about 235, 236
  editing 237-242
  working 236, 242
existing web link
  area, modifying 65

  editing 65, 66
  starting with 65
expand icon (>>) 12

F

flat database 49

G

global edit
  Copy Field option 197
  performing 196
  Swap Field option 197
  working 197
global templates 204
Google
  ACT! Calendar, synchronizing with 164-166
  ACT! contacts, synchronizing to 167-171
  Record History options, setting 172, 173
Google Authorization dialog window 163
Google Integration Preferences dialog box 175
Google Integration Preferences dialog window
    176
Google Synchronization Preferences dialog
    window 171
Group
  about 75
  creating 77
  creating, from current Lookup 84, 85
  creating, steps 78
  dynamic members, adding 82-84
  Show For
    drop-down, options 91
  similarity, with Contact 76
  Static Members, adding to 79-84
  Static Members, removing from 81
  working 79
  working with 88-90
Group Tab, Contact Detail view
  Group/Company tab, working with 88
  using 85, 86
  working 87

H

history and documents tab 106
History Tab
  about 74
  Website Link, adding to 72, 73
  working 73
hotfix 187
HTML (hypertext markup language) 206

I

incoming Outlook email
  linking, to ACT 146, 147
  working 147
Internet link
  about 70
  creating 70, 71
  Delete option 71
  Edit option 71
  managing 70
  Move Up or Move Down option 71
  working 71
Italicize icon 22
item, Sage ACT! Scratchpad
  adding to Scratchpad 20, 21
  changes, modifying 22
  entry, deleting 23
  marking, as complete 26, 27
  order, modifying 23
  To-Do item 25
  transferring, to ACT! database 24-26
  working 21, 26

K

keyword Search tab 43

L

list, Sage ACT! Scratchpad
  printing 27
  working 27
List View icon 13, 94

local library
  template, moving to 204-206
local templates
  about 204
  editing 206-211
  working 211
Lookup
  about 29
  Annual Event Lookup 35
  basic Lookup, performing 30
  by example 34
  creating, by Contact Activity 37
  creating, for campaign results 222
  creating, from company list view 109
  of company contacts, creating 109
Lookup by Example
  about 34
  creating 34, 35
  working 35
Lookup By Example dialog box 41

M

Manage Contact Sync Set dialog box 172
Manage Google Contact Sync Sets wizard 169
Manage List menu 27
Manage Outlook Contact Sync Sets dialog 156
Manage Smart Tasks dialog window 257
Marketing Results tab 43
Mark Item Complete tool 26
Microsoft Outlook. *See* **Outlook**
Move Down button 15
Move Up button 15
multidimensional cubes
  advantages 159

N

Navbar
  about 10
  Add or Remove Buttons option 16
  Current View 11
  customizing 15, 16

diagram 10, 11
Navbar buttons 11
Navbar Lookup area 11
Related Tasks 11
Show Fewer Buttons option 16
using 10
working with 12, 13
Navbar Options button 16
Navigation. *See* **Navbar**
new Outlook contact
creating 148, 149
requirements 148
Select Contacts dialog 149
task, scheduling from Outlook email Message
150
working 149
New Secondary Contacts button 56
new Web Link
about 67
creating 67, 68
multiple link, creating 69
working 69
notes 233
notes tab
contacts name, adding 105

O

Opportunities button 14
opportunity
about 111
creating 124-126
deal, closing 129
editing 127
existing price list, importing 120, 121
processes and stages, adding 114-117
product pricing 120
products and services, adding 118-120
opportunity fields
working with 121-124
Opportunity Graph
creating 132-134
opportunity layouts
working with 121-124

Opportunity List
columns, customizing 130
Excel, exporting 131
quick printing 131
reset button 130
working with 129, 130
opportunity view
working with 112-114
Outlook
as ACT! email client, working 140
setting up, as ACT! email client 136-140
Outlook, as ACT email client
default history option 141
requirements 136
setting up 136-140
working 140
Outlook Contact Sync Set Users dialog
window 156
Outlook Synchronization Preferences... button
150, 155

P

patch 187
Pending Smart Task Steps dialog window 255
plain text template
about 213
limitations 213
Purchase/Upgrade Services button 202

Q

queries. *See* **Lookup**

R

Record History options
Gmail managing, Outlook used 174
setting, in Google 172, 173
working 174
Record History tab 172
refresh ACT! 159
Related Contact
about 52, 54
adding 52, 53

features 53
multiple contacts, adding 54, 55
working 53
relationship
changing 55
Edit Relationship... option 55
removing 55
Relationships feature 49
Relationship Tab
about 50
adding 51
as system tab 52
unhiding 50
working 52
removal tool
old data, removing 190, 191
working 191
Remove Old Data dialog window 190
Replace Data dialog box 196
Restore Database dialog box 182
Revoke Access hyperlink 164
routine maintenance
about 178
performing 178, 179
working 179

S

Sage ACT! Database box 163
Sage ACT! Scratchpad
about 20
item, marking as complete 26
item order, modifying 23
items, adding 20, 21
items, modifying 22
items, working 21, 22
item, transferring to ACT! database 24
list, printing 27
opening, ways 20
viewing 21
Scan for Duplicate Contacts dialog 192
Schedule Automatic Integration button 175
Schedule Automatic Synchronization button 152

Schedule With field 26
Search box 46
search on keywords
about 42, 43
Contact by Access, searches 44
creating, steps 42, 43
Last Synchronized, searches 44
options 43, 44
Sync Set, searches 44
Users, searches 43
working 43
Secondary Contact
about 56
adding 50
adding, by duplicating 58
creating 56, 57
Lookup, creating 58
promoting 58
working 57, 59
Send E-mail option 248
service pack 187
Services Account tab 202
Show Details button 53
Show Dynamic Membership button 88
Show Fewer Buttons option 16
SideACT! 19
Sign Up Now link 17
Smart Steps feature 233
Smart Tasks
about 234
Birthday Reminder template 237
Closed Opportunity Follow Up 237
Contacts with No Recent Activity 237
Duplicate button 236
E-marketing: Birthday Greeting 237
E-Marketing: Incorrect/Missing Information 237
E-Marketing: New Contact Welcome 237
Enable Auto-Run button, working 252, 253
High Value Opportunity Alert 237
Manage Smart Tasks dialog window 235, 236
New Contact Welcome 237
New Contact Welcome template 236

Opportunity a Week from Close 237
running 234
running, manually 253-255
setting, to Auto-Run 250-252
status, checking 256
step, adding 246
step, changing 249, 250
using, with ACT! E-marketing 237
working 236
Smart Task template
about 243
creating 243-245
working 245
source record 192
Started drop-down 257
Startup tab 9
Startup View
about 8
modifying 8, 9
Startup options 8
Welcome Page, returning to 10
working 10
Static Members
adding, to Group 79-81
removing, from Group 81
working 81
Status drop-down 257
status, Smart Tasks
checking 256, 257
working 258
step, Smart Tasks
about 248
adding 246, 247
Add to Drip Marketing 249
changing 249, 250
Schedule ACT! Activity 248
Send E-mail 248
Send E-marketing E-Mail 249
Time Delay 248
working 247
survey
about 225
compiled information, checking 228
creating 225-227

inserting, into template 229
Swiftpage E-mail 200
Synchronize Calendar tab 164
Synchronize Now links 18
Sync Set Criteria dialog window 172
Sync Set Criteria window 170

T

target record 192
templates
column widths, determining 213
direct editing, from Internet 212
global templates 204
local templates 204
local templates, editing 206
moving, to local library 204-206
personal message, adding 213
plain text template, creating 213
working 206
template, Smart Tasks
creating 243
creating, steps 244, 245
translating 244
working 245

U

Undo button 196
universal search
about 44
features 45
special search characters, using 47
using 45, 46
updates 188

W

Web Form
about 229
List Builder 229
List Updater 229
Web Info tab
about 62
ACT! Business Info 64

adding 64, 65
example 62, 63
Internal Browser, manual resizing 65
options 63
User Links 64
using 62
working 63
Web Links
about 69
adding, to History Tab 72, 73
deleting 69
working 70
Welcome Page

about 5
changes, viewing 8
Import Data link 7
information category 6
modifying 8
starting with 6
using 6, 7
working 7
Workflow 233

Z

Zip file backup 181

Thank you for buying
Sage ACT! 2012 Cookbook

About Packt Publishing

Packt, pronounced 'packed', published its first book "*Mastering phpMyAdmin for Effective MySQL Management*" in April 2004 and subsequently continued to specialize in publishing highly focused books on specific technologies and solutions.

Our books and publications share the experiences of your fellow IT professionals in adapting and customizing today's systems, applications, and frameworks. Our solution-based books give you the knowledge and power to customize the software and technologies you're using to get the job done. Packt books are more specific and less general than the IT books you have seen in the past. Our unique business model allows us to bring you more focused information, giving you more of what you need to know, and less of what you don't.

Packt is a modern, yet unique publishing company, which focuses on producing quality, cutting-edge books for communities of developers, administrators, and newbies alike. For more information, please visit our website: www.PacktPub.com.

About Packt Enterprise

In 2010, Packt launched two new brands, Packt Enterprise and Packt Open Source, in order to continue its focus on specialization. This book is part of the Packt Enterprise brand, home to books published on enterprise software – software created by major vendors, including (but not limited to) IBM, Microsoft and Oracle, often for use in other corporations. Its titles will offer information relevant to a range of users of this software, including administrators, developers, architects, and end users.

Writing for Packt

We welcome all inquiries from people who are interested in authoring. Book proposals should be sent to author@packtpub.com. If your book idea is still at an early stage and you would like to discuss it first before writing a formal book proposal, contact us; one of our commissioning editors will get in touch with you.

We're not just looking for published authors; if you have strong technical skills but no writing experience, our experienced editors can help you develop a writing career, or simply get some additional reward for your expertise.

Oracle Siebel CRM 8 Installation and Management

ISBN: 978-1-849680-56-1   Paperback: 472 pages

Install, configure, and manage a robust Customer Relationship Management system using Siebel CRM

Oracle Siebel CRM 8 Installation and Management

Install, configure, and manage a robust Customer Relationship Management system using Siebel CRM

Alexander Hansal

1. Install and configure the Siebel CRM server and client software on Microsoft Windows and Linux

2. Support development environments and migrate configurations with Application Deployment Manager

3. Understand data security and manage user accounts with LDAP

4. Manage multi-server and multi-language environments

Sage ACT! 2011 Dashboard and Report Cookbook

ISBN: 978-1-849681-92-6   Paperback: 216 pages

Over 65 simple and incredibly effective recipes for creating and customizing exciting dashboards and reports from your ACT! data

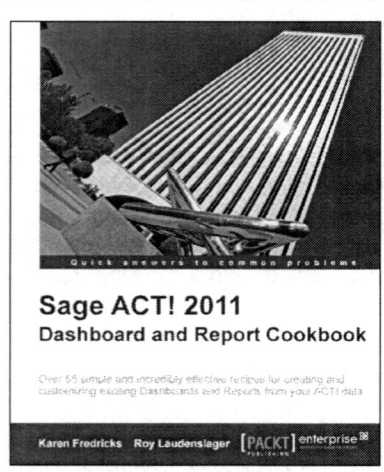

Sage ACT! 2011
Dashboard and Report Cookbook

Over 65 simple and incredibly effective recipes for creating and customizing existing Dashboards and Reports from your ACT! data

Karen Fredricks   Roy Laudenslager

1. Immediately access and fully understand the out-of-the-box ACT! reports and dashboards

2. Get to grips with filtering dashboard information

3. Customize existing reports and dashboards to make permanent changes

4. Create brand-new reports using the ACT! Report Writer

Please check **www.PacktPub.com** for information on our titles

Oracle Siebel CRM 8 Developer's Handbook

ISBN: 978-1-849681-86-5   Paperback: 576 pages

A practical guide to configuring, automating, and extending Siebel CRM applications

1.   Use Siebel Tools to configure and automate Siebel CRM applications

2.   Understand the Siebel Repository and its object types

3.   Configure the Siebel CRM user interface – applets, views, and screens

4.   Configure the Siebel business layer – business components and business objects

5.   Customize the look and feel of Siebel CRM applications

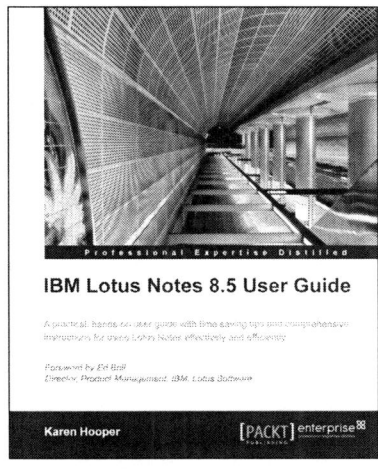

IBM Lotus Notes 8.5 User Guide

ISBN: 978-1-849680-20-2   Paperback: 296 pages

A practical hands-on user guide with time saving tips and comprehensive instructions for using Lotus Notes effectively and efficiently

1.   Understand and master the features of Lotus Notes and put them to work in your business quickly

2.   Contains comprehensive coverage of new Lotus Notes 8.5 features

3.   Includes easy-to-follow real-world examples with plenty of screenshots to clearly demonstrate how to get the most out of Lotus Notes

Please check **www.PacktPub.com** for information on our titles

Lightning Source UK Ltd.
Milton Keynes UK
UKOW040240060112

184796UK00002B/144/P